Praise for
Guided

'Laura Lynne Jackson's *Guided* is the kind of book that stays with you long after you finish reading. Her insights about the way we're all connected—especially to our loved ones who have crossed—and how that connection can lead us to our true purpose will inspire you to live more authentically."

—Kim Kardashian

'Laura Lynne Jackson's *Guided* is a luminous offering—deeply moving, exquisitely written, and imbued with both spiritual insight and emotional clarity. With her gift for storytelling and her extraordinary ability to perceive the unseen threads that connect us, Jackson reminds us of something vital: that we are never alone. The stories in these pages are both intimate and universal, drawing us into a world where love transcends physical boundaries and guidance is available—if only we're willing to listen. This book is not just a collection of stories; it is a gentle awakening to the truth that life is full of meaning, connection, and grace. I am grateful for the light Laura brings into the world."

—Gwyneth Paltrow

"In *Guided*, Laura Lynne Jackson shows how the connection to those we've lost is eternal. It's a reminder to live clearer, braver, and more connected, because you're never walking alone."

—Jay Shetty, #1 *New York Times* bestselling author and host of the *On Purpose* podcast

"If you want to feel more love and light in your life, read this book! Laura Lynne Jackson is love and light personified. *Guided: The Secret Path to an Illuminated Life* is your road map to feeling less alone, more alive, more connected, more inspired, and more certain that you are held, protected, guided, and loved in this lifetime."

—Jamie Kern Lima, *New York Times* bestselling author
and host of *The Jamie Kern Lima Show* podcast

"Laura Lynne Jackson radiates light, joy, and hopefulness, and *Guided* is the book version of who she is. It will help us all reach a deeper understanding of what we're doing here and how to light up the world. Read this if you want to walk away feeling more hopeful about the life you are living—and how connected you are to everyone who has come before you."

—Chelsea Handler, #1 *New York Times* bestselling author of
I'll Have What She's Having

"I inhaled every word of Laura Lynne Jackson's remarkable new book. As I finished reading, I exhaled with the certainty that our path is already waiting for us—we just have to take a deep breath and look around. This heartfelt book is an invitation to trust the journey and believe in the interwoven fabric of life."

—Amy Griffin, *New York Times* bestselling author of *The Tell*

"In *Guided*, Laura Lynne Jackson unveils the profound truth that we are all watched over and guided by a powerful Team of Light. Through captivating stories of miraculous connections and undeniable signs, she empowers you to recognize the subtle whispers from the Universe, leading you to a life filled with deeper meaning, purpose, and connection."

—Gabrielle Bernstein, #1 *New York Times* bestselling author of
The Universe Has Your Back

"Laura Lynne Jackson's gifts have the ability to reconfigure your understanding of life and what comes after. She may be one of the world's best mediums, but Jackson is first and foremost a teacher; the true beauty of her work is that she shows how you do not need her to stay connected to the Universe or your loved ones on the Other Side. In *Guided*, she shares the stories of real people who have followed the breadcrumbs of signs and synchronicities to a life of more meaning and connection. This book inspires us all to do the same."

—Elise Loehnen, *New York Times* bestselling author of
   On Our Best Behavior

BY LAURA LYNNE JACKSON

The Light Between Us

Signs

Guided

Guided

Guided

The Secret Path to an
Illuminated Life

LAURA LYNNE JACKSON

THE DIAL PRESS

NEW YORK

The Dial Press
An imprint of Random House
A division of Penguin Random House LLC
1745 Broadway, New York, NY 10019
randomhousebooks.com
penguinrandomhouse.com

Library of Congress Cataloging-in-Publication Data

Names: Jackson, Laura Lynne author
Title: Guided / Laura Lynne Jackson.
Description: First edition. | New York, NY: The Dial Press, [2025] |
Includes bibliographical references.
Identifiers: LCCN 2025026391 (print) | LCCN 2025026392 (ebook) |
ISBN 9780593729571 hardcover | ISBN 9798217154265 international | ISBN 9780593729588 ebook
Subjects: LCSH: Guides (Spiritualism) | Psychic ability
Classification: LCC BF1275.G85 J33 2025 (print) | LCC BF1275.G85 (ebook)
LC record available at lccn.loc.gov/2025026391
LC ebook record available at lccn.loc.gov/2025026392

International ISBN 9798217154265

Printed in the United States of America on acid-free paper

1st Printing

FIRST EDITION

BOOK TEAM: Production editor: Evan Camfield • Managing editor: Rebecca Berlant • Production manager: Sarah Feightner • Proofreaders: Emily Cutler, Susan McGrath

Illustrations: Getty Images, Alamy

The authorized representative in the EU for product safety and compliance is Penguin Random House Ireland, Morrison Chambers, 32 Nassau Street, Dublin D02 YH68, Ireland. https://eu-contact.penguin.ie

To my mom, Linda Osvald—
your love is a light that has guided me my entire life.
You are the root of all things good and kind and loving.
You inspire me every day.

To Garrett, Ashley, Hayden, Juliet and Cam—
you are my everything. My greatest gift in life was my soul
being guided to you. You each shine so brightly;
you illuminate my world.

To you, the reader—
You are more loved and guided than you can imagine.
You are right where you are supposed to be right now. You are safe.
You matter. You are made of light and you are magical.
May this book help you see that.

What you seek is seeking you.

RUMI

Contents

PART TWO

EXPLORING THE LIGHT
IN THE DARKNESS

PART THREE

OWNING THE LIGHT:
ILLUMINATING YOUR LIFE

PART FOUR

TURNING UP THE LIGHT

Introduction

Before we talk about wonderful things like love and light and creativity, I'd like to share two stories with you.

The first takes place in 1981. It's about a pediatrician and a premature baby. The tiny boy was born weighing only 3.2 pounds, and he was given only a fifty-fifty chance to survive. His condition was critical, and his first few hours on earth were touch-and-go. But his pediatrician didn't care about the odds. The doctor made it his mission to see that the little boy pulled through. Even though he had other cases and other concerns, the doctor sat with the premature child around the clock, checking his vital signs and cheering him on through the enclosed incubator. Night turned to day, and the doctor was still there, willing the boy to live.

And the boy *did* live.

The second story takes place thirty years later. A man was driving his SUV along the Pacific Coast Highway in California when, out of nowhere, a huge semitruck slammed into him from the side. His SUV was partially crushed and pinned beneath the truck. Then the SUV caught on fire. Luckily, a team of paramedics was nearby, driving back to their station after another call. They raced to the scene and found the SUV driver struggling to move as his legs caught fire. With almost no time to spare, the paramedics extinguished the flames and used the Jaws of Life to pull the driver to safety. Had they been a little farther away, the man might not have made it.

But he *did* make it.

Now, what if I told you these are not two unrelated stories, but actually *the same story?*

You see, the driver of the SUV was Michael Shannon—the doctor who saved the premature baby's life thirty years earlier.

And one of the paramedics who pulled Michael to safety was Chris Trokey—*the premature baby whose life Shannon had saved.*

The chance of such an amazing thing happening on a planet of more than seven billion people seems impossible, so much so that many believe the story of Michael and Chris is made up. It's not. They are real people who did indeed save each other's lives thirty years apart. Their journeys through life are intertwined to a degree neither could have known or expected or even understood. Yes, their story is an extreme example of the ways in which we are all connected. But the underlying essence of their unique bond, and how they were guided in their journeys, is universal.

That's because, as each of us sails forth on our individual adventures, we are not writing billions of separate stories.

No—*we are all part of the very same story.*

Sometimes it's hard for us to comprehend just how connected we are to one another. We cannot imagine how powerful our choices are in the context of our collective being. We ask ourselves, *How can any one person possibly make a difference against all the anger and neglect and injustice in the world?* We simply don't see how we could be a part of anything larger than our own sequestered individual lives.

The reason I wrote this book—and the reason it has found its way into your hands—is to help you understand just how loved, watched over, and guided you are, and how much impact you can have on everyone around you.

Each and every one of us has the power to absolutely transform not only our own lives but also our neighborhoods, cities, societies—even our planet. Every small positive action we take, every tiny bit of kindness we put out into the world, has a ripple effect. We can't possibly know how far that ripple will reach. In Shannon's case, the ripple reached through three decades and saved his life. In your case, the ripple could turn into a resounding tidal wave for change and betterment felt across the lives of everyone you touch, or even across oceans and continents.

It's easy for us to forget about this profound ripple effect, and to make choices we think matter only to us. But they don't—they never do. Each and every choice we make has the potential to yield great influence. The most consequential changes can often be measured in the smallest of increments—as small as a single, seemingly unimportant decision.

Think of it like going to the gym. You don't go to the gym for the first time and come home twenty pounds lighter and feeling fantastic. You come home exhausted and not an ounce lighter. But if you keep going to the gym every day, it adds up. Each minute of sweat and dedication builds. And the result—a new body, a new outlook, a new everything—can be transformative. Often, enormous shifts in our lives do not occur in concise aha moments. They occur in a series of small, rippling decisions.

We are never alone while navigating our lives and finding our paths. We are guided by loving forces imperceptible to the human eye but present and active nonetheless. I have come to understand that we each have a Team of Light made up of God energy, spirit guides (evolved spiritual beings who act as mentors and help guide us on our paths here), and loved ones who have crossed. These teams work hard to steer us on our life paths. They guided you to this very book. When we open our hearts and minds to this guidance, magical things unfold and lead us onto the secret path to living our best and highest life—a life filled with meaning, vibrancy, and engagement.

A *guided life. An illuminated life.*

Living a guided, illuminated life means understanding that our choices are powerful, that our influence is exponential, that no one's life or experiences are insignificant. Rather, all of us are connected to and responsible for one another.

It means living a life aligned with purpose—discovering what you were put here on earth to do, and doing it with clarity and passion. It means embracing the fullness of your experiences—being able to see meaning in the difficult moments, and to fully feel the joy in the happy ones. And it gives you the spiritual wisdom to value both. It is a life in which you have confidence in knowing you are never alone; you are always being guided onto your highest path. It is knowing that the Universe always dreams bigger for you than you can for yourself.

To grasp not only the beauty of these truths but also the daily implications and benefits of this way of thinking is to discover the meaning of our existence—and to live an illuminated life.

My name is Laura Lynne Jackson and I am a psychic medium. For nearly twenty years I worked as a high school English teacher and kept my psychic abilities largely under wraps. Then one day, I received what I call a *download from the Universe*, and the message was to spread what I had learned to a larger audience. So I took a deep breath, came clean to my high school principal, and wrote a book called *The Light Between Us: Stories from Heaven, Lessons for the Living*. It told the story of how I first discovered my abilities and how I came to terms with them.

A couple of years later, I got another download, and I wrote a second book, *Signs: The Secret Language of the Universe*, which was a guide to seeing and understanding the many signs our loved ones on the Other Side send our way. Both books were meant to share the many amazing lessons I've learned as a result of my "gift."

The reason I put the word *gift* in quotes is that the abilities I possess are not unique to me. This is one of the themes central to my books: What people think of as my gifts belong, in fact, to *all* of us. The things I see and hear and feel are things that swirl around us all; the connections I am able to make are available for all of us to make. It is just a matter of learning how to be *open* to these gifts, and to these swirling invisible cords of energy and the connections that bind us. *It is learning to see and trust the unseen.*

My first two books were intended to help readers open their minds and hearts to these hidden but very real connections—not only to one another on earth but also to our loved ones who have passed.

Then, after *Signs* came out, I didn't get another download—at least not right away. And I was okay with that. The work I do can be exhausting, and I'm not just talking about being a psychic medium—I'm also the mother of three children. Eventually, though, the download came. It didn't arrive as the first two did, which was all at once in a torrent of messages I couldn't write down fast enough. This time, the download was more like having a leisurely cup of tea with my guides on the Other Side. Something else was different: the sheer number of ideas that came through. It was dazzling! Apparently, there was quite a lot that the Other Side wanted us to know.

So that's what *Guided* is—a book of ideas. On these pages, I will share all that I've learned from the Other Side. *Guided* reveals the ideas that can change our lives—and change the world. It teaches you to recognize the signs leading you to your highest path, gifts you the wisdom and peace of trusting in powerful energies you cannot see, and reveals the beauty in recognizing how connected we all are. If you are reading these words, you are *already* being guided onto the secret path to an illuminated life; this book was placed in your path for a reason. It may change and shift not just your own life but also the lives of others you love, and even strangers whom you may influence and affect, even if you never meet them. I'm excited to go on this journey with you, as we are all guided toward the secret path to an illuminated life.

PART ONE

SEEING THE GUIDANCE

The Universe offers guidance to us all, gently steering us toward our best and highest selves. The Universe *illuminates* our path through life, like streetlamps suddenly turning on—except that the Universe's guiding light *never turns off.* It has always been there for us and always will be, and we don't have to do anything to activate it. There is no password, no secret handshake. We are born connected to one another and to the Universe, and we couldn't break that connection if we tried. Access to this illuminated path is our spiritual birthright. We are already members of the club.

But it's up to us to be open to this guidance so we don't miss it. And it's up to us to honor it once we see it.

Think of Part One of this book, Seeing the Guidance, as the Universe welcoming you and letting you know you're on the right path. In this part, you will read examples of how we can learn to see the guidance available to us through all the noise and fog of our modern materialistic lives. It's easy for us to become so consumed by the rigors and demands of life that our energy flows outward and gets depleted by obligations—which can dim the illumination on our paths. Sometimes we need to pull our energy back within us so that we can be more open to the guidance awaiting us.

In Part One, there are beautiful examples of the Universe's guiding light suddenly shining through the clouds and changing people's lives in big and small ways. These stories are about people who sudden y realize that the guidance they desperately sought was right there for them all along. Their stories can help us see how powerfully transfor- mative it can be when we open up our hearts and minds to the guid- ance around us.

The universe is full of magical
things patiently waiting for our
wits to grow sharper.

EDEN PHILLPOTTS

1

Unexpected Sparks

Every now and then the Other Side guides me to a specific place at a specific time for a specific purpose. That's what happened in 2022, when I was guided to central Florida on a scorching summer day.

Of course, I wasn't the only one being guided that day. There was another person who, because she was open to the forces that seek to steer us on our journeys, became a part of my story, just as I became part of hers.

Put another way—we were both characters in the *same* story, only we didn't know it.

And that story begins with a boy named Zach.

Zach Johnson-McDonnell and his younger sister, Makayla, were raised in Minnesota largely by their mother, Karleen Johnson, after she and her husband divorced when the children were young. Zach was one of those endlessly curious boys, a question machine, forever in search of his next adventure. "Oh, he was a ball of energy, all right," says Karleen, who lovingly called her son Scooter. "He was so full of life. He was the kind of person who could walk into a place and not know anyone and walk out with ten new friends and a plan to do something fun with them."

Zach burst with so much energy he could hardly be contained indoors, and his childhood was full of camping and four-wheeling and snowmobiling with his mother and family and friends. As a teenager, he took up hunting and became quite good at it. Zach's familiarity with hunting weapons led him to enlist in the U.S. Army at the age of eighteen, after they offered him a $25,000 signing bonus to become an infantryman—the soldiers who fight ground combat on foot. Zach wound up on the front lines of the grueling and bloody war in Iraq, often face-to-face with the enemy. What saved him were his courage and his fierce will to live.

"Not me," Zach would tell himself before rushing into battle. "Not me, not today."

What he did not know was that the worst danger for him lay ahead away from the battlefield, waiting for him when he came back home from two tours of duty.

The things he had to do in Iraq, the horrors he saw, the unimaginable atrocities and brutality of war—all of these "took a horrible toll on him," Karleen states. "He never actually told me what happened over there; he just said, 'Mom, I will always protect you because I love you so much, and there are things in life you just don't need to know.'"

Zach was diagnosed with post-traumatic stress disorder (PTSD). The disorder is characterized by intensely disturbing and recurring thoughts and feelings, sometimes through flashbacks, sometimes through nightmares, the trauma of war resurfacing in ordinary life. PTSD can be devastating; it often makes the people who suffer from it feel detached, estranged, cut off from the world, unable to sleep or concentrate or even have relationships. It can lock someone inside a prison of emotional numbness from which escape seems all but impossible. The grim, horrifying reality is that PTSD is particularly paralyzing for U.S. military veterans, and an average of twenty-two vets in the United States take their own lives *every day*.

Zach was determined not to be one of the twenty-two.

"He really tried to reintegrate into civilian life, but he just struggled with it so much," Karleen says. "Eventually he turned to drugs."

Zach battled a gripping addiction to different narcotics for fifteen years, never quite able to free himself from a dark, despairing loop.

"The drugs," says Karleen, "were his only way out of the pain."

Zach's mother and sister rallied around him at every chance, doing everything they could to pull him back into the light. Zach voluntarily entered a few drug rehab programs, with varying success, and Karleen and Makayla were always there to support and encourage him. "I kept thinking, *The kid is a warrior, front lines, infantry, he's got this new struggle and he will beat it,*" Karleen says. And yet, she adds, "there was always this imminent fear of the worst happening."

In November 2019, Zach booked himself for treatment at a Veterans Affairs medical center in St. Cloud, Minnesota. It was an encouraging sign. The night before his admission, he called Karleen and sounded agitated. "He was elevated and stressed," she recalls. "It was a tough call." Zach said he was hitting the road at 5:00 A.M. the next morning for the drive to St. Cloud, and right at 5:00 A.M. Karleen texted him.

Hey, Scooter, she typed, *are you on your way?*

Karleen checked her phone every few minutes for a reply, but she saw that her text remained unread.

In 2019, I began planning a big trip for my family to mark my husband Garrett's fiftieth birthday. Destination: Disney World. We'd traveled there before as a family, and we all loved going (particularly me; the energy there is truly remarkable), and one thing I'd learned is that to take full advantage of Disney, you have to do a lot of planning. Not planning down to the day or even the hour—you have to plan your trip down to the *minute*.

So that's what I did, buying plane tickets to Florida for July 2020, lining up which parks and attractions we'd be visiting each day, signing up for the right passes, getting reservations for the most popular restau-rants, and generally plotting out our every move. Months before Gar-rett's big birthday, our trip was thoroughly booked.

Then Covid hit in early 2020. We had no choice but to cancel our trip. Of course, I got right to work booking the same trip for July 2021, and eventually I nailed it all down again, but when 2021 rolled around, Covid was still a big problem, and once again we had to postpone the trip.

Undaunted, we tried once more. After much rearranging of plans, clearing of schedules, putting in for time off, and securing flight and hotel reservations, we were all set—nine days in Disney World in Au-gust 2022, each day packed with thrills and action. Did it matter that by then Garrett was already fifty-two? Not in the least. As a family, we have a lot to celebrate, and that's what we set out to do, two and a half years late.

My point is, I had no intention of being in Florida, at Disney World, in the summer of 2022—and yet there I was, rigid schedule in hand, bouncing from one attraction to the next with my husband and three children. Even more unlikely was what happened during our stay, when I got a sudden download from the Universe that led me to change my plans one morning, even though changing plans on the fly at Dis-ney World—especially reservations at highly popular restaurants—is all but impossible. As carefully as I had prepared our itinerary, I re-mained open to the Other Side and followed the little voice in me that told me to make the change.

Sometimes the Universe has its own rigid schedule for us.

Early on the morning of November 6, 2019, Karleen Johnson sent her son, Zach, a second text to see if he was still driving to the VA rehab center in St. Cloud as planned.

Hey bud, just checking in on you, she wrote. *You on the way to St. Cloud?*

Like her first text message to him at 5:00 A.M., her second text went unread. At noon that day, Karleen sent a more urgent message: *Zach, I'm losing my mind. Where are you?* Zach failed to respond to this text, too.

Perhaps Zach had decided not to check himself into rehab, Karleen thought, and was now somewhere confronting his issues and out of reach. Karleen did not hear from her son at all on November 6, and she didn't hear from him the following day, either. Three days after Zach was set to check into rehab in St. Cloud, his mother got a phone call.

Her worst fear had been realized. Zach had taken his own life.

His body was found in a basement laundry room of his then-girlfriend's home. The possibility had always been there, the terrible worst-case scenario, lurking in the back of Karleen's mind, yet when the actual news came Karleen wasn't prepared for the utter devastation she felt.

"I was always his rock, his go-to person," she says. "He knew he could call me at three in the morning to talk. Sometimes he just needed to know I was there, and I would stay on the phone and listen to him breathe."

Zach Johnson-McDonnell was just thirty-three years old.

After he was gone, Karleen found herself in a very dark place—a pitch-black tunnel without an entrance or exit. She constantly asked herself what she might have done differently to save Zach, agonizing over any chance she might have missed to give him the lifeline he needed. "I didn't just second-guess myself," she says, "I *fifty* times guessed myself." Things got so dark that Karleen turned to alcohol to ease her pain, and some days she simply couldn't get out of bed.

Finally, it was a phone call from Zach's former girlfriend, Lisa, whom Karleen considered her "bonus daughter," that provided Karleen with the lifeline *she* needed.

"Lisa said, 'Kar, I was listening to this podcast, and someone mentioned this book I think you should read,'" Karleen recalls.

This is how Karleen and I first crossed paths—Lisa was referring to my second book, *Signs: The Secret Language of the Universe*, which is about the many ways we can learn to look for signs sent to us by our Teams of Light on the Other Side, including our loved ones who have passed.

Lisa bought two copies of *Signs*, and she and Karleen committed themselves to reading it at the same time. As they both read it, they talked about specific signs they were each asking for and receiving. Karleen found herself choosing random objects or animals and asking Zach to put them in her path, as a sign that he was still with her and doing okay.

One afternoon, a couple of months after Zach had passed, Karleen asked him to send her a green ball. There was no reason why she asked for a green ball—it was, as usual, a completely random object. Karleen was in the kitchen of her parents' home, having coffee with her mother, when she suddenly looked out the window above the sink and gasped.

Out of nowhere, a big green ball had come bouncing into the yard.

"Are you okay?" her mother asked.

"Mom, I asked Zach for a green ball, and there it is!" Karleen said. "Zach sent it to me!"

Karleen tried to find out where the green ball came from—some neighborhood kids kicking it around?—but she was never able to figure it out. Somehow, the ball just magically appeared out of thin air. Which, for Karleen, only confirmed what she already knew.

"I asked for a green ball, and Zach delivered it," she says. "I asked for it and there it was, the sign. It was Zach saying, 'Hey, Mom, I'm okay. You asked for it, here I am.'"

Not much later, Karleen and Lisa spent a weekend together in Nashville, Tennessee. Karleen chose another random sign for the weekend—this time, she asked Zach for a rabbit. For dinner, Karleen and Lisa chose an Asian fusion restaurant, and when they were seated at a table by a wall Karleen glanced over to her right. "There on the wall, right in front of me, a giant painting of a rabbit," she says. "A *big freaking giant rabbit* right where we were sitting! It was astonishing."

As if to drive home the point, the restaurant's menu featured a specialty drink called Bull in a China Shop—the exact phrase everyone used to describe Zach during his childhood.

"The two signs hit me like a slap in the face," Karleen says. "It was like Zach was saying, 'Mom, Mom, I'm right *here!*'"

Slowly, over time, Karleen began to see glimpses of light in her dark tunnel, many of them sent to her by Zach. In 2022, two years after Zach's passing, Karleen decided she wanted to celebrate her son's life in a big, festive way. She wanted to do something her son would have enjoyed, something immersive and full of light and love. And because, like me, Karleen is a Disney fan, her choice of destination was obvious.

Karleen booked herself a solo trip to Disney World in Florida, to coincide with what would have been her son's thirty-sixth birthday on August 27.

"One more trip around the sun for me and my boy," she told herself.

That is how a plan neither Karleen nor I were ever aware of began to fall into place.

In August 2022, my family and I touched down in Orlando to begin our nine-day Disney adventure. Because our schedule was so tightly packed, we could only spend a single day at Animal Kingdom, one of the popular parks at Disney World.

We'd been to the park before on previous vacations, and normally we ate dinner at a lovely restaurant there called Tiffins. But a few months before the trip, Garrett and I had dinner with friends who recommended we choose a different restaurant, Yak & Yeti. Apparently, it was a hugely popular place to eat, and I worried that even with a few months' notice I might not be able to make a reservation that fit our schedule. Luckily, we were able to book a table for noon on our one day at Animal Kingdom.

The night before our visit to the park, in our hotel room in Orlando, I received a strange but urgent download from the Universe. It was very specific: *Change the time of your lunch reservation from noon to one o'clock.* I turned to Garrett and told him about the odd download, and he said exactly what I was thinking: "Well, that will never happen." Getting a reservation at Yak & Yeti was hard enough, but changing it the night before?

Now, *that* would have been some real Disney magic.

Still, I logged on to the Disney website and gave it a shot. And to my astonishment, I saw that there was, improbably, one single lunch slot still available at Yak & Yeti.

At precisely one o'clock.

I booked the reservation and went to sleep, both confused by the strange instruction and amazed I was able to pull it off.

Many years earlier, Karleen Johnson had lived in Tampa, Florida, about an hour's drive from Disney World, and the theme park became her outlet, her refuge, her place to escape. She bought an annual pass and visited two or three times a month for more than ten years. She was, in other words, a seasoned Disney veteran.

That's why traveling there alone in August 2022 did not faze her; she knew her way around. She spent the morning of August 25 at Animal Kingdom, enjoying all the exhibits and trying to stave off the oppre-sive summer heat. Later on, she had a thought: *An adult beverage might be nice around now.* So, she recalls, she left Animal Kingdom, "popped into the Rainforest Café, bellied up to the bar, and ordered an ice-cold Blue Moon beer with an orange slice on the rim."

As it happened, Karleen sat next to a group of three women talking and laughing and heartily enjoying themselves at the bar. After a few minutes, one of the women, Shay, turned toward Karleen.

"Hey, how are you?" Shay asked her. "Are you here by yourself? Do you come to Disney often? Want to join our little group?"

Shay was friendly—"super crazy friendly, like we'd known each other forever," Karleen remembers. "We all sat there at the bar for the next hour or two just talking and having the best time."

After a while Shay suggested Karleen join her and her friends, Mary

Lou and Connie, for lunch. "Come with us, we're going to the Yak & Yeti!" she said excitedly. Karleen knew how popular that restaurant was, and she also knew that getting a reservation there, on busy summer days, was basically impossible. Yet Shay casually insisted that getting a table there wouldn't be a problem.

"We have a Landry's card!" Shay exclaimed, referring to Landry's Select Club, a nationwide loyalty program that provides access to restaurants like Yak & Yeti without a reservation.

Regrettably, Karleen informed the group, she didn't have a Landry's card of her own.

"Oh, girl, we need to get you one!" Shay said. "Come with us!"

Just like that, Shay and her friends took Karleen under their generous wings and arranged for her to get a Landry's card, and before she knew it Karleen was in Yak & Yeti, flashing her new card and waiting only ten minutes to be seated. A hostess led Karleen and the group up the stairs to their table on the second floor. "Ordinarily, I would never have been at the Yak & Yeti on that day at that time, never ever," Karleen says. "It just wouldn't have been possible."

Karleen and her new friends took their seats at a table and ordered a bunch of food: lettuce wraps, Korean ribs, a handful of sides.

When the food arrived, Karleen happened to glance at the clock to her right.

It was shortly after 1:00 P.M.

Just a few minutes earlier, I'd arrived at Yak & Yeti with Garrett and our two youngest children, Juliet and Hayden. The restaurant, designed to resemble a two-story inn by the same name in Kathmandu, Nepal, was vast and sprawling, with room for hundreds of diners. The kind of place where you could get lost looking for the restroom. The menu made our mouths water—miso salmon, chicken tikka masala, firecracker shrimp, and on and on. A hostess, possibly the same one who later led Karleen to her table, led us to ours on the second floor, by the railings that overlooked the main dining area on the first floor. I sat facing the back of the restaurant, which meant I couldn't see anyone coming up the stairs, and all they could see of me was the back of my head.

A waitress came by to take our order, and just as Garrett was ordering I felt a firm pull—a pull to the table next to ours. I turned my head slightly to the left and saw a woman at the table looking at me. I locked eyes with her, and she locked eyes with me.

"Excuse me," the woman said. "Are you—"

"Laura Lynne Jackson," I said, interrupting, "and I feel like I've been sent here as a sign for you. I feel like I need to give you a hug because I think I am your sign."

I got up and went over and hugged the woman—Karleen Johnson.

"You know, I just happened to look over to my right, and I saw this woman sitting there, and I thought to myself, *Is that Laura Lynne Jackson?*" Karleen recalls. "I did a triple take. I knew you from the photo on your book jacket, and suddenly there you were, and I took a chance and leaned over, and before I could even ask you, you told me you were my sign."

Karleen and I hugged each other, both of us essentially strangers but both of us entirely sure that we were meant to be precisely where we were at that exact moment.

"You saved my life," Karleen told me. "My son left on his own terms three years ago, and your book saved my life."

Karleen was crying and I was crying, and I told her, "Your son put me in your path. He's been with you all day, and he brought you here. This is him showing you that he's still with you every step of the way."

By then, Karleen's new friend Shay was crying, too, though she had no idea why. She asked Karleen what was going on, and Karleen explained the circumstances of our unlikely meeting.

"I read this book about signs, and Zach has sent me all these signs, and then I came here to celebrate him and now here she is! This is Laura! She wrote the book, and now she's right here!"

"Oh my gosh!" Shay said. "I can't believe this is happening!"

In fact, I explained to Shay, Karleen's son, Zach, was actually guiding Shay, too. He'd been guiding her actions, steering her into position, making this crazy meeting possible. As I explained all this, Karleen's face just lit up.

"That's when it hit me," she says. "Shay and her friends had been so instantly friendly, so immersed in making sure I had a good time and so insistent on being with me, and *that's exactly how Zach was with people*. He could walk into any place and make new friends and become the ringleader who made sure everyone had fun. Zach had a plan to pull us all together!"

Karleen and I sat down and talked for a while. It wasn't a reading, because there was no need for a reading—Zach had made his presence, and his intentions, readily apparent. He'd done it in a way that Karleen couldn't possibly have missed even if she'd tried. And, as if all his machinations weren't enough, Zach pulled out one last bit of magic from his bag of tricks.

It happened toward the end of our meals when Shay opened her fortune cookie. There, in tiny black type, this message:

> *Our brightest blazes of gladness are*
> *commonly kindled by unexpected sparks.*

Shay had been the spark. She had kindled a blaze of gladness for Karleen. Zach and the Other Side used her—guided her—to play a part in a truly miraculous moment for Karleen, the most powerful affirmation she'd ever received that her beautiful son was still with her, every day.

"Well, now Zach's just showing off for you," I told her.

Even our waitress, who witnessed our emotional meeting and learned the details along the way, left a wonderful note for me at our table:

> *Thank you so much for being open and sharing kind and positive*
> *energy with others. I hope you and your family have*
> *a beautiful rest of your day and a wonderful trip.*

At the bottom of the note the waitress drew a tiny butterfly.

. . .

Without question, meeting Karleen in Yak & Yeti was one of the most profound and meaningful experiences I've ever had with the Other Side. I've thought back on our meeting quite often, and it *still* amazes me that it happened. Think about it: I was *not* supposed to be at Disney World in August 2022 (my original plan was for July 2020). And I was *not* supposed to be at Yak & Yeti (our usual spot was a different restaurant). I was not supposed to be able to get a reservation there, and I definitely was not supposed to be able to push that reservation back one hour on almost no notice. And once all of that happened, the hostess could have led us to a table anywhere within the cavernous two floors of the restaurant—conceivably to a spot a football field away from Karleen Johnson.

And yet—

—I *did* end up at Disney World on August 25, 2022. And I *did* get a reservation to Yak & Yeti. And somehow I *did* manage to push it back one hour at the last moment. And then, at precisely 1:00 P.M., I was guided to a table that wound up being *directly* next to Karleen Johnson's table.

That all happened.

Remember, too, that Karleen wasn't supposed to be at Yak & Yeti either. She had no reservation, she was at Disney all alone, and she'd already left Animal Kingdom to grab a beer at the Rainforest Café on her way out and had no intention of fighting her way back into the park. It was only after a trio of exceptionally friendly strangers literally swept her back into the park to dine with them at Yak & Yeti that she, too, found herself on the second floor of a massive restaurant, just a few feet away from me.

What did this all mean?

It means that we are all angels to one another. It means we are all being guided through our journeys here on earth, just as Karleen and I were magically guided to each other. Karleen's son, Zach, didn't just tug on a string or two to make the meeting happen—*he put boots on the ground and enlisted a whole team of helpers to pull it off.* What it means is that we can all play roles for each other in our lives as long as we honor and trust the pulls we feel from the Universe.

As long as we remain *open to being guided.*

It means that none of us are truly strangers, and none of us are ever alone. It means that we are all connected—*all part of the same big story.*

For Karleen Johnson, our meeting in Yak & Yeti helped ease some of the pain she felt at losing Zach. The way in which it happened was just so perfect, so unlikely—so *Zach.* "When his girlfriend Lisa and I were reading *Signs,* I remember feeling that the book was saving my life and getting me out of that dark tunnel. I said to Lisa, 'What I wouldn't give to meet this woman,'" Karleen says. "And so Zach said, 'You wanted to be in her presence? Well, here she is.' Just like that. He knew it was something I really needed, and he made it happen. Zach wanted to leave a legacy."

Zach Johnson-McDonnell did indeed leave a legacy, and he is adding to it every day, from the Other Side.

Zach's legacy is one of intense connection, of the unbreakable bonds of family, of providing solace and comfort, of deep caring and unending love. It is a legacy of enduring consciousness, of faith and trust in our ability to communicate with our loved ones wherever they are.

It is a legacy of signs and messages, chief among them this:

Stay open to being guided. Because a guided life is an illuminated life, and such a life is beautiful—full of meaning and connection and love.

After writing this chapter, I was guided to share the names of these organizations that give dogs to veterans suffering from PTSD. I encourage you to look into them and help if you can:

- Canine Companions

- K9s For Warriors

- Pups4Patriots

- Paws Assisting Veterans

- Paws of War

For it matters not, how much we own,
the cars . . . the house . . . the cash.
What matters is how we live and love
and how we spend our dash.

LINDA ELLIS

2

72

Have you ever had this experience?

A number pops up in the course of your day, and you start seeing that number everywhere. Maybe it's your thirtieth birthday, and for the rest of the day you see the number 30 on signs, receipts, license plates, over and over. Maybe you randomly open a book to page 30, or you hear someone say the word *thirty*, or you find a quarter and a nickel in a drawer.

Then you think, *Wow, that's really weird.*

Some people call that occurrence *frequency illusion*, which is a combination of selective attention (our brains are really good at noticing information we deem relevant) and confirmation bias (we prioritize things that confirm our beliefs). In other words, you see the number 30 a lot because that number is on your brain that day.

People who think this way might dismiss the sudden prevalence of that number in their life as illusory.

But there *is* another explanation.

What if the Universe is putting that number in your path as a way to send you a message?

The idea that numbers have a significance beyond their numerical value is actually a very old one. Back in the fourth century, Saint Augustine of Hippo wrote, "Numbers are the Universal language offered by the deity to humans as confirmation of the truth." He believed numbers conveyed secret relationships that could only be interpreted by our individual minds. That kind of thinking still exists today, and is often referred to as *numerology*.

I believe that certain numbers reoccurring is not always a coincidence or an illusion. In my experience, our Teams of Light often use numbers as signs, as a language of sorts, because numbers are clear and direct and specific—and because numbers are everywhere. I've been part of hundreds of readings in which numbers have played a major role.

Being open to the secret relevance of numbers is part of living an illuminated life. My good friend Tara, whose experience with the number 72 is a truly astonishing story, is proof of that.

Tara's story begins with her father, Michael, as loving and devoted a family man as there ever was. "He was incredible," says Tara, a Long Island native and the mother of two children. "He was strong, smart, hardworking, a man of integrity, a big guy at six-foot-three, but a sweet, gentle giant who loved staying active. And he loved us all unconditionally."

Not once can Tara remember her father coming through the front door after a day of work without a big smile on his face—evidence of his genuine happiness at being with his family. "Many years later my mother told me that if my father ever had a bad day at work he would wait outside the front door for ten minutes so he wouldn't bring his bad day to us," Tara remembers. "And he was always the one dad who would get off the train and come straight to all our games still in his suit, just so he could cheer us on. He was always there for us."

Sadly, in his later years, Michael was diagnosed with Parkinson's. After a bad fall, he moved to a nursing home with around-the-clock care. Tara's mother, Lynn, sat with him at the nursing home every single day, without fail, and they even celebrated their fiftieth wedding anniversary there. But as time went on, Michael began to slip away. "It was a gradual decline into a world of Parkinson's and dementia," Tara says. "We all lived in that world with him, in his world. He could barely speak and no longer knew where he was. My aunt would say, 'He's half in heaven.'" Yet right up to the day he passed, his gentle, loving nature was on vivid display for everyone who crossed his path.

"At his funeral, in addition to all his family and friends, half the nursing home staff showed up," Tara recalls. "Two head nurses, two aides, the people that ran activities, the office workers, the nutritionist, you name it. That's the kind of man he was, and so many people showing up was a testament to how he impacted everyone around him."

Tara's connection with her father on the Other Side began the very night of his crossing.

She was on her way to the nursing home when she had a strange feeling that her father had passed. "When I got there, I was ten minutes too late to see him, but I already knew he was gone," she says. That night, as she sat in her living room grieving and crying, a driveway light began flickering like a strobe light, flashing throughout the house. It flashed that way for a long time.

Great, Tara thought at first, *now I need to get a new bulb.*

But her second thought was completely different.

He is trying to talk to us, Tara thought. *After being trapped in that condition for so long, I'm sure he has a lot to say.*

Sure enough, Tara found the driveway light wasn't broken, and a new bulb wasn't needed. But after that night, it never flickered again.

The lights in her kitchen, however, started blinking two weeks later. "I have eight high-hat lights recessed in the ceiling, and all of a sudden they just turned off," Tara says. "Two minutes later, they turned back on. My son was there, and I told him, 'That's your Pop Pop.' But he was skeptical, so I told him if he didn't believe me he should just tell Pop Pop to turn the lights off again."

Her son did just that—and the kitchen lights turned right off.

"We tried it a few more times, and each time we said it, my father did it again," says Tara, "and when we stopped, the lights stayed on the rest of the day."

The electrical messages turned out to be just the opening act.

At her father's funeral, Tara's uncle Bob, a little old man in his eighties, asked if he could read a poem at the gravesite. The poem, by Linda Ellis, was called "The Dash," and it was about how the dash between the dates of birth and death on gravestones symbolized the quality of the lives we led. "Uncle Bob talked about how my dad lived his life and made the most of his dash and of every single moment he had," Tara says. "Whether he was traveling the world or shopping at Costco, my father really knew how to live."

Tara had never heard the poem before, and it moved her deeply. She resolved to live her life the same way her father lived his, making the most of the dash.

A month later, her mother, Lynn, was in Tara's home going through Michael's paperwork when she collapsed and fell into Tara's arms. She was suffering a stroke. Years of caring for her husband had taken their toll. Had Lynn not been with her daughter at the time, she might have died. But after a hospital stay, she was given a clean bill of health—something she hadn't had in all her years of caring for Michael instead of herself. "We believed it was my father who made sure we all stayed close to each other after his passing, so that I could be there and call 911 and get my mother the help she needed," says Tara, who, in the weeks that followed, was there to drive her mother on all her errands and doctor visits.

One day soon after, Tara and her mother spent the day going through paperwork related to her dad's crossing. There were a lot of issues to tend to, and they both felt overwhelmed and deflated and especially crushed by Michael's passing. The reality of his loss hit them deeply. But still, they had to get the paperwork to the post office and run other errands, and they got in the car with heavy hearts.

While doing part of their errands, they drove past a post office neither Tara nor her mother usually went to, and decided to stop there. As Tara was patiently holding the door open for her mother, her attention was suddenly drawn to something on the ground off to the side. Tara moved in for a closer look.

What had caught Tara's attention was a small decorative stone on the sidewalk. Tara could see something written on it in yellow and white. She picked up the stone and read what it said:

"MAKE THE MOST OF YOUR DASH"

Tara and her mother looked at each other and started to cry. "We knew we had just received an incredible message from my father," Tara says now. "And the message was 'I am free now, free of all my medical problems, and so are you.' It reminded us that he was right there with us, guiding us in our lives, just like he guided us to that stone. His love hadn't gone anywhere. It was his way of saying that he wanted us to live engaged, beautiful lives."

Yet the most impressive and consistent signs from Michael involve a number.

I spoke with Tara after her father's crossing, and I advised her to ask him to send her a specific sign. Tara knew her father's college football jersey number was 72. So she and the rest of her family asked Michael to send them a 72.

He started small. "I ran out to get some grab-and-go cold cuts, and the weight was .72 ounces," Tara says. Later, when she turned on the TV, a basketball game was on. "The score," she says, "was 72–72." She got an email advertising a sale—"a 72-hour blowout sale." A Facebook post she looked at had 72 likes.

On and on it went. She flipped on the radio and heard a DJ say, "That song was written in 1972." She randomly bought a box of coffee cups—a 72-count box. The number of online reviews for a product—72. The battery life on her cell phone—72 percent. The temperature readout in a store—72 degrees. The bus in front of her as she sat in traffic—No. 72. And a receipt from a store that featured her father's first name—*Michael* Kors—was for a grand total of $172.72.

Then there was Tara's nephew, Shaun.

At high school, Shaun signed up for the football squad. "He asked for his Pop-Pop's jersey number, 72," says Tara. "He really, really wanted it, but they went through the entire box of available jerseys and didn't find that number."

Shaun was ready to give up when he heard someone say, "Wait a minute, there's a whole other box of jerseys over there." Sure enough, a second box was mostly out of sight in another part of the room. When they opened that nearly overlooked box, the jersey on the very top of the pile was 72. "I now have a picture of Shaun in that jersey, just like my dad," says Tara. "I knew my father wouldn't let him down."

When I was invited on *The Dr. Oz Show* to talk about how our loved ones on the Other Side are still with us and show us this by sending us signs, I asked Tara to come on the show with me, so she could tell the story of the dash. Tara was nervous, but she wound up doing a really great job. After the show, we left the studio and Tara said, "Dad, if you're listening, I hope you're proud of me."

Just then, Tara says, "I turned around and saw a street sign."

The enormous sign said:

M72—FREEDOM PLACE

Tara and I looked at each other, and we both started to cry. She was always saying that in death, her father finally found freedom from his disease, so Michael sent her a sign with both the number 72 and the word *freedom* in it. And also a dash.

"I knew right then, and I know every day, that my father is always with us," Tara says. "We feel him in our hearts. He continues to find ways to be part of the family, which was all he ever wanted, and is *still* all he wants. And we are forever grateful to him for that."

More than anything, Tara's story serves as a reminder that we are all connected to, and guided by, our loved ones who have crossed. They find ways to show us and communicate with us, so that we may not be stuck in our grief, but rather be free to go on living our best dash. They are always urging us to pursue lives of joy, meaning, connection, and love, illuminated by the knowing that they are right there at our side for every step, celebrating it all with us.

3

Wrong Number

I'm not an especially tech-savvy person, beyond making sure our router is plugged in so my kids can play video games or watch shows on their iPads. But I do marvel at the ways we share information in this speed-of-light technological age. And the basic system at the heart of it all—the data network—is, I believe, a pretty good analogy for how the Universe works.

A data network is a system that figures out how to send information from one point in the network to another—from, say, a movie-streaming site to its customers. The information, or data, can be delivered in many different ways—through circuit switches, leased lines, packet switching networks, point-to-point transmission, and on and on.

For our purposes, let's say the massive information hub at the heart of the data network is the Universe itself.

And we, the people, are each an access point in the network.

So—how does the Universe transmit its steady stream of data to us, the access points?

The answer is the same for the Universe as it is for any data network—the information gets sent to us in *lots* of different ways.

In my book *Signs*, I wrote about all the various worldly things our Teams of Light (God energy, our spirit guides, and loved ones who have crossed) can and do use to send us messages. Birds, coins, license plates, electrical disturbances, purple elephants—the list is practically endless. The point is that, as a data network, the Universe is exceptionally clever and resourceful in getting its data to us.

But the network doesn't work unless we, the access points, are fully open to receiving new information.

In other words, we have to be *plugged in.*

The story I'm about to share is a story about how to stay open to our hardworking Teams of Light, no matter how utterly strange or absurd the delivery method they choose.

It's a story about how to plug into the guidance.

Growing up in Farmingdale, Long Island, Joseph M. never thought about getting messages from the Other Side. He had an uncle who claimed his house was haunted, "and another uncle who said he could see family members who passed in his dreams," he says, but other than that, communication between the two sides just wasn't on his radar.

That changed after he got married and had two daughters, Emma and Sarah. In 2008, Joseph, a real estate attorney, and his wife, a paralegal, noticed that their younger daughter, Sarah, then five, began having stomach troubles. She'd lost weight, was often pale, and just didn't feel well. Still, after multiple tests, her pediatrician insisted nothing was wrong with her. "All we knew was that Sarah kept having the problems and they kept getting worse," Joseph says.

Around that time, Joseph also began receiving an unusual number of phone calls on his cell phone that were wrong numbers. The messages left were all roughly the same: "Hi, Cathy, I saw your flyer. I'm trying to get in touch with you. Please call me."

Who was Cathy, and why were the people trying to reach her by calling Joseph's number?

Meanwhile, Joseph's daughter's condition worsened. She lost more weight and looked ashen. There were more tests but still no diagnosis. Joseph was running out of ideas.

One day, he got yet another phone call from someone trying to reach Cathy. He happened to answer this call, and the caller asked about some kind of group meeting. Joseph asked what number she meant to call. Finally, he solved the mystery—the caller was off by one digit. Joseph's area code was 516, while Cathy's was 561.

Then Joseph called Cathy and told her about the repeated mix-ups, and asked her to check her flyers for typos.

"By the way, what kind of group are you running?" he asked.

Cathy said, "It's for people with celiac disease. It's a gastrointestinal issue. People who have it can't digest gluten, and they lose weight and show a failure to thrive."

Joseph was astonished. *Those were Sarah's exact symptoms.*

(In 2008, unlike today, celiac disease, an autoimmune disorder in which the protein gluten damages the small intestine, was considered rare and diagnoses were not common.)

Yet even after speaking with Cathy, the message didn't quite get through. "For whatever reason," Joseph says, "it just didn't click with me." So, in quick succession, two more messages for him arrived.

First, Joseph went to a business dinner and sat across from a woman who randomly volunteered that she'd just been diagnosed with something called celiac disease. "Then she recited all the symptoms, and they were the same as Sarah's," Joseph says. Now he was beginning to turn this over in his mind.

Then, two days later, another person who crossed paths with Joseph mentioned having celiac disease.

"After that," Joseph says, "I knew someone was looking out for me."

Joseph and his wife took Sarah to a gastrointestinal specialist, who quickly diagnosed her with celiac disease.

"And from that day on," Joseph says, "I never got another wrong number asking to speak with Cathy."

The specialist prescribed a medication and advised a gluten-free diet, and within months Sarah's condition improved dramatically. "Her skin tone changed, she put on weight and grew four inches, and she became a totally different kid," Joseph happily recalls. "All the issues just peeled away, and she had this beautiful glow to her."

So how did Joseph, a rational attorney who never entertained thoughts of supernatural phenomena, explain what happened?

"For me, there was no other way to explain it but to say that someone was directing me to look into this disease," he says. "There is no other way to put it all together—the wrong numbers, the two other people who had celiac disease. We thought about my wife's father, who had passed away right around the time we started dating, and we finally understood who was behind all the calls and messages. It was Grandpa Fred, looking out for his granddaughter from heaven."

Those messages from Grandpa Fred forever changed the way Joseph looked at the world. In fact, he looked back in time to reconsider old events from his new, illuminated perspective. When his firstborn daughter, Emma, was just sixteen months old, Joseph saw her huddled in the corner of the living room of their new house, giggling at something.

"Who are you talking to, sweetie? What's so funny?" Joseph asked.

"Mr. Peter," Emma answered. Joseph had no idea who Mr. Peter was—he figured she was making up a little imaginative game.

But the same thing continued to happen. Emma loved playing in that same corner, always seeming to happily chat away with an imaginary friend named Peter. But then Joseph needed to look at the deed to their house to handle some paperwork. When they had purchased their home, Joseph and his wife dealt with a widow, Mrs. N. After looking at the deed, Joseph was stunned to learn that Mrs. N.'s first name was *Emma* and her deceased husband's was *Peter.*

Apparently, Peter's conversations with his wife had not ended when she sold the house.

A few months later, Joseph caught his daughter Emma speaking to someone in the back seat of the car.

"No, Emma a good girl," he heard her say about herself. "Yes, Emma do that."

"Who are you talking to?" he asked her.

Matter-of-factly, Emma said, "Grandpa Fred."

"She had never met him or known of her grandfather," Joseph says now. "Yet there she was having a full-blown conversation with him."

One year later, Joseph was with Emma in a Costco when suddenly she blurted out, "Nanny is here." Nanny was her great-grandmother, Joseph's grandmother, who had passed a few weeks earlier after a long battle with Alzheimer's disease. While they had often brought Emma to visit Nanny, Joseph was never really sure that Nanny understood that Emma was her first great-granddaughter.

Startled to hear Emma mention Nanny, Joseph asked, "Emma, what do you mean?"

The child pointed at the ceiling.

"Nanny's up there."

Joseph looked up and saw a single, solitary balloon directly over them, clinging to the ceiling. As soon as he spotted it, the balloon began to move across the ceiling and then fly out of sight.

Joseph knew what this message meant: Nanny *did* understand that Emma was her great-granddaughter.

"My wife and I have accepted that we have family looking over and guiding us," Joseph says. "We are now open to these things happening. The line that separates us from the Other Side is much, much thinner than we think. There are people looking out for us, and they are trying really hard to point us in the right direction. The same people who watched out for us when they were alive—they are still doing it, guiding us."

When I speak of being guided on a path to an illuminated life, Joseph's frame of mind is what I mean. He decided to be open to the possibility of such communications, and because he was, he found a way to help his daughter beat back a very serious illness.

I have a special appreciation for Joseph's story, because a very similar thing happened to me. When my daughter Ashley came down with a crippling, destructive illness that no one could diagnose, it was a message from the Other Side—in the form of a medical brochure I came very close to not reading—that pointed me in the right direction and helped begin the process of healing for Ashley.

"That is the trick: Once it begins to happen, you have to be open to *anything*," Joseph says. "In fact, focus on the elements in your life that you don't normally pay a lot of attention to. The balloon on the ceiling, for instance. If you do that, those loved ones who are watching over you will get you the messages you need."

If everything around you seems dark,
look again, you may be the light.

RUMI

4

The Accident

This chapter tells the story of a miracle disguised as a car crash But it's also about a person who exemplifies living an illuminated life as well as anyone I know.

Her name is Sarah Lewis, and she is someone with a brilliantly creative and expressive mind whose every step seems to light a beacon for others to follow. She is the John L. Loeb Associate Professor of the Humanities and Associate Professor of African and African American Studies at Harvard University, and she also received graduate degrees from Oxford and Yale. She has held curatorial positions at the Museum of Modern Art in New York City and the Tate Modern in London, serves on several prestigious boards, and was a part of President Obama's Arts Policy Committee. Her 2014 book, *The Rise: Creativity, the Gift of Failure and the Search for Mastery* (one of many books she has written or is writing), was an extraordinary bestseller translated into seven languages, and in 2010, Oprah put her on her annual *O Power List*, calling Sarah "a person who seeks out different angles to questions."

Did I mention that when I met Sarah, she was only forty-two?

Sarah is a uniquely gifted thinker who focuses on the intersection of visual representation, racial justice, and democracy to champion the power of art. What's most remarkable to me, however, is how she manages to do all this without ever sacrificing her childlike excitement. "Sometimes I say, 'I don't research, I just *search*,'" Sarah explains. "It happens with a sense of wonder and curiosity."

There is another part of Sarah's life that she doesn't talk about all that often—the feeling that her connection to the Universe allows her to access information in nontraditional ways.

"I've always believed my mother had psychic abilities, and I believe I do as well," she says. "As a scholar, that can be hard to integrate into your life, but I have learned to trust that my instincts are a force for good and are there to protect me."

Sarah points to many instances throughout her life when she has felt an "impulse" to do something—call a friend, hail a taxi, wear a sweater—and wound up on an unexpected journey of discovery and affirmation. She has also had many moments of what she calls knowing—feeling certain that something that hadn't happened yet was going to happen. Like the time when Sarah was in her early twenties and decided to be late for an event she was attending with her boyfriend just so she could stay on the phone a bit longer with a close friend. "My boyfriend thought it was rude of me to make us late, but I knew I needed to talk to my friend that day," Sarah says. "I just *knew* it. Two days later, my friend died."

It was these experiences, many of which are familiar to me (I also remember "knowing" a close friend was going to pass before he did), that eventually brought Sarah and me together. And then, when I gave Sarah a reading in 2021, I learned about the car accident.

Actually, there were *two* car accidents.

The first one happened in January 2020. Sarah, who lives in both New York City and Cambridge, Massachusetts, made plans to meet a friend for coffee and called an Uber to pick her up. Her driver arrived in a Honda Civic, and when she got in, "I could tell right away the driver was distracted by something," she says. As Sarah sat in the back and texted her goddaughter *Happy New Year*, a yellow taxicab T-boned the car at an intersection. "I blacked out for a while," Sarah remembers. "My doctor said I'd be fine, but I felt a little off, and months later I slurred a word during a speech and felt a very bad headache." A top neurologist diagnosed a concussion that took Sarah several months to recover from.

The second car crash—what Sarah calls "the miracle"—happened later that year, on July 10.

The story of that accident starts a week earlier, when Sarah bought her very first new car. "The first thing I did was christen the car by sitting in it in the garage and putting my hand on the dashboard and saying, 'Thank you for protecting me,'" Sarah recalls. It wasn't something she'd planned to say; it just seemed like the right thing to do at the time.

Then something odd happened. When she left the garage, she saw what looked like an exact duplicate of her car—the same make, model, and color—parked across the street. This car, however, "had all of these duct-taped dent marks all over it because it had been in a collision and was still under repair," she says. "I remember seeing that and thinking, *This is a sign about something that is on my path.* And I was unnerved by it."

One week later, on a warm Friday evening, Sarah got ready to drive from New York to Cambridge, a roughly four-hour trip. She'd just come back from physical therapy on her neck and she felt good, and the rain, which had been coming down all day, had finally stopped. Everything was in place for the trip. Just before she left, she says, "I heard this voice say, 'Well, if you're going to do this, at least put on a sweater.'" It was July, and the evening wasn't particularly cool, but even so, Sarah slipped on a black long-sleeved sweater and set off.

Because it was a Friday, the weekend traffic on Manhattan's Henry Hudson Parkway was heavy and slow. The parkway was still partially flooded along the narrow shoulders. There was a break in the traffic, and Sarah was in the middle of three lanes driving around 30 mph. She glanced to her right and saw another car hurtling toward her.

"The car was hydroplaning," she says. "The driver had lost control of his car and was coming into my lane from the right."

The car began to pinball, as if it had hit a railing, but it was still on a collision course with Sarah. In that moment, she says, "it was clear I was going to crash, and so I swerved to my left to get out of the way, and now I am headed straight into a concrete divider."

The next several events are what Sarah believes constitute the miracle—and they all happened in less than two seconds.

"I remember I cried out," Sarah says. "I made this decision, or maybe a declaration to God, that it wasn't my time to go. I don't think I've ever felt as clear about wanting to live, and I basically said, 'God, both you and I know this car is out of control, and we have to make this right. We need the outcome to be okay.' Not like I was directing God on what to do, but, in a way, I sort of was."

Suddenly the front and side airbags deployed, and Sarah's car plowed into the concrete divider.

Inside, Sarah did not feel the brunt of the impact. Instead, "I felt like I was in this cloud as I crashed. And when I hit the divider, my vision split. I could still see the highway and every earthly thing happening. But at the same time, just as clear and just as real and valid—I could see these remarkable bands of light."

Sarah describes the bands of light as resembling a cosmic nebula—a massive cloud of gas and dust that serves as a nursery for new stars. Nebulas look like giant swirls of multicolored cotton candy. "These bands were coalescing and emanating toward me, suspending me, connecting to me, supporting me, and it was clear all these bands of colorful light were different dimensions of other moments in time, other experiences, all rooted in love," Sarah says, still sounding awed by the spectacle. "It was like a mammoth bird in the sky unfurling its wings and saying, 'Oh, you need me? I'm happy to lift you up.'"

And as these bands of light filled the left side of her vision, on the right side she saw boxes that held images—"images of things I have lived the past year and of things awaiting me in my future. And all of that happened in maybe the span of 1.5 seconds. An entire conversation between all there is, and all there is to come."

Sarah's car came to a shuddering stop. She'd been on a handless call with a friend at the time of the crash, and her friend, a doctor, told her to stay calm and reminded her the car was designed to absorb most of the impact. Which is precisely what happened. Still, the car's engine was smoking, "and I realized I needed to get out of the car because it might catch fire," Sarah says. "But what if I got out and another car hit me? Should I stay or go?" Sarah pushed open the driver-side door and stepped out onto the parkway.

Miraculously, no car struck her during or after the crash. Another car did pull up and stop in front of her, and a man stepped out.

"Do you need help?" he asked. "Are you okay?"

Sarah answered, "No, I'm not okay. I need help."

From that moment on, the mysterious man "literally took care of everything," says Sarah. "He called for EMTs and he talked to the police when they arrived and he got the license plate of the other car and gathered what I needed for the hospital, and he protected me as I stood there on the open road. It was like, when he looked at me earlier, he and I just communicated and downloaded everything he needed to know to be my caretaker. Even a paramedic who came up to me asked if my husband was going to come with me to the hospital. I had to say, 'I don't even know this man.'"

Much later on, Sarah got the chance to ask the man—whose name is Benjamin—why he stopped to help her.

"I looked at you and your face answered that question," he told her. "Your body was there, but your spirit wasn't."

The front of Sarah's car was completely pancaked, like a flattened accordion. The rest of the car was a total wreck. One paramedic asked Sarah if there was anyone else in the car. "I realized they asked me that," she says, "because based on the crash and the condition of the car, they assumed there must have been a fatality, and there I was walking around on my own. The other EMTs and police stared at me in disbelief that I'd survived."

In fact, doctors at St. Luke's Hospital in upper Manhattan found only a single scratch on Sarah's right arm, caused by the airbag. The pinky on her right hand, struck by a piece of metal on the airbag, was sore and didn't bend properly. But otherwise there were no lacerations, no internal injuries, no broken bones. "The doctors were surprised by how little damage there was," she says.

Sarah, however, was more shaken by what she'd experienced in those 1.5 seconds. "After the crash, when my car stopped, I stopped seeing those beams and bands of light," she says. "And I kept looking around and saying to people standing there, 'Did you see them? Did you see that?' But they were gone."

The experience had a deep and profound effect on her. "I could not have had a more powerful response in that moment," she says. "The intensity and the force of my desire and intention to live, to survive the crash, brought forth an equally powerful response from the Universe, and somehow I was able to maneuver that vehicle to have the outcome that I did, and avoid what could have clearly been a fatal crash."

What, exactly, happened to Sarah on the parkway that night? Why did her vision suddenly split? What were those bands of light? How did she make it out of the wreck in one piece?

Sarah believes she has the answer.

"When I saw the bands of light connecting to and supporting me, I understood that our spirit guides are right here—*right here next to us*," she says. "I will never forget the intensity of the grace I felt, or my disbelief at the proximity of the guidance we have."

One other oddity stood out for Sarah. When she was young, she had a friend who lived in an apartment complex that overlooked the very same stretch of the Henry Hudson Parkway where the crash occurred. What, she wondered, were the chances of that?

"I remember sitting there looking out that window and just staring at the highway," she says. "It was as if, as a girl, I had a sense that something important would happen to me in that exact spot."

When Sarah told a close friend and colleague about the crash, and about what happened in those 1.5 seconds, the friend remarked that it sounded similar to the way I described my own psychic process in my first book, *The Light Between Us*. Later on, after a mutual friend introduced Sarah and me, I went back and reread some passages in that book, and I found that Sarah's friend had been right.

I explained how, during a typical reading, "a field of vision emerges. It is a blank rectangular field that appears in my mind." On the screen's left side, "the sitter's spirit guides appear as points of light. Spirit guides are evolved spiritual beings who act as mentors and help guide us on our paths here; our spirit guides aren't people we know from our lives here; they are assigned to us before we arrive here on earth and they guide us always. I see the sitter's core aura, which is a color map of the person's soul path here."

The right side of my screen, I explained, was reserved for "letters and words and names and images" sent by our protective loved ones on the Other Side. These images and names and words arrive as their own points of light, and they represent "the energy of our visitors from the Other Side." I even described one particular reading during which the left side of my screen/vision was filled by "a dazzling array of colors, like a rainbow, only fuller and more intense, infinitely more intense, colors upon colors upon colors, white, blue, pink, green, all of them pure and vibrant and explosive"—a description similar to Sarah's recollection of her bands of light as "coalescing and emanating toward me, suspending me, connecting to me, supporting me."

The very title of my first book, in fact, is a reference to these brilliant bands or beams of light, which I have also called *cords of light*. These cords, I wrote, "tie us to those we love and can never be broken, not even when we cross. They don't even fray; in fact, they can even be strengthened."

Perhaps the simplest way to put it is that these cords of light represent a beautiful, powerful energy that binds us to our guides and loved ones on the Other Side.

When Sarah reached out to me through our mutual friend and asked me for a reading, she did so because "I was still in a place of needing to process this trauma or miracle, whichever you want to call it," she says. "I went in very open and excited to talk about what I saw as the post-event chapter of my life."

As for me, I went into the reading knowing nothing about Sarah's past or family, or about her accident. But during the reading an incredible amount of information came through. In fact, the reading went on for two and a half hours and morphed into more of a deep conversation than a reading, as together we explored the remarkable events of the crash, how they had affected her, and what it all meant.

"During the call I was in my apartment sitting by the window with a big moon in the sky, over the Hudson River, and Laura would bring up people close to me as if she knew precisely who they were, right down to the color of their shoelaces," Sarah says. "I just sat there listening with my mouth hanging open. I guess I have a ton of guides, because it was like an entourage showed up."

Most of what I shared with Sarah was merely an affirmation of what she already knew. It was clear to me that she was, as she believed, highly intuitive and empathic, and that the experience of the crash was something she saw as a valuable tool to explore the many dimensions and connections that make up her life on earth.

"The reading was a confirmation of what words alone could not express for me," Sarah says. "Laura's download, what she was describing to me, I already knew it. She even said at one point, 'But you know all of this better than I do.'"

I also told Sarah that the trauma had not swallowed her up, and that she was now stepping into it and seeing it for the miracle it was. And to be able to see it that way, Sarah later explained, "helped me get over the trauma of it."

Sarah understood that the crash was something that was destined to happen along her path. "I mean, I already knew it was going to happen seven days earlier, when I thanked my car for protecting me, and when I saw that other, damaged version of my car on the street," she says. "And the night I set out on the trip, and my guides said, 'Get a sweater' and I needed that sweater because I had to stand out in the open on the highway for a long time. It was one of those things that I had on my heart that I have sensed was about to happen."

The question is, *Why* did the crash have to happen at all?

"Well, one wishes that it didn't always have to take a crash to do it," Sarah says. "But I now understand why some people who have experienced trauma like this say they would have it happen all over again. That they wouldn't trade the experience for anything. That is how I felt. I remember thinking, when the car stopped and it was smoking, *What am I going to do?* And in that moment, I walked out of a burning car to save my life. And once you have done that, it changes what you think is worth your energy on the planet. Even when I got out of that car and I was standing there on the road, I remember thinking, *Do you see what a miracle just this one second of your being is?* It gave me a new freedom and liberation."

Sarah now sees the crash as both a demarcation—an event that separates one part of her life from another—*and* a continuation of what she was already doing and thinking. "Yes, I have been profoundly changed," she says. "But there are ways to get to this state without the trauma, and in a way what occurred is just a continuation of all the work I had done up to that point."

The work Sarah refers to is beautifully encapsulated in her book *The Rise*, an explosion of energy and creativity that to me also serves as a primer on how to live an illuminated life.

Sarah's book touches on an incredible array of vibrant and vital top-

ics that reflect the messages I receive from the Other Side—the wisdom meant to guide us onto our highest life paths. She discusses how
failure is a requisite part of the creative process; how childlike wonder
often leads to innovation; how vulnerability is the strongest part of us;
how surrendering "to the fact of death, not the idea of it, [gives us] license to live more fully, to see life differently" (words Sarah wrote before her accident).

Here are Sarah's insights into just three of those topics—topics that
are part and parcel of living an illuminated life.

Creativity

Sarah believes that failure—or what she calls a "near win"—is essential
to the process of creating anything meaningful.

"It's about the *propulsion* that comes from the near win—having a
sense of productive incompletion," she explains. "Look at Cézanne.
Cézanne didn't sign 90 percent of his paintings. Michelangelo thought
the Sistine Chapel was horrible. Faulkner had envisioned a different
ending for *The Sound and the Fury*. They saw their work as near wins."

In fact, when one interviewer asked Faulkner what criterion he used
to rank America's best writers, he replied, "The criterion is failure. My
feeling is that we all fail, that none of it is as good as we all wanted it to
be. None of my stuff is as good as I wanted it to be. That's why I keep
writing another one." Faulkner believed his classic and challenging
novel *The Sound and the Fury* was "the most gallant, the most magnificent failure" of his career.

Why is it so important to embrace our failures as we aspire to be
better? "There is a spiritual dimension to the creative process, a greater
plan in mind," Sarah says. "What we produce within ourselves, and
how we are propelled down the path, represents a connection to the
world that we should honor. It's like how the magic of the everyday
encounter is part of a grander narrative that we are all a part of. There
is a larger force at play."

In Sarah's view, one person's creative work is similar to the way musicians surrender their individual talents and prowess to the greater power and force of the entire orchestra.

"Everyone is playing their part, but there is an additional quality, a grandeur, that is just *there*," Sarah says. "Living an illuminated life requires a certain humility—the idea that you are playing your part in a much grander scheme."

Sarah offers a wonderful example of embracing failure in her book—the four-hundred-year-old Japanese art of kintsugi.

Kintsugi is the art of putting broken pottery pieces together again using lacquer mixed with precious metals such as gold. The gold is intended not to hide the break, as glue might, but instead to *highlight* it. The gold also ensures that the pottery *will be stronger at the broken spots*. "The cracks are what make it even more glorious," Sarah says. "Part of what makes creativity so inspiring is this theme of light passing through the most unlikeliest of places. A crack is just something that lets the light pass through. That is what *The Rise* is all about—all these innovations that come out of unusual and improbable foundations. Being open to these larger plans and larger forces."

In other words, we can embrace each failure as a unique opportunity to create something even more beautiful. If we work on viewing failure this way, we become open to seeing the light of inspiration that passes through the cracks and broken spaces.

Childlike Wonder

Another way of thinking that can help us lead illuminated lives is to embrace the childlike wonder we all had when we were younger but may have lost along the way—simply *searching*, like a kid in a toy store, instead of *researching*, like a scholarly academic.

"It's the contrast between expertise and amateurism," says Sarah. "You want that sense of play and curiosity." In her book, Sarah cites the example of two scientists, Andre Geim and Konstantin Novoselov, who together won the 2010 Nobel Prize for Physics—perhaps the highest accolade in the field of science—for a discovery they made during a session of what they called Friday-night experiments, or evenings devoted to pursuing wild and fanciful ideas.

On one such Friday, when Geim and Novoselov allowed their minds to roam freely, they figured out how to isolate the world's first two-dimensional material, graphene. The key insight came when Novoselov remembered seeing lab workers cleaning graphite to use as samples by putting strips of Scotch tape across the top of the graphite and then pulling them off. The used Scotch tape was then simply thrown away. Novoselov was inspired to use these discarded strips of tape with graphite particles on them to create an experimental transistor device that might help in understanding how to create graphene. "We made our first device very quickly, within a half an hour of picking up that Scotch tape," Novoselov said. "We tried it, it failed and we almost forgot about it."

But a year later, the two scientists succeeded in isolating graphene—and went on to win their "accidental" Nobel Prize.

"Accidents are important in science, but accidents never happen accidentally," Novoselov explained. "You actually need to create an environment for those accidents to happen."

That is where nourishing our innate sense of childlike wonder comes in. "Often, when you keep a viselike grip on what you're doing, you are prevented from seeing the full range of what is available to you," Sarah says. "There is a real importance to just *playing*, because childlike wonder leads to innovation."

Blankness

The idea of blankness—of wiping the slate clean to make room for new ideas and innovation—is, for both Sarah and me, another important component to living an illuminated life. As Sarah explains t, "We're talking about the importance of embryonic space, private do-mains, places we can go to be within ourselves in order to receive new ideas. Because ideas are always coming to us, and we need to let them coalesce, to give birth to them, in a way."

By aspiring to this blankness—a private place or state of mind where we can free ourselves from the judgments of popular wisdom and ev-eryday life—we can create an environment that is receptive to new input, new brainstorms, new insights, in a way that may not be possible while we're at work.

"It's a balancing act," Sarah says. "Knowing when it is time to unveil your work to the public and knowing when you need to be in your own private domain."

Ask yourself: Do *you* have such a private domain in your life? A specific room, or a block of time, or whatever condition is necessary for you to step out of the spotlight of your life and allow a blankness, a wip-ing clean, to occur?

As an example of such a private space, Sarah brings up dreaming. "Dreaming is a blankness," she says. "When they studied jazz improvi-sation, they realized that you cannot critique yourself while you are playing. The brain activity during improvisation was as close as we could get to REM-state dreaming." Blankness is a state of nonjudg-mental openness that invites innovation. By relaxing our analytical minds and slipping free of norms and expectations, we welcome cre-ative breakthroughs.

What a beautiful and liberating observation this is by Sarah, espe-cially considering that she spends so much time in the often rigid and restrictive world of academia and scholarly study. What this shows is that no matter where you work or what you do, it is always possible to create a private domain where you are free to swim in the beautiful flow of your own soul energy. As I wrote in *The Light Between Us*, achieving this temporary blankness does not require that anything "about our lives has to change, except for our perception." It is simply about looking at our lives in a different way.

. . .

Sarah Lewis is a radiant example of what it means to be open to being guided toward an illuminated life. This was true before her two accidents, and it is even more blindingly obvious now. The car crashes have only expanded Sarah's broad and generous view of human existence, as well as her appreciation of the brilliant beams of light that swirl around us all, all the time. The way Sarah embraces alternate explanations, different perspectives, and decidedly non-mainstream concepts is inspiring. Her thought process allows her to see the first accident as preparation for the more serious second crash—and both accidents as an illumination of how we, as humans, are guided through our lives here on earth.

"They have made me think about the nonlinearity of time," Sarah says, "and the ways in which our paths here are ordained."

After hitting her head in the first car crash and suffering a concussion, Sarah often slept for twelve or fourteen hours a day in the ensuing months. The long recovery process, she found, lessened the impact of 'that inner critic that suppresses impulses and pushes away the guidance we might receive" through signs and inclinations. Instead, she says, "I was very attuned to my different impulses. They were always very gentle, but they were also very clear, and they were not *from* me, but they were connected *to* me."

One such impulse guided her to go to Ellis Island on a Sunday.

Sarah hailed a taxi and traveled to downtown Manhattan, and from there a ferry took her to the legendary island where many millions of immigrants were screened on their way into New York and New Jersey. She had no idea why she was there, but at one point she decided to look through the ship manifests that list more than sixty million immigrants, passengers, and crew members who passed through Ellis Island. She found a listing for her great-grandparents—the parents of her beloved grandfather Shadrach Lee. She brought home a copy of the manifest and put it away, but weeks later another impulse told her to dig it up and read it more closely.

"And when I did, I found the exact address where my grandfather Shadrach Lee had lived in Manhattan," she says. "It was only six blocks from where I live now."

Sarah walked over to the address, stood before the building, and thanked Shadrach Lee for the part he plays in her existence.

Here was yet another cord of light binding Sarah to her past, to a loved one who guides her and watches over her still. Here was another timeline overlapping with hers, another dimension blending into her own.

Just like the beams of light she saw in the moment of her crash—"these bands of colorful light all rooted in love . . . these different spheres and periods of time coalescing to create a miracle"—Sarah's beautiful moment with her grandfather Shadrach happened somewhere outside the boundaries of ordinary thinking, in the bright glow of a truly illuminated life.

> The spiritual life does not
> remove us from the world but
> leads us deeper into it.
>
> **HENRI J. M. NOUWEN**

5

The Material World

In the previous chapter, Sarah Lewis spoke eloquently about the concept of blankness—creating a private place or state of mind where you can free yourself from the judgments of popular wisdom and everyday life. The popular wisdom about reality is that only those things we can see, measure, and explain scientifically are real. This view of the world is called *materialism* or *physicalism*, and its overriding idea is that all consciousness originates in the brain and is the result of a neurophysiological process. Which means that when the brain dies, consciousness dies with it. Any story or anecdote that contradicts that is simply not to be believed.

One of the themes of this book is that, like Sarah Lewis, we must challenge this conventional view of reality, given the seemingly inexplicable occurrences—Sarah clearly seeing bands of light on the Henry Hudson Parkway—that do not fit into the materialistic model.

Materialism is already being challenged by brilliant scientists, researchers, and psychologists who don't believe the physical world is the only world. In the last forty years, there's been a revival of interest in what is called the *idealism model*, which holds that the ultimate nature of that which exists is formulated in the *mind* rather than in the physical world, and that consciousness is *not* just the product of brain activity. One of the goals for these brave thinkers is to formulate a model of existence that encompasses both what we know about the physical world and what are known as *psi phenomena*—experiences that are not explained by physical or biological mechanisms.

"I think we're on the verge of being able to display a kind of theory that would allow psi phenomena to occur and not be incompatible with what we know about physics," says Edward Kelly, a professor at the Division of Perceptual Studies at the University of Virginia. "And when that happens, it changes the game."

You'll hear more from Professor Kelly later in this book. I met him when I was one of five subjects in a mediumship study he conducted, and I've since learned he's one of the leading voices in challenging the materialistic model. One of the areas he's most interested in is the endurance of consciousness after death, which materialists believe isn't possible because they hold that there is no realm beyond the physical from which it could arise. Personally, I'm aware of hundreds, maybe thousands of experiences that prove consciousness is not just a function of brain activity or biology. Take, for example, the story of Vicki Noratuk.

Vicki became blind shortly after birth due to receiving too much oxygen in the incubator, destroying her optic nerve. She had no sight memory at all—no real idea of what things in the world look like. "I've never seen anything like light or shadows, even in my dreams at night," Vicki said in one interview. "It's all just taste, touch, sound, and smell."

But at the age of twenty-two, Vicki was in a bad car accident that fractured her skull and broke her back and neck.

"It was then," she said, "that I saw for the first time."

On the surgical table in the hospital, Vicki felt her body float in the air and drift so that she was looking down on the scene of her accident.

"I saw the crumpled van, having never seen anything before, and it was quite frightening and strange," she said. "Then I was looking at what I realized was my body in the hospital. I recognized my wedding ring and my long hair."

How was it possible for Vicki to "see" any of these things when she'd

been blind all her life? Vicki also saw childhood friends and recognized them, even though she'd never seen their faces. She saw herself
lying on grass and seeing the trees and flowers. Her descriptions prove
that she saw things she'd never been able to see before—but how was
that possible? If all reality is a product of the physical world, known to
us only through the biological process of eyesight, how was it that a
blind person saw all of these physical things, too?

Is there something else going on akin to *mindsight*?

Vicki's story is only one of *millions* recorded in history that cannot
be explained by the materialistic model. In the same way, Ed Kelly's
research is part of a growing body of work in the field of paranormal
phenomena. The first four chapters of this book provide numerous
examples that support a broader, more encompassing view of consciousness. As you read the chapters to come, maintain a healthy skep-
ticism about the strictly materialistic model of existence. Let go of
conventional ideas about what constitutes reality. Create space for
yourself to experience the blankness Sarah Lewis talked about—the
permission to believe that we are more than just physical beings.

In that beautifully open space, you will be able to clearly see the
guidance the Universe wants you to have.

6

Omega

This is a short note to introduce you to a place the next two chapters have in common—the Omega Institute for Holistic Studies, a nonprofit organization founded in 1977 in pastoral Rhinebeck, New York. One of its co-founders, Elizabeth Lesser, is an amazing author and spiritualist who has turned the institute into a prominent center for holistic education through its many workshops, conferences, classes, and retreats. For the past few years, I've offered a three-day workshop at Omega once a year called An Illuminated Life, and its sprawling wooded campus ninety miles north of New York City, which used to be a summer camp, has become, for me, a place that holds truly dazzling energy.

When I walk around the Omega campus, it literally glows. That's because I'm not just experiencing it in a physical way, I'm experiencing the incredible *energy* it holds. I've been in many spaces and places that have a special light and energy coming from them, and they are almost all places of learning—libraries, museums, universities. When groups of people all come together as a community to pursue their highest selves, to push the boundaries of their experienced lives, that place becomes a magical portal into another world with uncommon vibrational energy and a beautiful sense of exploration.

When I hold my workshops at Omega, I feel this divine orchestration of people arriving from all walks of life, with their own life fingerprints, and forming a whole that is much, much greater than its individual parts. I guess you could call it collective energy. It's like a scene in the movie *Finding Nemo*, when all the fish are struggling to swim out of a net on their own, until one fish suggests they all swim together to one side and pull the net down so they can all break free.

Once they're free, the fish will disperse and swim off to their separate lives, but by then they've been changed. Because now, as they swim off, *they take the community with them.* That's what happens at Omega: After three days, the hundreds of participants scatter out into the world, but by then they've already shifted their interior landscapes to make room for the collective energy they experienced. They have, as I mentioned in the previous chapter, carved out space to embrace a non-materialistic view of the world.

So as you read these chapters—one about two sisters whose lives were changed by goats and pies, and one about a nurse whose life was illuminated by her late grandmother—pay attention to how collective energy can help you see the guidance in your life.

Do not be dismayed by the brokenness of the world.
All things break. And all things can be mended.
Not with time, as they say, but with intention.
So go. Love intentionally, extravagantly, unconditionally.
The broken world waits in darkness for the light that is you.

L. R. KNOST

7

Goats and Pies

When Elaine Rubenoff was five or six, she often had trouble falling asleep because of a question that kept rattling around in her brain, over and over, unanswerable, inescapable:

Where do we go when we die?

In the morning, she'd wake up and ask her parents, *How can you go to work and not know what happens when we die? How can anyone live their lives without dwelling on this endlessly?* Most nights Elaine simply gave up and squeezed into the furry dog bed alongside her yellow Lab, Cody, and eventually fell asleep there.

I don't think too many of us have allowed existential anxiety and perplexing cosmic questions to drive us into furry dog beds (although I could be wrong), but I'm sure many of us have, at some point, asked ourselves these kind of deep questions:

Where do we go when we die?

If all we do is live for a while and then cease to exist, what's the point?

Do all the lessons we learn in our lives add up to anything?

Are we connected to our ancestors, or even to our own past?

Do our lives mean anything, or is everything just random?

To be honest, I don't think I can answer these questions for you.

What I mean is, I don't think there's anything I or anyone else can simply *tell* you that will satisfy your curiosity about the afterlife.

What I *do* believe is that the answers we seek are most convincingly delivered not through words but through *experience*. The Universe reveals itself to us, and gives us the answers we are seeking, through our experience of it—*if* we know what to look and listen for.

Which brings us to the magical road trip a grown-up Elaine Rubenoff and her sister Natalie took in 2022, from Rhode Island to New York, a two-hundred-mile drive on a crisp fall day with an audiobook playing and the trees turning red and orange, and both sisters feeling unusually excited, almost giddy, for the weekend that lay ahead, as if they knew something very special was about to happen.

Which it was.

Elaine, thirty-one; Natalie, thirty-five; and their older sister, Lauren, thirty-eight, grew up in a rural town near New Hartford, Connecticut; their mother, Marta, was a teacher and artist, and their father, Glenn, took over the family business selling industrial hosing. Both parents were "always so kind and loving to us," says Natalie, explaining how their mother wound up staying home to raise the three girls and their father often drove two hours so he wouldn't miss any of their soccer, volleyball, or basketball games. There were trips to Disney World, lots of family outings, and a deep sense of love and affection. "They used to call us Nanny Goat and Lainey Pie," Natalie says. "We always felt such warmth and safety at home."

But the relationship between the sisters was complicated by the different pressures and emotional challenges each faced, many of which were painful to deal with. As a result, their relationship was sometimes marked by tension and disconnect. "We didn't always see eye to eye," Natalie says of Elaine. "I'd lock her out of our room sometimes because I just wanted to be with my friends."

Natalie was bullied as a child and often felt sad and depressed. Her moods could turn dark.

Her sister Elaine experienced similar feelings of isolation and being targeted. "I was an extremely sensitive kid, very in touch with my emotions," she remembers. "What I yearned for most was finding somewhere that I felt I belonged." Luckily, their mother was an artist who filled the house with artwork and music and encouraged the children not to repress their emotions, but instead to find a way to *express* them. "She always had crafts and materials lying around, and she helped us find ways of exploring how we were feeling, and I developed a real love for painting," Elaine says. "The healing of my younger self became a project that I've been working on most of my life."

For the Rubenoff sisters, their childhoods lingered in their minds as a warm and wonderful time that was also fraught with unresolved questions, relationships, and feelings.

Then, in 2008, their father was diagnosed with stage 4 prostate cancer. He had always been athletic and active, an avid golfer and sports fan, and seeing him progressively weaken over the years he fought the illness was brutal. Natalie and Lauren were living in Chicago for the later part of his struggle, but Elaine, who was in high school, was there for it all. "I was trying to be normal and going out with my girlfriends, but all the time I was thinking about my dad dying," she says. "Seeing him go through multiple strokes, and seeing this strong, vibrant, charismatic guy deteriorate and turn into a more negative person, was shocking to us all. It made me grow up really fast, and I wasn't ready to grow up."

After fighting bravely for four years, their father passed away in 2012. Elaine took the loss hard and hoped to talk about it with her mother and sisters, but that wasn't possible. "Our family wasn't ready to face what happened together," she says. "I wanted to talk about dad all the time, but no one else did. It could have been a bonding time, but instead we kind of handled it separately. We were trying to stay afloat in our own ways."

Looking back, Natalie says, "I didn't process my father's loss the way I would now. I didn't allow myself to feel my feelings. And I just compartmentalized his passing. I believed our dad was still there, still with us, but I had no way of feeling his presence or getting guidance from him, and that was devastating."

Not long after their father's passing, their mother was diagnosed with stage 4 ovarian cancer. She, too, fought valiantly, and there were more long years of ups and downs, chemo and radiation, getting better and getting worse—a roller coaster of emotions. Natalie returned more often to be with her mother than she had when her father was ill—"she was my best friend and I felt like I just couldn't lose her," she says—but because of the Covid pandemic, their mother spent much of her illness at her home by herself, isolated from her daughters. When the pandemic eased, the sisters spent as much time as possible with their mom. Lauren, her husband Vince, and their baby Mia even lived with her for a year while waiting for their new house to be finished, and their presence—especially that of little Mia—gave their mother a huge boost.

As for Elaine, "I interviewed her every night, asking her all these questions I wish I'd asked my father," she says. "It was great to hear all these stories she shared with us. It was a heartbreaking time, more like taking care of a child than being with a parent. But she needed us there, and it turned out to be the most wonderful thing."

During that time, their mother told each of the sisters what sign she would send them once she crossed, so that they'd know she was still with them. Lauren's was a rabbit, Elaine's was a nest, and Natalie was given a rainbow. The sisters were right there with her, on December 20, 2021, when their mother took her final breath and crossed. As fortunate as they felt to be there with her, seeing her pass was traumatic. The sisters had lavishly decorated their mother's house for Christmas, her favorite holiday, and on Christmas morning they opened the final gifts their mother had left for them. In their stockings, they each found a Christmas ornament depicting the sign she gave them. "It was the last but also the best Christmas present we all opened that day," Natalie says.

The months that followed were a reflective but confusing time. "We'd been in this constant fight-or-flight mode for ten straight years, always waiting for the other shoe to drop," says Natalie. "It was like we never stopped mourning, and when our parents were gone, we both needed to know where to go from there."

Where they went, it turned out, was on a road trip.

During her mother's illness, Natalie read my second book, *Signs*. In the spring of 2022 she came across one of my Instagram posts and was reminded of how my book helped her through her difficult times. My post was about a weekend workshop at the Omega Institute for Holistic Studies. The institute is a remarkable place that "awakens the best in the human spirit and cultivates the extraordinary potential that exists in us all," its website tells us. I have been affiliated with the institute for many years, and I can testify to its extraordinary power as a place of healing and guidance. In fact, I would be the teacher at the fall 2022 weekend workshop that caught Natalie's attention.

"As soon as I read about it, I called Lainey and said, 'I have this urgent feeling we both need to go to this and it will change our lives,'" Natalie recalls. "And Lainey said, 'Yes, no question, let's do it.' It wasn't the kind of thing I would ordinarily do, but I felt motivated to try things that were not common for me. I was listening for what my spirit was telling me to do and what I felt compelled to do."

She was, Natalie says, *"allowing myself to be guided."*

Elaine, too, didn't hesitate to sign up. "I've always been down to try new things and I've always believed I think differently from other people," she says, "and this felt like a new way of looking at the world."

Natalie gassed up her reliable gray 2019 SUV and drove from Rhode Island, where she lived, to the airport to pick up Elaine, who flew in from Chicago. Together they drove west to Rhinebeck, New York, and—knowing I was teaching the workshop—replayed the audiobook of *Signs* so they could listen to it on the drive. "So we're in the car listening to the book on the way, and at one point it suggests that we ask our loved ones who have crossed for signs," Natalie says. "We talked about it and we decided we wanted to ask for a sign from *both* our parents, and that I would ask for one and Elaine would ask for one. We were asking for two signs that we could see together."

"It wasn't just that," Elaine adds. "We also decided that we wanted to be able to see both signs *at the same time.*"

The signs they asked for were easy to come up with.

Natalie, or Nanny Goat, asked to see a goat.

And Elaine, or Lainey Pie, asked for a pie.

Pies and goats, an animal and a dessert, somehow grouped together, on demand.

Hey, if you're going to ask the Universe for a sign, you might as well shoot for the moon.

Literally thirty seconds later, as the sisters drove along the rural, two-lane New York State Route 308 West, through rolling countryside of woods and fields, they came over a hill and saw an astounding sight—to their left, a cluster of fifteen goats lazing behind a fence and staring at them, and to their right, a small country store with a big sign propped up outside that read:

PIE SHOP

"We were both, 'Whoa, wait a second, are you seeing this?'" says Elaine. "I mean, there they were, pies and goats, on opposite sides of the road, showing up at the same time. We just looked at each other and we both said, 'We don't even need to go to the workshop!'"

They went anyway and shared their amazing story with other participants, who all marveled at the speed, timing, and completeness of the signs the sisters received. "We became the Pie and Goat Girls!" says Natalie. Some attendees even provided further evidence that the sisters were, indeed, connecting with the Universe. "One woman told us she was reading a book and the chapter she was currently on was called 'Nanny Goat,'" Natalie says. "On top of that, her daughter Piper's favorite stuffed animal was a nanny goat, and she'd dressed up as a goat for Halloween! She wound up becoming a great friend." (The woman and her mother even attended Elaine's wedding the following year.)

The three days the sisters spent in Rhinebeck, sitting with me and the other attendees in a large room and sharing stories about the unending bonds of light and love, were full of such profound moments that they shared, and that had a huge impact on their lives. "I'd been yearning for something that made me feel connected to my mom, to know that she still existed, and when we got the pie and goat signs, we both felt this really strong, instant connection to our parents," says Natalie. "Since then, I've felt like I'm connected to this higher, bigger source, and I feel like I know certain things, with conviction, things I don't even remember learning. It's like I'm receiving downloads from the Universe, and every time I get one, I get shivers."

Elaine, too, feels a seismic change in her life, stemming from her new sense of connection to her parents. "It's like I changed my lens, my perception, the way I look at the world around me," she says. "I feel like I can live a freer, more loving life, and make choices that are guided not by fear but by love. And the more I connect to my past experiences, the more they teach me about who I am and where I belong. The idea that things didn't just happen to me, they were *meant* to happen. Life is intentional, not random, and the past comes full circle.

"It's like we're all living a curated existence."

Elaine says she has brought everything she felt and learned that magical weekend to her practice as a psychotherapist and professional artist. "I encounter people who are struggling through life's challenges, and I think I learned how to help them process their emotions and release what is holding them back from feeling more connected, like I do now. Sometimes we can overcomplicate it, but in the end being connected is really just about love. Because when you feel connected to loved ones who have passed, you feel stronger."

Natalie, who works in marketing technology, has also taken what she experienced at the workshop at Omega and introduced it to her colleagues and friends. "I feel like I'm able to bring a new dimension of trust and empathy to the corporate world just by sharing my spiritual experience in Rhinebeck," she says. "I used to have really high anxiety and work these crazy long hours, but that's not me anymore. Now, my anxiety is much better regulated." Natalie has also begun exploring creative outlets—almost, she says, as if she were channeling her mother. "She always loved decorating, and I think that's why I've found a new love and passion for interior design," she explains. "I feel like my mom has helped open me up to being more creative from the Other Side."

Both sisters have kept in touch with several women they cried and shared signs with at Omega, and this new spiritual community they are part of has been, as Natalie puts it, "life-changing." The members of the group meet once a month and are even planning a workshop of their own. They also reach out to other friends and relatives, creating a ripple effect of love and goodness—all these new lightworkers out in the world helping others. You can imagine how immensely satisfying it is for me to hear about the new lives and communities Natalie and Elaine have created since attending the workshop. Those kinds of results are an expression of my very wildest hopes.

Of course, it wasn't me who caused these changes to happen.

As I often point out, and as the Rubenoff sisters more than confirmed, no one needs me to make these connections happen in their lives. As Natalie explained, all she had to do to put herself in position to experience such a life-altering weekend was listen to what her spirit was telling her and *allow herself to be guided.*

All I do is help people understand the many ways that they, too, can live such guided lives.

I am sure not every question that Natalie and Elaine struggled with was answered at Omega. But I do believe, now that I've heard the stories of their time in Rhinebeck—and especially of the incredible confluence of goats and pies on New York State Route 308 West—that they understand the answers they seek are accessible to them through

their *experiences* of the Universe. After all, it wasn't me who empowered them to feel more connected to their parents than ever.

It was the goats and pies.

No one needs a psychic medium, or even a three-day workshop
(though if you can possibly attend such an event, by all means do), to
tap into what Natalie called "a higher, bigger source" of energy. That
powerful stream of light and energy flows like a mighty river just above
us all, and there are many, *many* ways we can all learn to simply reach
up and access it. Natalie and Elaine found ways to do it, just like everyone you are reading about in this book. The only requirement is that
we open ourselves to the prospect of an illuminated life and acquaint
ourselves with the many ways we can connect to the Universe. There
is no trick, no secret password. There is just a language of love and
light we can all learn.

One of the exercises I introduced at the workshop had to do with
manifesting our dreams and wishes so that our loved ones and teams of
light on the Other Side can help us make them reality. Among other
goals, the Rubenoff sisters manifested something that had to do with
me. They wrote on their pads of paper that, somehow, they wanted to
be able to collaborate with me in some way in the future, and specifically to have their story told in my next book.

I was not aware of their manifestations when, months later, I bumped
into the sisters at another workshop and told them I'd been trying to
reach them but could not find their contact information. Then I asked
them to share their story of goats and pies with each of you, on these
very pages.

And so here they are, and here you are.

And, somewhere in the world, waiting for you, are your own goats
and pies.

As you start to walk on the way,
the way appears.

RUMI

8

Grandma C.

The Universe brought Beth C. and me together so I could help her answer a fundamental question:

What is my purpose in this life?

Most of us have grappled with this and other questions like it at some point in our lives, and Beth, a nurse from Cape Cod, Massachusetts, was having an especially hard time finding any answers. She'd always wondered what happens when we die, and because of her profession, she'd been exposed to more death and dying than most people, especially during the Covid pandemic. She'd reached a point where she needed wisdom and guidance from someone or somewhere to help her decide what to do with the rest of her life. She just didn't know where that guidance would come from, or if it would come at all.

You see, Beth never really wanted to be a nurse. In fact, while growing up in Kansas, nurses terrified her. When she was five, she needed to have her tonsils removed, but she was spooked by the nurse with the needle. "I was screaming and thrashing, and the nurse said, 'If you don't calm down, I will send your parents out of the room,'" Beth recalls. "Well, I didn't calm down and she sent out my parents, and then she sat on me and gave me the injection. After that, just the rustle of a nurse's polyester uniform freaked me out."

Ever since that traumatic experience, Beth would faint while getting a shot, having blood drawn, or even just seeing blood. "I'd see stars, and before I knew it people were tending to me on the floor," she says. "It happened so often that whenever I'd see stars I'd know what was coming and I'd tell the adults around me, 'I'm gonna faint.'" Somehow, she managed not to faint while having a mole removed in sixth grade—but when she saw the mole in a jar afterward, she passed out on the spot. Even as a teenager, she snuck out of her uncle's pediatric office rather than have blood work done.

"One of the doctors in his practice told me to go downstairs to the lab to have blood drawn, and instead I walked right out the front door and drove home," Beth says. "I did not like *anything* about medicine."

Which is why it was so surprising that she voluntarily signed up for a biology class in junior college and found she didn't at all mind dissecting a frog. "I actually *loved* that class," she remembers, "and it didn't make me faint." When it came time to pick a profession, Beth had two criteria—a field that required only two years of training and that allowed her to escape Kansas. "I almost went with dental hygienist," she says. "But then I saw a nursing program, and I realized it was good money and I could live anywhere. When I told my parents I had signed up for it, they both just said, 'What????'"

That's how the girl who hated blood wound up in nursing school.

It wasn't all smooth sailing. On her very first day a teacher sat seventy-five nursing students in an auditorium and showed them a film about surgery. The old familiar feeling of seeing stars and getting wobbly rushed back, and Beth slipped out of the classroom and lay down on the floor in the hallway. "Other students would walk past and say, 'Are you all right?' and I'd say, 'Oh, yeah, sure, I'm fine, just go.' I snuck back in just as the film ended, and no one knew I was gone. That was the first time I said to myself, 'Wow, Beth, good job signing up for nursing school.'"

But then, as the weeks progressed, she settled down and discovered she was good at certain nursing skills, particularly giving shots and starting IVs. "I got lucky," she says. "Out of all the people in my class I was never picked to be the student who received injections. I was always the one practicing shots. So I never once fainted *and* I got good at handling needles."

Her two-year nursing program required clinical work in hospitals right from the start, and Beth excelled and passed her nursing board exam on her first try. Just like that, she was a registered nurse. She packed up her tiny white Geo Storm and drove to Florida, where she took a job in an orthopedic clinic. She lasted only nine months, however, before heading back to Kansas. "The doctors were mean and had huge egos," she explains. Soon after moving home, she married her high school sweetheart; they moved around the country while Beth paid for him to attend three graduate schools. She worked in many different areas of medicine and found she could handle any nursing job just fine.

And yet—she found she lacked the passion she recognized in some other nurses. She loved caring for people, and she received high marks from her supervisors and many thank-you notes from her patients, but "I didn't have that personality where I would say, 'I am a nurse! That is my identity!'" she explains. "I mean, I didn't even tell people I was a nurse. I tended to get bored, and I tried seven different kinds of nursing work in seven different jobs. There was always that little bit of distance between me and the profession."

A few years ago, after getting divorced and moving to Cape Cod, Beth settled into the specialized field of home infusion—administering IV medications to patients with chronic health issues who can't make it to the hospital. Her patients included some people with amyotrophic lateral sclerosis (ALS), a fatal nervous system disease that weakens muscles and can make communication difficult. Back in nursing school, she'd secretly hoped she wouldn't wind up caring for ALS patients; watching their lives slowly and agonizingly slip away was hard for her to bear. Yet her skill for easily starting IVs and providing infusions—

some of which take six hours to administer and cost $30,000 a dose—carried her through, and she became a specialist in the field.

But when the infusion pharmacy she worked for took advantage of a promising new ALS drug, Radicava, and sent more and more ALS patients her way, Beth felt the familiar uncertainty about being a nurse resurface.

Her only comfort was a scrappy stray dog with a broken hip found wandering the streets in Puerto Rico. Through an agency, Beth adopted the mangy but animated Chihuahua mix in early 2020. She chose the dog—whom she named Margarita, or Rita for short—because she felt she was the one to patch her up and make her whole. "I spent so many hours rehabbing her, making her put weight on her back legs, walking on the beach in winter, building up her strength," Beth recalls. "She had the most beautiful spirit and I loved her so much."

Sadly, later that year, in the midst of the Covid pandemic, Rita went in for oral surgery and passed away in the recovery room, after only ten months with Beth. "I was shattered," Beth says. "*Shattered.* I felt like I'd lost my very best friend."

The pandemic, her new ALS patients, and the tragic loss of Rita all combined to create a crisis point for Beth. She felt lost and overwhelmed by death, and she knew she needed help and guidance from somewhere, only she didn't know who or where to turn to for it. Finally, she read a book about how dogs end up in heaven, and it helped her realize whom she needed to turn to for help.

Her best friend, Rita.

A week after Rita died, Beth took her other dog, Munchkin, for a walk along the Cape Cod Canal. "We sat down and I said, out loud, 'Rita, if you're around, give me a sign to let me know you're still with me,'" Beth says.

That very moment, something appeared above the waterline—something she'd never before seen in three years of living on the Cape.

"It was a shark fin," she says. "Right in front of me. This shark swam right past just as I asked Rita for a sign."

And yet it wasn't enough for Beth.

"I said, 'Rita, if that really is you, can you send me another sign so I can be sure?'"

Right on cue, a *second* shark fin appeared in the water.

That wasn't enough, either.

"I needed to know it wasn't just a coincidence," Beth says. "So I said, 'Rita, can you send me just one more sign?'"

There was a big splash, and out of the water popped a seal, shiny and black, with big whiskers and curious eyes. It stayed there, bobbing in the water, staring at Beth, and holding eye contact for a long while.

This time, all Beth did was say thank you to Rita, and cry.

After that, Beth wanted to learn more about the afterlife. The mother of one of her patients had read my book *Signs,* and she referred it to Beth, who read it and then felt guided to sign up for a three-day workshop I was teaching at the Omega Institute in October 2022 (the same workshop I mentioned in chapter 7).

Among other things, the workshops I lead help people open up to their own psychic and intuitive abilities, connect with their Teams of Light on the Other Side, and become more comfortable with asking for and receiving signs from loved ones who have crossed. Throughout the weekend workshop Beth attended, I guided the participants through exercises in clairvoyance, clairaudience, and mediumship, with the intention of showing them how to open themselves more and more to the powerful secret language of the Universe around us.

Beth, feeling absolutely burned out as a nurse and grappling with the loss of Rita and some of her ALS patients, arrived at Omega with two pressing questions:

What is my purpose in this life?

What happens when we die?

To get ready for the conference, Beth practiced asking for signs at home. She thought of her beloved step-grandfather, Julius, who had passed twenty-six years ago. She asked him, "Give me a sign. Let me see one of those old-fashioned, turn-of-the-century bicycles with the giant front wheel. Show me the bicycle."

Two nights later, Beth watched a random documentary on Netflix. "It was about a group of people in Argentina who were bakers," she recalled, "and I have no idea why I picked it to watch, but I did."

As Beth watched the opening credits, the logo of one of the production companies involved in the documentary caught her eye. She had to reach for her remote and pause the show. Then she moved closer to the screen and stared at the design. The last letter in the name of the company was an O, and it was represented by a circular image. Could it be?

Yes, it was—a high-wheel bicycle, also known as a penny-farthing, from back in the late 1800s.

"There was even a little man riding the bicycle, who of course I took to be Julius," Beth recalls. "He not only sent me the sign, he even sent himself as part of the sign!"

The next week Beth traveled to Rhinebeck for my Omega workshop. From the start, she felt the urge to share her story with everyone she met, even though she was a natural introvert who rarely approached strangers. "It was just so *invigorating* to be there," she says. "I told everyone about my signs from Rita and Julius, and everyone laughed at me for asking Rita for three signs."

One of the exercises we did during the workshop was a guided meditation session, during which I tried to help everyone enter into a highly receptive place of openness and tranquility. The idea was that, in that quiet, contemplative time, we would try to meet our own personal Teams of Light who guide us from the Other Side. The truth is, no one ever needs a psychic medium to connect to their loved ones who have crossed. That ability belongs to us all. We just have to create the space for it to happen. The guidance and love are ever present. I asked everyone to close their eyes as I guided them on a meditation to connect with their spirit guides and loved ones on the Other Side.

Beth closed her eyes and soon felt like she was in a blank white space, which transformed into ethereal cloudlike puffs of light pink. Everything was soft and a bit blurry. Julius appeared, of course—there was no question he was part of Beth's Team of Light. "He was this tiny little man with big glasses that took up half his face," Beth says. "The other half was his big smile. Glasses and smile. When I saw him, I was just so happy to know he was there."

Before long, someone else appeared in Beth's soft pink ethereal space—someone Beth hadn't expected to see at all.

It was her Grandma C.

That's what Beth used to call her when she was little, all the way up through Grandma C.'s passing eleven years ago. Grandma C. spent her life working as a labor and delivery nurse, and when Beth decided to go to nursing school, her grandmother was very proud of her.

Even so, Beth never connected her grandmother's passion for nursing to her own seemingly random decision to become a nurse. That is until Grandma C. appeared to her in Rhinebeck.

Grandma C. came through with a clear, audible message for her grandchild. "She said, 'Beth, you were always meant to be a nurse. Just like I was meant to bring people into this world, *you were meant to help bring people out of it.*'"

It was a moment of profound emotion and meaning for Beth, who for the longest time had believed being a nurse was anything *but* a calling for her. "All of a sudden I just *got it*," Beth says. "I was part of this beautiful circle of life, my grandmother ushering people into the world and me easing them out. It wasn't random. It hadn't been naive of me to think I could be a nurse. It had nothing to do with needles or anything like that. It was all meant to be. It was my purpose. *I was meant to be doing exactly this on earth!*"

In the course of just a weekend, Beth's perspective of her life and mission changed completely. She came to Omega mourning the loss of her beloved pet Rita and unsure about her career of the last three decades. These were difficult, complex, existential issues, and Beth did not expect to be able to wrap them up neatly in the span of just two and a half days.

Yet Beth *did* find answers to the two most pressing questions she arrived with: *What is my purpose in this life? What happens when we die?* She left Rhinebeck believing that crossing over to the Other Side does not mean our existence ceases—on the contrary, our loved ones who cross become a part of our personal Teams of Light, striving always to guide us along our worldly paths.

Indeed, it was Beth's Grandma C. who showed up to help her answer her questions, and in particular the question *What is my purpose in this life?* Somehow, it had escaped Beth that her path through life could have been connected in some way to her grandmother's path, even though both chose to be nurses. In my experience, I have seen how some people can come to believe that their existence is solitary and untethered to anyone else's. But this is not true—it is *never* true. None of us live small, solitary lives.

We are *all* tethered to others, and to those who came before us, in the majestic tapestry of light and energy that is existence.

After the conference, Beth drove all the way back home to Cape Cod in silence—no radio, no music. "I wanted peace and quiet to think about what happened," she says. "To think about how amazing it was that I got the answers I was looking for. And how they weren't vague or ambiguous, they were so specific—I am meant to help people transition out of this world. I am good at it, and I know how to do it. And now I know that all along, it was what I was meant to do."

Since the conference, Beth has volunteered at a new hospice house that was built on Cape Cod, where her experience is greatly welcomed. She looks at people crossing over differently, not as a depressing end or something to be afraid of, but as part of a bigger journey that we all share. Beth has also remained close to some of the people she met at the workshop, traveling with them to other events and staying in touch. This often happens at my workshops, and I believe the people who attend are guided to be there and are meant to meet.) Beth shared that they call themselves the Fox Family, because so many of them asked to see a fox as their sign from a loved one, and sure enough a fox kept magically appearing to participants and also right outside our workshop classroom. After that, a fox became our collective workshop sign. Beth later wrote me a letter to tell me she felt instructed by her Team of Light to make a large Fox Family quilt to commemorate how much their weekend at Omega meant to them all.

The quilt was magnificent: a dazzling patchwork of some six hundred bright pieces of fabric depicting the striking red fur and the piercing green eyes of a fox. The image and effect were overwhelmingly powerful. Beth shared that it took her around eighty or ninety hours to finish the quilt, and it shows—the craftsmanship is astonishing (she's a veteran quilter). She also said that if I didn't care much for quilts, she would be perfectly fine with me gifting it to someone else. Of course, I kept it. It is stunning and so incredibly meaningful to me, and I even displayed it at Omega the following year.

Only now as I write this chapter do I realize that the quilt that Beth gave me as a gift represents the intricately woven, brightly colored, intertwined fabric of all of existence, binding us to one another and to the larger Universe, turning our disparate lives into one common pageant of love and light. Creating a picture of something greater. Those connections between us are why Grandma C. was able to convey such an important and life-changing message to Beth—and why any one of us can receive the same kind of life-altering sign from the Other Side, if only we open ourselves up to the possibility.

"Never in a million years would I have thought about Grandma C.'s path and my path as being connected like that," Beth wrote to me in her letter. "But now I know. Nothing in life is random. I am where I am supposed to be."

All Beth needed was a little push, a little guidance, and suddenly her world made sense. And now it is she who provides the push and guidance for others, sharing her experience and her belief in the power of signs with as many people as she can.

"That weekend changed my life," Beth says. "I told all my friends and patients about it, and I keep telling people and bringing them around to this way of thinking. That is part of my purpose now, part of helping others on their paths. I guess that makes me a Light Worker, too!"

I am out with lanterns,
looking for myself.

EMILY DICKINSON

9

The Unspoken Language
of Energy

The concept of collective energy—the idea that living organisms share energy, even at a distance—has been around for thousands of years. When considering the concept of collective energy, think of how fish in a school turn in perfect tandem, how voices in a choir come together to create something more powerful and melodious than a single voice, how studies have shown that audiences attending the theater together have their heartbeats align, and how, in quantum physics, the phenomenon of entanglement proves that particles are a part of one another's energy field, no matter how far apart they physically might be (which Einstein referred to as "spooky action at a distance"). Although some in the scientific community insist we need more proof, there are others who feel we've accumulated enough evidence of shared energy to accept it as a fact of our existence.

Among that evidence is the story of an especially sensitive *Dracaena* plant.

It was a bored scientist named Cleve Backster—a polygraph expert and interrogation specialist for the CIA—who cooked up a whimsical experiment to measure the length of time it took for water to travel up the plant's long, thick stem and reach its leaves. During a coffee break from his regular research, he connected two sensor electrodes from a polygraph to one of the plant's curved leaves, hoping to measure the leaf's electrical resistance to the incoming water and thus how long it took for the water to travel up the plant's stem. But instead of an increase in energy, the polygraph detected a decrease, followed by a quick blip upward, the same pattern produced by human subjects who fear detection while they're strapped to a polygraph.

This struck Backster as a strangely emotional reaction from a plant. "He decided that if the plant really was displaying an emotional reaction, he would have to come up with some major emotional stimulus to test that response," wrote the journalist Lynne McTaggart in her remarkably valuable book *The Intention Experiment*, a journey through the "furthest reaches of consciousness," as she describes it. Backster knew he had to somehow threaten the plant's existence to fully stimulate an emotional response, and he had the thought to burn off its leaves with a match. But the very instant he had that thought—before he ever reached for any matches—the plant reacted. "The recording pen swung to the top of the polygraph chart and nearly jumped off," McTaggart wrote, meaning the polygraph had registered an emotional response from the plant. Mind you, Backster hadn't *done* anything, other than have a thought about what he would do. The plant reacted as if it had understood Backster's thought about doing it harm. The leaf fitted with the electrodes, targeted for destruction only in Backster's mind, essentially flipped out.

Backster concluded that the reaction could only have occurred through some sort of sophisticated extrasensory perception (ESP). He then decided to study whether the *Dracaena* plant would react to other organisms being threatened. Could it somehow know and feel empathy for other organisms in danger? To do this, Backster conducted an experiment to measure the plant's energy output when thousands of brine shrimp were dropped in boiling water in a different room.

Do you know what happened? At the moment the shrimp hit the water, the polygraph spiked several times. Somehow, the plant *had* registered the death of an organism three doors away. What did that mean?

It meant that all organisms are somehow in tune with one another, and that they share energy to the point where even a thought can impact another being. Even though plants and other living organisms don't have the capacity for a verbal language, there is clearly *some* kind of language that allows them to connect with other living things.

But what could that language be? When Backster conducted these experiments in 1966, he was ridiculed by the scientific community. But just a decade later, a Russian professor of quantum physics, Konstantin Korotkov, conducted experiments in an attempt to capture this mysterious life energy on film, or at least measure it in some way. Do living beings really emit energy that can alter another being's reality in some way? Through his research Korotkov was able to record what he called the biosphere around living organisms—the emission of photons, known as biophotons, or tiny particles of electromagnetic light radiation that are imperceptible to all but the most sophisticated recording equipment. Korotkov's focus on these minuscule electric fields traveling through space "made sense of Backster's findings," McTaggart wrote. "If thoughts are another stream of photons, it is perfectly plausible that a plant could pick up the signals and be affected by them."

In this way, Backster was able to discover a hidden interaction—an unspoken language of light energy—shared by all beings. His research also strongly suggested that our thoughts—which are a language made up of strings of light perceptible to the human eye only through technology, yet also felt energetically—can significantly impact other beings. This finding further solidifies the idea that we are all connected to something larger than ourselves. In the next chapter, you'll read about a groundbreaking researcher who is examining how nonverbal children and teenagers with autism are capable of reading this secret language of light energy—even more proof that shared collective energy truly is a fact of our existence.

We do not need more material development, we
need more spiritual development . . . We do not
need more of the things that are seen, we need
more of the things that are unseen.

CALVIN COOLIDGE

10

Challenging the Paradigm

More than four hundred years ago, William Shakespeare had the main character in his play *Hamlet* insist to his scholarly, skeptical friend Horatio that the existence of ghosts—and life after bodily death—was not all that far-fetched. In Act 1, Scene 5, Hamlet explains, "There are more things in heaven and earth, Horatio, / Than are dreamt of in your philosophy."

In the hundreds of years since Hamlet first spoke that line, our knowledge has dynamically expanded. We have come up with computers, combustion engines, space travel, gene splicing, string theory, quantum mechanics, and artificial intelligence, to name just a few major breakthroughs. Even so, one of the smartest humans who ever lived believed our understanding of ourselves and of the universe remains, at best, elementary. "We still do not know one thousandth of one percent," said Albert Einstein, "of what nature has revealed to us."

In other words, we've still got *a lot* to learn.

Some people resist this idea. They prefer to rely on cold, hard empirical evidence of the existence of anything, and if they don't get it, they're content to write the thing off as impossible. *We know enough,* they seem to be saying, *to assume that such a thing cannot happen.*

Of course, most humans once felt that way about the possibility that the earth was round.

Others aren't quite as quick to shut down the inexplicable. For them, life is a constant exploration of the hidden blessings of existence— a roller-coaster ride of discovery. It's as if they are saying, "We cannot hope to know but a fraction of the boundaries of reality, so why not dive into this deep knowledge gap and see what miraculous wonders we uncover?"

Diane Hennacy Powell, the subject of this chapter, is one such explorer.

Powell has been many remarkable things—a student of ancient wisdom traditions, a scientific theoretician, an integrative medical doctor, a neuropsychiatrist, a psychotherapist, an author, a researcher, a public speaker. That, however, is just the start of her résumé. She is also an expert on autism and savant syndrome whose ongoing studies of autistic savants and their extraordinary abilities are breaking new scientific ground. Specifically, Powell is researching what she calls the "potentially highly psychic abilities" of nonverbal autistic children. (Many of you will be familiar with Powell's work from her involvement in the wildly popular podcast *The Telepathy Tapes*.) I first met Powell in 2013 at a Forever Family Foundation conference we were both presenting at and felt instantly drawn to her and the work she was doing.

"People think these children lack empathy, when in fact they are very empathic," she says. "It's almost like they see and absorb too much information, which makes them kind of withdraw. But the more time I spend with them, the more I realize how aggressively misunderstood they are, and how they have abilities that are also misunderstood."

Powell is a visionary who sees *what might be* rather than *what can't be*. She is someone who, in her own words, is "challenging the paradigm"—the generally accepted norms and limits of science and psychiatry. Her work with children who are autistic (neurodivergent) strikes me as a perfect illustration of remaining open to all the known and unknown wonders of existence. In this way, Powell not only lives a beautiful, illuminated life but also advocates for others to be more accepting of seemingly inexplicable phenomena.

"With the children I work with, we don't have a full understanding of what they do, but that doesn't mean we should deny it," Powell says. "It's something that is happening. It's a reality for a lot of people. So why not accept that it's possible and explore it more?"

This spirit of adventurous inquiry has steered Powell throughout her diverse and unique career. She has often switched disciplines and areas of study when some new way of seeing the world came into view. "When I was in medical school and interacting with different people, I came to have a totally different sense of how everything works," she explains. "What I saw is that a lot of people get put on medications that have toxic side effects simply because they said something that goes against the current paradigm and that is therefore considered magical thinking."

As an undergraduate, Powell was a neuroscientist doing research on crayfish; however, she realized that what she was really interested in was the human brain and human behavior. So she went to medical school at Johns Hopkins to become a neurosurgeon. While doing her clinical rotations, she was inspired by the chairman of the psychiatry department, who was both a psychiatrist and a neurologist. She felt guided by this and became a neuropsychiatrist who studied child psychiatry, and she spent six months at the London Institute of Psychiatry. There, she worked closely with Sir Michael Rutter, a renowned autism expert who was knighted for his work.

Powell hoped to continue working with children with autism, but in the late 1980s, there simply weren't very many reported cases or patients available. Instead, she joined the faculty of Harvard University and served as the clinical director of the consultation liaison service, where she was responsible for consultations on the medical and surgical floors of Cambridge Hospital. Part of her job was helping doctors evaluate patients' mental states. It was at Harvard, Dr. Powell says, "that I met the patient who blew my mind and changed my life."

By then, Powell had shown a strong instinct for pushing past tradi-tional diagnoses in search of some hidden underlying issue—finding what others had missed. "I'd often get called in to talk to patients whom the doctors couldn't find anything wrong with," she says. "They'd say, 'We think it's in her head, can you confirm it's psychological?' I just wanted to make sure they'd done a sufficient evaluation and thought of every possibility before sending a patient down the wrong path."

One patient, who had been injured in a car accident, complained of numbness and paralysis below the waist, and difficulty with bladder function. "They thought it might be emotional, not physical," Powell says. But her training and instincts led her to dig for a physical underly-ing cause. The patient's symptoms matched those of cauda equina syn-drome (CES), which occurs in the cauda equina, a sac of nerve roots that fan out like a horse's tail at the very lower end of the spinal cord. The doctors "were focused on the spine, but this patient had damage of the central nervous system that was just *below* the spinal cord," Pow-ell says. "She needed immediate surgery." After consulting with Pow-ell, the patient's doctor reexamined her scan and realized the CES diagnosis was correct. He ordered the patient to be taken directly to an operating room, where emergency surgery saved her from permanent paralysis.

Another woman who had heard Powell on a podcast called her and explained that her husband was dying in a hospice. "She said he'd been diagnosed with dementia, even though, as she told it, he had brief moments of lucidity," says Powell. "The fact that the dementia seemed to come and go made me think that the patient might have delirium, on top of or instead of dementia." Delirium is a sudden re-duction in orientation that usually lasts only days or weeks, while de-mentia is the more gradual, more severe long-lasting loss of cognitive functioning. The woman spoke to her husband's doctor about delirium and, sure enough, she says, "he had an infection that was causing his loss of function. He got on antibiotics and was sent home from the hospice."

When the man's dementia continued at home, along with a broad-based gait and frequent incontinence, Powell recognized the symptoms of normal pressure hydrocephalus (NPH), a known complication of brain radiation undergone to treat brain cancer. The MRI can look just like a case of Alzheimer's, so it's easy to mistake the diagnosis. NPH is the result of the buildup of cerebrospinal fluid in the ventricles of the brain. The man's wife took Powell's advice and found a neurosurgeon who performed a spinal test on her husband, and the test revealed he did indeed have NPH, which is often accompanied by urinary incontinence. Surgeons inserted a shunt, and the man's cognitive functions returned. "She told me he was suddenly himself again," Powell says. "Too often patients are shuttled into one or another category prematurely after a quick diagnosis. I think that happens to thousands and thousands of people. So you have to dig deeper and have a broader perspective to start. You kind of have to be Sherlock Holmes."

The patient who changed Powell's life when she was on the faculty of Harvard was admitted to the Cambridge Hospital with a possible heart attack. Back then, the tests confirming whether or not someone has really had a heart attack took two days to come back; in the meantime, Powell was asked to evaluate the patient. "The doctors thought she was crazy," Powell says. "They told me, 'She's hallucinating and delusional, she's on another planet.'" Because the doctors didn't believe the patient, and because the patient said she saw ghosts in her room, she wanted to leave the hospital immediately, while the doctors wanted her to stay the two days until the tests came back. Powell was in a position to make the final ruling. All she had to do was sign a paper confirming that the patient was insane and the patient would be committed against her will.

Powell took a different approach. "My preference was always to win a patient's cooperation," she says. During their talk the patient suddenly looked at Powell and said, "You have this bright white light around you. I get a good feeling about you. I have a reading for you. Do you mind if I tell you what I see?"

Powell told her to go ahead. Much of what followed did in fact sound somewhat delusional, but Powell had never had a reading or heard of auras and was willing to hear her out. "You're married to a chemist," the patient said; in fact, Powell's husband had a PhD in biochemistry and was applying for a postdoctoral position in biochemistry that very week. This was long before Google, so there was little possibility of the patient knowing anything about Powell, whom she'd just met.

The patient then said, "Your husband is applying for a job in two different cities, and his heart is in one place, but you'll end up in the other place." She even identified the city they'd wind up in: San Diego. This, too, proved to be true. Several other statements were also startlingly accurate. "I was blown away," says Powell. "I told her, 'Okay, if you're seeing ghosts in your room, I understand how scary it would be for you to stay. But I'm concerned because, if you did have a heart attack, I'd feel bad if you went home and something bad happened to you."

The patient thought about it and said, "If you promise to come see me again tomorrow, I'll stay."

The cardiac tests came back normal, and the patient was discharged without the trauma of confinement or being classified insane.

For Powell, the encounter had a profound, life-altering effect. "I was just two years out of training and suddenly my entire paradigm had been blown away," she says. "It set me on a journey of trying to understand just what happened that day."

Her journey of inquiry and exploration led her to write a book, *The ESP Enigma: The Scientific Case for Psychic Phenomena*, a beautiful rumination on consciousness and the evidence for psychic phenomena long ignored by mainstream science—specifically, telepathy, psychokinesis, clairvoyance, and precognition. I believe Powell's book made a real difference in proving to skeptics that psychic phenomena are not just some whimsical invention of mystics and spiritualists, but rather have a firm grounding in scientific research.

Unfortunately, Powell's book did something else, too—it led to her medical license being revoked.

.   .   .

Less than two years after *The ESP Enigma* was published, a psychiatrist in a different medical community from hers—where she was highly respected—notified the medical board that Powell had written a book about ESP and therefore, as Powell puts it, "must be psychotic." The emergency meeting to strip Powell of her license left her unable to make a living at a time when she was divorced and supporting a daughter in high school. Powell sees the loss of her license as a direct result of her challenging the paradigm—posing questions that many found troubling. "I simply asked, how can we be so certain these things are impossible," Powell writes on her website, "especially when telepathy and precognition have been reported across all cultures, and throughout recorded history."

Powell was forced to undergo extensive psychological and neurological testing, after which a psychologist concluded she was "an eccentric genius willing to think out of the box." Three months after taking away her license, the board restored it. Powell wondered what it was about her book that so threatened the psychiatric establishment. In the wake of the incident, she resolved to bolster her case even more thoroughly and to "find the most compelling evidence that I could for psychic phenomena," she said at the time. "Which is why I chose to do research with autistic savants, whose abilities are so similar to ESP they are almost indistinguishable."

Which brings us to Vishal.

Even before she dived into her intense study of children with autism, Powell formed a theory that she presented at a Science of Consciousness conference in 2005 and included in *The ESP Enigma*. "I believed the autistic brain fits the profile and activity pattern for psychic abilities," she explains. "There were many parallels between some of the savant skills I was aware of and the right-brain functions that you see in dreaming."

Powell's book and theory caught the attention of Mythily Chari, a founder trustee of the Commandur Foundation and a vice president of the Autism Society of India. Chari invited Powell to come to Chennai, India, to visit with three young savants with psychic abilities, including a remarkable five-year-old autistic savant named Vishal.

Those who knew him described Vishal as a "walking Wikipedia" who "knows without studying"—someone with a staggering depth of knowledge that simply could not be explained. Socially reticent but playful and joyous, Vishal was just six when his ruminative and whimsical first book, *Meadow of Moods*, was published, challenging the stereotype that those with autism cannot also be introspective. He wrote letters to top scientists and mused about ways to harness nuclear energy. Powell traveled to India to meet Vishal (and his watchful mother Vidhya) and test him for savant skills—in particular, knowing information without any prior exposure, and solving a puzzle with a thousand pieces all the same color.

"I asked him scientific questions, and since he was nonverbal he typed out his answers on a computer, and he basically got most of them right," Powell remembers. "He was showing a broad knowledge of science that neither he nor his mother had been formally trained in. The question was, How is he getting this information?" In other words, was Vishal able to peer into Powell's mind and psychically retrieve the answers from her? Or was he somehow tapping into a universal invisible stream of knowledge and wisdom swirling around us all but accessible only to a few?

Back home, Powell worked with several other autistic savants in an attempt to solve this confounding variable. Did Vishal psychically get the answers from Powell, or did he mysteriously just know them?

Powell then met with another remarkable five-year-old autistic savant named Ramses. She found him through Facebook, where his parents had posted videos demonstrating his uncanny telepathic abilities. "His mother had a whiteboard that he couldn't see, and she wrote random numbers and figures on it, and from across the room with his back turned to her, Ramses would call out the numbers every time," Powell says. "My first thought was, *Wow, I have to meet this kid.*"

Powell learned that Ramses could recite the alphabets of at least eight languages, including Hebrew, Arabic, Russian, and Japanese. Unlike other savants she'd met, Ramses was verbal, allowing Powell to experience his inexplicably expansive vocabulary. "He used these little magnetic letters to leave notes and clever messages all over the house," she says. "The refrigerator wasn't working, and Ramses left a note that read, 'Fridge on vacation.'" Ramses's mother told Powell that her son spontaneously began reading at the age of four months.

Powell sat with Ramses and performed tests similar to those she'd seen on Facebook. She picked cards from a deck and hid them from Ramses and asked him to name the card—which he always did. She wrote random numbers on the whiteboard and, once again, Ramses could somehow see them in his mind. "It became very clear to me that Ramses was genuinely and highly telepathic," says Powell. "I concluded that if you accept autistic savants have other special skills, you should also accept that telepathy and ESP are among those skills."

But Powell has also seen children with autism exhibit one additional skill—mediumship.

"Many of these children are exhibiting a wide range of psi abilities—precognition, clairvoyance, past life recall, communicating with an angelic realm, and mediumship. They are highly psychic," she says.

In fact, I was privileged and honored to be invited to connect and communicate with one teenage girl with autism in an attempt to help her understand and manage her mediumistic abilities.

Through Dr. Powell's introduction, I met Mia, who is nonverbal and uses a talking board to communicate. Besides being telepathic and able to access information about numbers and objects from an unseen source, Mia shared that she could see and communicate with spirits of those no longer in a physical body. She also communicated that she found it distracting and overwhelming, and didn't know how to manage it.

On a recent trip with her mom to the doctor, Mia communicated through her talking board, which is a wonderful device developed using something called the Rapid Prompting Method, which allows nonverbal people with autism to have a voice. (If you know anyone who is nonverbal and autistic, please encourage their loved ones to look into the Rapid Prompting Method, or RPM for short; it can be life-changing for everyone. People who use this method of communication are referred to as "spellers.")

Mia shared that the spirit of her mother's friend, a little boy named Luke who had crossed from cancer at age six, was present. He wanted her to let his mom know that he was okay and in a beautiful place of love, and was with her still and loved her so much. To validate how present he was, the boy gave specific information about some changes his mother had just made to her home that Mia had no way to know about. He shared that he didn't want his mom to worry about him, and that he wanted her to laugh and have fun and feel joy in life. And so Mia became the messenger. Why did Luke choose Mia? Because she could see and perceive his energy! Our loved ones on the Other Side always look for any opportunity to let us know they are guiding us.

I believe that people with autism—a form of neurodivergence— have the ability to perceive the unseen energy that the brains of neurotypical people filter out. I have always been shown by the Other Side that our brains are really like dunce caps that keep us from remembering who we truly are on a soul level; they block us from seeing all the energy and cords of connection that are there. I believe the reason for that is so that here on Earth School, we can grow our souls in powerful ways. If we always had all the answers, we might not do the collective work.

With individuals with autism, however, the wiring, or rather filtering, system in the brain is a bit different. It's kind of like how, if you jail-break an iPhone, it can do all sorts of things the phone wouldn't otherwise allow. Individuals with autism often have trouble communicating in this earthly, heavy vibration; however, their personalities are vibrant and fully formed.

I was asked to connect with Mia for two reasons. The first was that Mia was highly telepathic and had expressed frustration that no one could "talk back to her" telepathically. We wanted to see if, in time, I might be able to. The second and more pressing reason was that she was overwhelmed by her mediumistic abilities and had no one to turn to who would understand and possibly help her navigate them.

Because we live in different countries, we connected over Zoom. On the Zoom with me were Mia, her mother, a translator, and another researcher that Dr. Powell works with. I watched as Mia was faced away from the camera. The researcher had a picture of a giraffe hidden on a piece of paper that Mia could not see. Mia was asked to tell us what was on the paper the researcher was holding.

Without missing a beat, Mia spelled out a word on her talking board: *g-i-r-a-f-f-e.*

Next the researcher wrote down a random six-digit number, with Mia still turned away from the camera. When she was asked what number was written down, Mia immediately tapped the correct number on her talking board.

How can you make sense of this using the accepted parameters of scientific thinking in the world today? Quite simply, you can't.

When Mia and I met on Zoom, we clicked instantly. Mia shared that she liked my energy and was glad to meet me. She then shared something interesting—she told her mom, through her talking board, that she (Mia) had thirty-nine antennas coming off her own head, and that she saw I had them, too! This fascinated me. I think what she was describing was energy cords, or feelers if you will, that we both have as a way of reading and connecting with unseen energy around us. It's the same energy that's around all of us. It's just a matter of finding a way to tune in to it.

I then spoke to Mia about ways she could manage her mediumistic abilities as she shared that she felt overwhelmed and scared by all she was experiencing. We spoke about how she had the power to not always have to be fully open to her abilities. I spoke to her about surrounding herself with a white protective light, and about envisioning a volume switch that she could use to turn down the energy when she needed quiet time.

I applaud Powell for being a critical thinker and for opening her mind and heart to the truth of these connections. It is not easy, especially in the world of science and academia, to stand up and walk a path that bucks the norm. (Remember how that went for Galileo and other forward-thinking seekers?)

Recently, a speech therapist in the Midwest reached out to Powell. The therapist was new to the world of unseen energy but was thrust into it when she began working with children with autism. These children, during the speech therapy sessions, spontaneously started performing unprompted psychic and mediumistic readings on her. They would know all sorts of things about her: what she ate for breakfast, that she had a dog, and even what the dog's name was. They talked about loved ones of hers who had crossed, and passed along messages of love and guidance from them. And it wasn't just one or two of the children—it was the *majority* of them. Flabbergasted and dumbfounded, the therapist reached out to faculty at the University of Virginia's Division of Perceptual Studies, who then directed her to someone they thought might have information to help her, who then directed her straight to Powell because she is known for this research. In other words, this speech therapist was *guided* to Powell. "I felt like I was going crazy before speaking to you," she told Powell. How fortunate for us all that Powell has chosen to break the taboo barrier of the materialistic prism of belief.

The truth of all this is powerful and far-reaching, not just for those children with autism, their families, and the researchers, but for all of us. Because the truth is something beautiful and profound, and something that belongs to us all: We are all connected. We are all loved. Those we love who have crossed are with us still, watching over us and guiding us.

Our lives are important and meaningful—not only because we have our own spiritual path but also because we are intertwined with the great fabric of collective energy. We just need to learn ways to open our minds and hearts to perceiving and feeling the unseen energy all around us—to tune in to the love and guidance—for it will illuminate our paths.

Powell's research led her to believe that children with autism "are more in touch with whatever the source of information is that's interconnected to us all. Whether you want to call it the collective unconscious or the hypersoul or whatever, these children are simply more tapped into it, likely because many of them have sensory processing disorders and as a result are less seduced by material distractions, less tethered to the material world. They are more attuned to the here and now."

The ultimate goal of her studies of children with autism, says Powell, "is for these kids to be recognized as the intelligent, introspective beings they are. And to have more of an overall acceptance that some people can do these remarkable things that most of us just can't understand."

That is Powell's holy grail, the big question she poses at the top of her website: *What is the full human potential?* What is possible and what isn't? Are we capable of vastly more than modern paradigms allow for? The questions keep coming, and Powell plans to keep asking them—to keep challenging the paradigm. "What if telepathy and other psychic abilities are innate to us all and expressed most highly in our infancy, but then disrupted by our development and language learning and pulling away from our parent-child bond?" Powell wonders. "What if these are abilities that we can all still access somehow?"

Powell, for one, has trained herself to be open to information received through all sorts of venues—including her own dreams. Years ago, she had a small mole on her leg and began having vivid dreams that she had melanoma. She showed the mole to her husband, whose specialty was oncology, and he told her it wasn't melanoma. "Then I had another dream, and another," Powell says. "So I went to see a doctor."

But the doctor, too, told her she most certainly did *not* have melanoma. Powell, however, chose to believe what her dreams were telling her. "I said, 'Doctor, I know it doesn't look like melanoma, but it's

really bothering me, so can you remove it and send it for a biopsy?'"
The doctor did so, and a week later phoned Powell with the test result.
"She told me the pathology report was positive for melanoma," Powell
says. "My dreams were right."

This special intuitiveness is what initially drew me to Dr. Powell,
and to now share her incredible insight with you. When I met her for
the first time at that Forever Family Foundation conference in 2013, I
got a quick download that she was going to be a truly important and
groundbreaking scientist and thinker in her field—"the Jane Goodall
of children with autism" is how I referred to her during our brief reading. But now I realize that what she's really doing, as she lives her
guided, illuminated life, is helping us all to be more dismissive of artificial limits and more accepting of whatever our true human potential
may be.

"What I've seen," Powell says, "is that if you start convincing people
that these abilities are real, and you demystify them and put them in a
strong scientific context, and sort of normalize them in a way, it's like
giving people permission to start recognizing these abilities in themselves. I've seen people begin to discover and accept the reality of these
abilities, and I've seen them begin to develop their own intuition and
see that it can be an extremely useful tool. It is about accepting that
there is so much more for all of us to explore."

Powell's openness and trust in her own intuitive pulls, knowings,
and dreams have guided her onto her highest path. And while there
will always be naysayers and obstacles in the academic arena and elsewhere, when it comes to researching and exploring psi phenomena,
the most important thing is to remain open and inquisitive—to be a
true explorer! That is what living an illuminated life is all about: trusting the guidance from your Team of Light, allowing them to reveal
your true purpose to you, and following the secret path that leads you
to the people and experiences that will expand and deepen your life—
and theirs.

A mystic is not one who sees God as
an object, but one who is immersed
in God as an atmosphere.

KEN WILBER

11

Holy Truth Begin Again

One of the keys to living an illuminated life is the understanding that our relationships do not end when a loved one crosses over.

In fact, these relationships can deepen and even feel more authentic and loving after someone has crossed. That is why I urge people to keep the lines of communication with loved ones open, so they can receive signs and messages and assurances from the Other Side. This continuing bond is so strong and vivid, it can even lead to the healing of earthly wounds and trauma.

Holly Ruth Finigan, an author and meditation leader, is a beautiful example of someone who understands the nature and power of these eternal bonds and uses them every day to lead a brighter, more vibrant life.

Holly is the middle of three daughters nicknamed "Small," "Medium," and "Large" by their mother, Ruth. "So even back then I guess I was a kind of medium," she says with a smile. Her parents, she believes, married too young and split up when Holly was just five years old. She was raised mainly by her mother, with whom she was exceptionally close. "My mother told everyone that I spent the first six months of my life literally attached to her hip," Holly says.

Holly spent every other weekend with her father, whose side of the family was Catholic. Yet Holly never felt much connection to the church. "Looking back, I realize I was a spiritual child rather than a religious one. No one ever gave me an understanding of what it meant to be spiritual, but I would get goose bumps and I believed that spirits were close by. I thought goose bumps meant something special was going to happen to me." Then someone told her, "No, goose bumps just mean you're cold," so Holly grew up thinking her body temperature was just lower than everyone else's. Even so, "I kept thinking, *This has to be something else,*" she says.

Eventually, Holly came to her own conclusion about her goose bumps.

"All the constant shivers—I now know that was feeling a spirit," she says. "I believe goose bumps are how the spirits announce themselves." At first, Holly didn't shape her life around her spirituality—which, back then, she only partly understood. She worked in restaurants and helped care for her mother, who fought off cancer for twelve years. It was only after her mother crossed, ten years ago, that everything changed for Holly—a change that her mother was very much involved in. "I have to say that my mother has been far more inspirational in my life in the decade since she crossed over," she says, "than during the thirty years I got to spend with her."

Holly's mother was diagnosed with leiomyosarcoma, a rare type of soft tissue cancer that began in her uterus, in July 2002. She had a full hysterectomy and was declared cancer-free for eight years. But in 2010, doctors found a large tumor on Ruth's lung. It was surgically removed, but over the next four years the cancer kept returning and doctors kept scooping out smaller tumors. "For me, I felt like the Universe kept knocking on her door, trying to get her to heal from something beyond cancer," Holly says. "Sadly, she just didn't have the tools to do it."

In early 2014, when her illness was all but incurable, Ruth began the journey to crossing over. "It was winter, which is the off-season on Nantucket, where I lived," Holly says, "so I spent a lot of time with my mother in Vermont. That was one of the greatest gifts of my life, that I got to be present with my mother at the end of her life."

Ruth crossed over on April 8, 2014. "The loss of my mother was the greatest loss of my life," Holly says. "My life giver was gone, and that seemed so unnatural. But even then, I didn't believe my mother just disappeared. I felt her death was just as much of a beginning as it was an ending."

The only problem was that Holly wasn't quite ready to explore the lessons in her mother's passing. Instead, she loaded up her schedule and overbusied herself so she wouldn't have to deal with the loss. She spent the next four years creating a strong social media presence and building a prominent online brand. She had a successful blog and founded the first social-media-based guide to Nantucket.

Only later did Holly understand what was really happening during those hectic years. "I stayed busy so I wouldn't have to confront my broken heart," she says. "After losing my mother, I did everything I could to avoid dealing with my grief."

Four years after her mother's passing, it was finally Holly's turn to confront her own mortality—and her broken heart.

Holly was born with Marfan syndrome, a connective tissue disorder that affected her heart. For most of her life she understood she would eventually need surgery to repair or replace a defective heart valve. In 2018, four years after her mother crossed, Holly finally decided to address the problem. She checked into Brigham and Women's Hospital in Boston and prepared for open-heart surgery.

The surgery was successful, but it sapped Holly of energy. She understood she would need time to heal and, slowly, she did. When she finally got her strength back, she discovered she had changed.

"I felt like some old version of myself had died," she says, "and the wise woman in me had woken up."

And because she is a writer, Holly began to write. A lot. "After the surgery it was almost like my hands started to write these answers instead of me deciding," she says. "I would ask, 'Who am I? Why am I here?' I was asking myself all these big questions, and the answers came pouring out." She was being guided.

This was when Holly embarked on a healing journey that continues to this day—a journey that led her to a truly illuminated life.

To mark her healing journey, Holly booked a trip to Bali, the magical Indonesian island known for its spiritual scene and enlightened Hindu culture. (Bali is where Elizabeth Gilbert, played by Julia Roberts in the movie *Eat Pray Love*, spends several months during her journey of self-discovery.) There, Holly wrote down her thoughts and experiences in her journal, including what she saw as a sign of assurance from her mother—a beautiful yellow butterfly. "I knew this was her coming to me and telling me I was on the right path," she says. Not long after, Holly went to see a gifted kirtan master, meditation teacher, and energy worker named Punnu Singh Wasu, who did his work out of the Yoga Barn, in the town of Ubud. Holly wasn't entirely sure why she was there—until she arrived at Punnu's door and saw a yellow butterfly flitting about.

"That's when I knew I was always meant to meet Punnu," she says. "They say when the student is ready, the teacher appears. I was definitely guided to him."

Her experience learning meditation and studying chakras with Punnu, and indeed all of her time in Bali, "opened everything up to me—all the truths I'd been seeking," she says. "It wasn't easy. It wasn't as simple as seeing a butterfly and thinking, *My mom is still here.* It involved a lot of work, particularly the meditation. But once you start the work, you realize that turning within is the most beautiful journey you can ever take in your life." Turning within, in fact, is how the secret path to an illuminated life can be discovered.

Why, exactly, did Holly believe her journey was so essential?

"Because it helped me discover who I am," she says. "Especially who I am when no one else is watching."

Holly's journey allowed her nothing short of a complete reevaluation of her life, her place in the Universe, her purpose going forward, and the very meaning of her existence. One of the things she discovered was that her whole life had been far more spiritually inclined than she'd previously believed.

"I'll give you an example," she says. "For many years I served as a bartender, which in the old days could be called a *spirit tender*. People would come in and order beer, wine, and cocktails, and I would serve them drinks—the spirits. But for my whole life I'd been looking for a connection to the *other* spirits, on the Other Side. Finally, I realized you didn't need to serve people liquor in order to help them to connect to the spirits. We can all go on a transformative spiritual journey just by focusing on our breathing.

"What I realized was that I was in fact a spirit tender. My whole life, I had been tending to the spirits all around me. And I still do that today."

Holly's bartending days are behind her, and since her mother's passing, she has devoted her life to helping others find healing through spiritual work. The first person she helped, however, was already on the Other Side—her recently crossed mother, Ruth. "My mother never really challenged herself in her life," she says. "She was a wonderful mother and a great success at being a mother, but she didn't go on her own journey to seek the truth of who she was and why she was here. She carried so much shame and guilt within her about different events and failings in her life, and she never just sat down and meditated and discovered her real self. Now I feel like I am doing the spiritual work with her, doing the work I believe she wished she'd done."

Imagine that—believing you can help your mother heal from her trauma even *after* she has crossed over. What a powerful, sustaining, beautiful belief that is! It acknowledges that our relationships with loved ones not only continue after a crossing but can be deepened and strengthened as well. "What I learned is that we are here to be both human *and* spirit," Holly says. "To embody what I call the big Self and the little self: a human self with all the social conditioning *and* a divine Self that never changes and never goes away."

The writer in Holly leads her to see words and names as symbols she can use to convey her spiritual beliefs. Her human name, she explains, is Holly Ruth Finigan. But as she delved deeper and deeper into her spiritual self, another name emerged—Holy Truth Begin Again.

"Holly is the daughter, the sister, the partner, the friend; she is all the roles and archetypes, and I love her," Holly says. "But Holy is who I really am. Holly follows the rules and conditions of mortality. Holy is timeless and eternal—a connected source and a part of everyone else."

This subtle bifurcation between her human and spirit selves helped Holly understand how to shed some of the trauma her mother never confronted and thus passed along to her. "What I was doing," she says, "was unpacking all the stories that weren't mine so I could begin life again and work my way back to my authentic self." In essence, Holly was trying to integrate everything that happened to her in her life in order to see where something got blocked and prevented her from living the rich, fulfilling life she wanted.

"One of the traumas I knew I had was deep abandonment," she says. "The trauma you go through between the ages four and seven imprints itself on your heart. So if your parents get divorced when you are five, you may end up living with a closed-off heart and attachment issues."

To learn how to feel empowered, Holly focused her work on chakras. The word *chakra*, which means "wheel" or "disk" in Sanskrit, refers to one of the centers of spiritual power and energy in the human body. There are seven chakras: a root chakra; a sacral chakra; a solar plexus chakra; heart, throat, and third-eye chakras; and a crown chakra. Holly's studies allowed her to understand her own power to heal not only her trauma but also any buried trauma her mother Ruth had never addressed.

"We all have opportunities in our lives to go back and heal the trauma for those who didn't heal it," Holly says. "I felt like I was healing my mother through healing myself. I recognized how my mother carried all her guilt and fear and shame, and how they could have been passed to me like a toxic torch. But by healing my own heart chakra, I was able to stop it from happening." Doing this, in energy terminology, is called doing *constellation work*.

Or as Holly loves to say, "To heal it, you gotta feel it."

Holly seeks to discover the divine name for everyone she crosses paths with, but these names to her aren't just clever wordplays attached to idle spiritual beliefs. They are, Holly believes, the key to understanding who we are and where we belong in the Universe—the most important questions of all. "We all have this other spirit side to us; it's just that not all of us do the work to tap into it," she says. "Put your hand over your heart. Feel the heartbeats on your palm. I believe those heartbeats are our higher selves knocking, telling us, 'I am here, I am here, I am here.' If your heart is beating, you are alive, and if you're alive, your divine Self is inside you, relentlessly reminding you that you are part of something much bigger than just yourself, guiding you onto your highest path."

Which brings Holly to another powerful word—*alone*.

"To me, *alone* means 'all one,'" she says. "We can't ever be alone because we are connected to everyone else in existence—we are *all one*."

What Holly is doing is searching for the meanings *behind* the definitions we've been given and mostly accepted as, well, definitive. She is looking for the divine truth of what these words are trying to describe—the vast network of love and light and connection that exists just beyond our capacity to aptly describe it, as well as the immense well of healing power and energy that exists within us all. Your name was given to you and is your name, but it's *not* all that you are. Neither are the parameters others have built around your life—in Holly's mother's case, the all-consuming obligation of being a mother apart from her spiritual self. Holly—ever the spirit tender—wants to help others access the much deeper truth of who they are and how they fit in.

Today, Holly uses her gifts as a spirit tender to empower others

through her meditation and chakra healing workshops. She emphasizes that not everyone needs to dive into their healing journey as con-
sumingly as she has. What matters most is that we open the door and
have the courage to *begin again*.

"No one is too busy for this," Holly says. "Spirituality does not have
to be this arduous ordeal. It can be as simple as meditating a few minutes a day."

What matters, Holly says, is that we simply *start* the journey—much
like you are doing right this moment by reading this book and taking
these words to heart.

12

Hindsight Is 20/20

The stories you've read so far show that often we can't see the big picture of our interconnectedness—the magical threads binding us—but sometimes after many years have passed, we gain a better understanding of how we have impacted each other's paths. We may go through rough times in our lives, and it's only ten or fifteen years later that we think, *Oh, wow, if I hadn't gone through that I wouldn't have met this person or found this job.* Or we reflect on how some small event from our past helped us avoid a tragedy in the future.

This phenomenon is sometimes called the butterfly effect, a facet of chaos theory that holds that small changes in a system can eventually result in large differences. It was a meteorologist, Edward Norton Lorenz, who developed the theory after seeing how small, sometimes imperceptible early changes to a weather model could, several weeks later, lead to a violent tornado. He likened these early actions to the gentle flapping of a butterfly's wing, a mere wisp of energy compared to the 200 mph winds of a severe tornado. Today, the butterfly effect doesn't just refer to weather; it's about any small event that leads to significantly larger consequences.

Another way to think about this phenomenon is the way that tossing a tiny pebble into a lake causes a series of ever-widening ripples that dwarf the pebble's size.

The same is true of the invisible light and energy that guide us through our lives. We cannot always see or feel this light when we go through an experience, but in hindsight it's clear we were always being steered onto a higher, safer, and better path. The small events of the past shape the larger realities of our present. I find it greatly reassuring that even in our darkest moments, we are being guided toward a brighter light. Often, we are doing powerful work, growing our souls, expanding with love. I hope you feel reassured by that as well.

Frequently in my readings I see timelines of people's lives, and sometimes in those timelines I see a certain period of time bracketed off. I've come to call these periods *soul cycles.* By that I mean that we can get locked into a cycle of behavior or circumstances that we don't quite understand at the time, but that, years later, make sense. Some of my sitters will describe being stuck in what they perceived to be a bad relationship—a cycle they found difficult to break out of. I tell them what I see—that the relationship was a *soul contract* meant to help someone's soul grow. They were never stuck—they were where they needed to be for their own growth and for their partner's growth, too.

Past events had ripple effects that changed the future.

I'd like to share the story of a lovely man who has sat for readings with me. His name is Danny, and in the space of three years he suffered the tragic death of his son followed by the passing of his ex-wife (who he was extremely close to). When I read for Danny, I could see that energetically he was in the midst of a painful and powerful cycle of soul growth. I saw that he was doing the work and *not* off his path.

On the phone Danny told me that his body was falling apart, and that life had only become rougher and rougher in the past months, and that he couldn't believe that God or the Universe was throwing more painful suffering his way after all he'd been through. "I've already lost my two favorite people way before their time," he said. "It's too much. I'm losing faith."

During the reading, I picked up a message to Danny from his son,

who took his own life. His son shared that the fifteen or so months leading up to Danny turning sixty were going to be a very, very difficult
time, and that in fact that cycle had already begun. I told him he was
about to face a series of life lessons—the highest master class of
lessons—that he'd need to find a deep strength to face. Finally, I told
Danny what his son was insisting I say: that, through it all, there was
one thing, one vital truth, he absolutely had to remember: *Everything
that happens to you is happening for you.*

Six weeks later, Danny went through what he called "a scary and
emotionally traumatic event." The next day, another deeply stressful
thing happened, and on the third day, there was yet *another* traumatic
event. This went on for five days in a row. Despite the message from his
son—that everything that happened to him was happening for him—
this accumulation of traumas pushed Danny to the edge.

"I was driving home on the fifth day when I started to lose my mind
a little," Danny told me. "I started to yell at God out loud. I was screaming at the top of my voice, 'How can you do this to me? How can you
keep doing all this stuff to me?'" Just then—*just then*—Danny felt a
strange calm, as well as the urge to look to his left. Out the car window,
he saw the license plate of the car driving by him.

It read, *4 U DANNY.*

Danny then remembered the message from his son that I'd shared.

"I started laughing," he says now. "I felt my son laughing with me,
his beautiful, trademarked loud laugh. And I felt this extraordinary
emotion, like I was being held in the hand of God. The next morning
I sat down at my desk and looked out the window at nature, at a tree
swaying back and forth in the wind, and in an instant, I knew what
those five stressful days had meant, what the lesson in each of those
days was. Each event became a slice of wisdom for me."

We can't always see it at the time, but the Universe and our Team
of Light are guiding us through our very darkest hours—and eventually
we'll see just how our paths were always illuminated. That's what the
next part of this book is about—finding the light of guidance in the
darkness that can sometimes overwhelm our lives.

EXPLORING THE LIGHT IN THE DARKNESS

As I was writing this book, I tried to imagine someone reading it while they were in the darkest period of their lives. Someone who had lost a child or a spouse, someone whose world had been shattered. What would they get out of it? Would they say, 'Well, all this stuff about a secret path through life is a nice little fairy tale, but what am I supposed to do with that when all I feel is grief? When I can barely breathe?"

I kept that thought in mind as I wrote Part Two. The people in these chapters have gone through impossibly difficult times, when all they could see around them was darkness. A sister who lost a brother. A wife who lost a husband. Parents whose child died mysteriously.

What they all discovered is that, even in the pitch-black darkness of loss and grief and confusion, there is light.

The light is there for us to see and feel, like the sun breaking through clouds. That bright light of guidance is *always* there for us, especially in the hard times. Our connection to each other and to the Universe is unbreakable, and it endures even when we feel like we've been victimized and forgotten by the Universe. These stories show that while our Teams of Light on the Other Side cannot always prevent us from experiencing suffering and grief, they are always right there with us as we go through the trauma, loving us and guiding us and helping us navigate the seemingly dark path.

What our Teams of Light need us to know is that *everything we experience in life is tied to love.*

But how are we supposed to see losing a loved one as an experience that's somehow tied to love? How can we look at it as anything other than a meaningless tragedy?

As you'll see from the stories in this section, making an adjustment and seeing tragic events as part of our soul path is not easy. Most of the time, it's extremely difficult, especially when we're still going through the heartbreak of loss.

But what I've learned from the Other Side is that being alive is like being in Earth School, and in this school, hardship is part of the lesson plan. None of us are exempt from pain and suffering. But I've also learned that every single thing we experience here *is meant to grow our love.*

Sometimes on our paths through life, we find that we've signed up for a particularly hard soul experience, the purpose of which might elude us at the time. What we need to cling to in these times is the understanding—the reassurance—that *all* our soul tests are meant to grow our capacity to love. Nothing is random and no one is forgotten. We are always being guided toward a higher, richer path.

Think of what happens when we walk out of the bright sunlight and into a darkened room. For a moment, we can't see anything at all because our eyes need time to reacclimate. But once we make that adjustment, the darkness lifts, and we begin to see the light that was always there.

When terrible things happen to us, we need time to reacclimate too. At first there is only darkness, but in time we will see the light that was always there. We need to trust that this will happen in our lives, that things won't always be dark, even when grief consumes every face of our lives. Because even then, when all seems lost, there is light in the darkness, illuminating our path out of the woods.

Lead

Here is a story
to break your heart.
Are you willing?
This winter
the loons came to our harbor
and died, one by one,
of nothing we could see.
A friend told me
of one on the shore
that lifted its head and opened
the elegant beak and cried out
in the long, sweet savoring of its life
which, if you have heard it,
you know is a sacred thing,
and for which, if you have not heard it,
you had better hurry to where
they still sing.
And, believe me, tell no one
just where that is.
The next morning
this loon, speckled
and iridescent and with a plan
to fly home
to some hidden lake,
was dead on the shore.
I tell you this
to break your heart,
by which I mean only
that it break open and never close again
to the rest of the world.

MARY OLIVER

13

Always and from the Start

Though nothing can bring back the hour
Of splendour in the grass, of glory in the flower;
We will grieve not, rather find
Strength in what remains behind.

WILLIAM WORDSWORTH, "ODE: INTIMATIONS OF
IMMORTALITY FROM RECOLLECTIONS
OF EARLY CHILDHOOD"

They were students at Syosset High School, on the north shore of Long Island. She was a sophomore, he a junior. They went on a single date, and a few days later he asked her to marry him. But she had another boyfriend and she didn't want to date two boys at once.

"Come back in ten years," she told him.

They went their separate ways, married other people, started careers, led their lives. And then he did what she told him to do.

He came back in ten years.

What happened next, and long afterward, is the story I want to share with you now.

Believe me, it's a love story.

. . .

Their history together actually predates high school—Liz Rosenberg, who would become a writer and professor at Binghamton University, and David Bosnick, an aspiring middle school teacher, attended the same summer day camp on Long Island when she was seven and he was eight, though neither made an impression on the other at the time and only later realized they had been campmates. (Liz remembered a girl who used to stand too close on the monkey bars and breathe down her neck, and years later she recognized that girl in David's summer camp photo.)

Nor was their first conversation, at Syosset High School, an auspicious start. Liz knew David by reputation: He was a state champion wrestler and football player who went into the folders of his fellow English class students and left witty or brutal notes on their poems. "I heard he wrote horrible things under the name Mephisto, things like 'Grovel in your own infinite hypocrisy, worm,'" Liz recalls. On one of Liz's own poems, the message was even more direct:

You call this poetry?

"I was *really* mad about that," she says. "And he was a year ahead, so he wasn't even in our class. I thought, *Who is this David Bosnick guy and what gives him the right to pick apart our poems?*"

Liz vowed to do something about it, and one afternoon she confronted David in the library. Summoning up all her fury and resolve, she slammed her poem down on the table in front of him. David calmly picked up the poem, studied it for a moment and looked up at Liz, hovering above him.

"I didn't write this," he said.

"What?"

"Wasn't me."

He wasn't lying; David had *not* written the remark. "God, that was embarrassing," Liz says. "It was supposed to be my big moment, and this guy is just calmly sitting there looking at me like I'm crazy."

She and David wound up sitting at the table and talking about poe ry for the next two hours straight. Later she found out he had skipped wrestling practice so he could stay with her.

Then came David's ill-fated wedding proposal and Liz's polite "ten years" rejection. David accepted his fate but stayed in touch. He made expensive long-distance calls he was afraid to tell his parents about. In his typewriter he always kept a sheet of paper with a letter to Liz in progress. Liz went on to publish stories and poems and to earn a master's in creative writing and a PhD in comparative literature, taking a professorship at Binghamton University in upstate New York. David earned a master's in English and in teaching, as well as a PhD in creative writing at Colgate University before creating and running independent bookstores in Binghamton and on Cape Cod.

In the mid-1970s, Liz lived with the well-known American novelist John Gardner. Through that courtship, she and David continued to keep in touch. When Liz and John went through a rough patch, Liz escaped to North Carolina to spend some calm time with David. "It just felt like a safe place to be," she explains.

At the end of her stay, David drove her to the airport, where he briefly met John Gardner. "They talked for a minute or two, very friendly, and then David just turned and ran away," Liz says. "I mean, he was an athlete and he ran full-speed away from us. He didn't want to hang around and make small talk." John watched him dash away and later told Liz, "You know, that may be the only man in the world who loves you more than I do."

The friendship endured. It endured when Liz married John in 1980, and when David married someone else and started a life with her. "I remember calling his sister to see how he was doing, and she told me he had a wife," Liz says. "I thought, *Good for him. I want him to be happy.*" She and David spoke less often, sent each other fewer letters, but they never broke the connection between them. It just kept going.

And then, as sometimes happens in life, both Liz and David grew apart from their spouses. As they went through the process of their divorces, they resumed their calls and talks. The timing, it seemed, was right, and once again, David proposed. "This match is what David wanted," his mother later commented. "It's what he *always* wanted."

As David put it, "I never stopped loving her."

It took a few months, but they finally set a wedding date for the spring. As it happened, they actually married in winter. And when they stood shivering in a freezing trailer and exchanged vows in front of a justice of the peace who memorably stuttered, Liz realized the significance of their wedding date.

It was ten years after she first turned him down.

As fated as their nuptials might have seemed—and each of them described the other as their bashert, or fated one—Liz and David had to get married not just once, not twice, but *three* times to get it right.

Their first wedding, that small affair presided over by the justice, had only six guests. It took place on the final day of classes at Binghamton, and Liz wore a purple wool dress to her last class. David wore a dark blue suit with white sneakers. They exchanged rings, and on the ring David gave Liz he inscribed the words *Always and from the start.* The ceremony was short and sweet and joyous.

Ten years later, David's ex-wife asked him to send her a copy of their divorce papers (she was planning to remarry). David looked for them but couldn't find them.

It turned out his mother, who worked for a lawyer, had accidentally misfiled the paperwork.

Liz and David's marriage, technically, was null and void because he'd never been divorced.

They laughed it off, but when the family's lawyer learned about it, he insisted that Liz and David have a formal ceremony right away. This time, they chose to have a large traditional Jewish wedding. Their eight-year-old son, Eli, helped hold up the chuppah, the wedding canopy. A rabbi they both knew well presided, and they received a beautifully illustrated scrolled ketubah, a Jewish marriage contract.

A few years later, the couple decided to adopt an infant from China. They filled out dozens and dozens of forms and spent eighteen months on a waiting list before, finally, being cleared to adopt a baby girl. They already had a name picked out: Lily. With just a few days to go before the paperwork would be finalized, Liz and David got an urgent call from their adoption agency.

"Where's the paperwork from your second marriage?" they asked.

David immediately called the rabbi who had married them.

"Where did you file our paperwork?" he asked.

"I didn't file any paperwork," the rabbi responded. "I thought *you* were filing the paperwork. All I gave you was the ketubah."

As far as official marriages went, Liz and David were zero for two.

Unlike the first foul-up, this time there was a real sense of urgency—they needed to produce a legal wedding certificate, or they would not be permitted to complete the adoption. They hustled down to their local city hall on a Saturday and—needing to send out the proper paperwork that Monday—waited for their turn in front of the clerk.

The clerk looked over their application and said, "You do know there's a forty-eight-hour waiting period from the time you come in to file the papers before you can actually get married?"

Liz and David looked at each other in a panic. A forty-eight-hour delay meant they would not get the adoption paperwork in on time. After spending eighteen months on a waiting list, they might lose their one chance to adopt Lily.

"We don't have forty-eight hours," David said, explaining their situation.

The clerk held his ground. There was nothing he could do.

Just then, the secretary working in the office got up from her desk and asked the clerk to follow her into an adjacent room.

Liz and David watched through a window as the secretary scolded the clerk, waving her arms and pointing back at them. They heard her say, "You're going to do this for them, and you're going to marry them today, and that's what you're going to do!"

The clerk returned and performed the ceremony. When he asked

Liz the fateful question, she said, "For the third and final time, I do!" After fourteen years and a child together, Liz and David were finally, *finally* married for real.

Not much later, they met their beautiful daughter in China, and their family was complete.

When Liz was offered a Fulbright Scholarship at Queen's University in Northern Ireland in 2013, she and David moved to Belfast for a semester. By then Eli was twenty-four and off on his own, but ten-year-old Lily went with them. Liz took the winter off from Binghamton University, while David took a sabbatical from his eighth-grade English teaching job. They settled into a lovely rental home near the Belfast Botanical Garden, within walking distance of Lily's school and David's gym. It was a wonderful time, new and different, full of promise and adventure.

One morning David walked Lily to school, holding her hand as always, before heading to the gym for a workout. Later that day, as Liz was in a cab on her way to pick up Lily, her cell phone rang. She was running late, and she didn't answer the call. Her cell rang again, and then a third time, and Liz finally answered it. The female voice on the other end said, "Are you connected to David Bosnick?"

"Yes, I'm his wife," Liz replied.

There was a pause. "Your husband has been brought here to Royal Hospital and he's . . . very seriously ill."

A thousand scenarios played out in Liz's head, none of them good. "Well, is he alive?" she finally asked.

"He's very gravely ill."

Liz thought, *Well, that can't be good.* Then the woman on the phone told her to come to Victoria Hospital right away, and asked if she had someone who could drive her home.

"When she asked me that," Liz recalls, "that's when I knew."

David had just been warming up on a stationary bicycle at the gym when suddenly he bowed his head and collapsed. A doctor happened to be working out nearby and rushed to his side. By then, the doctor would later tell Liz, David was already gone.

He'd suffered an aneurysm. He was fifty-nine years old. Physically, David was a bear of a man, strong and fit from years of wrestling, capable of bench-pressing three hundred pounds. He had muscular arms and a dark golden beard that "made him look like Hercules," Liz says. He ate only healthy foods and worked out regularly, and he'd recently had a checkup and was deemed in peak condition. "What I used to tell people was that he was the healthiest dead man I ever knew," Liz says.

David's sudden passing shattered everyone he knew. "He was an amazing man," Liz says. "His students adored him and never forgot him, not to this day. He was a great storyteller, he was funny and wise, and he cared about everyone who crossed his path. He was guided by the idea that we are here to manifest our goodness in the world."

The high school boy who'd been a bully had shed his youthful bravado and become a man of great humility, exuberance, and love for humanity. "Everyone who knew him was elevated by the acquaintance," read one obituary. "He made a difference in the lives of countless students, and he lives in every person he touched," read a condolence note. Another good friend and mourner said, "Touch football in Rec Park, working at the bookstore, swimming at the lake, birthday parties with the kids, dinners at Bingham's, hanging out at your house with his warmth, humor and deep caring filling the room: during difficult times, his encouragement, generosity and wisdom gave us all strength. As he always liked to say, 'There is hope in action.'"

Liz remembers one of his students leaning out the drive-through window at McDonald's to greet David with utter elation: "Hey, Dr. B., how you doing? So good to see you, Dr. B.!"

"When I asked David who that was, he told me it was a student whom he'd given a C in his class," Liz says. "I thought, *Wow, if the kids he gave Cs to feel this way about him, how much must the A students love him?*"

At the end of every class David taught at West Middle School in Binghamton, he inspired his eighth-grade students with the same impassioned exhortation: "Go forth you angels of eighth, you wizards of West, you acmes, you geniuses—get out there and light the world!"

That was David—a giver of light and life and love. And then, in an instant, he was gone. But even then, in the darkest hours of her life, Liz experienced a sensation that was raw and real and unexpected and, most of all, hopeful. "From the very start of losing him," she says, "I had the sense that he hadn't just disappeared into the ether. I felt very strongly that he was still near."

On the day of David's funeral Liz gazed out a window overlooking the parked hearse and remembered a line of poetry.

Let there be no severing of our love.

The line comes from an 1807 poem by William Wordsworth, "Ode: Intimations of Immortality from Recollections of Early Childhood"—a beautiful meditation on the purity of our childhoods and the loss of our innocent connection to nature, and the poem that includes the well-known lines in this chapter's epigraph. In the poem, the actual text reads:

And O, ye Fountains, Meadows, Hills, and Groves,
Forebode not any severing of our loves!
Yet in my heart of hearts I feel your might;
I only have relinquished one delight
To live beneath your more habitual sway

"That was my most fervent prayer," Liz says. "That the love between us, the intense connection, not be severed."

For the first year after David's passing, it wasn't. Liz constantly heard David's voice in her head, advising her on family matters, chiming in on decisions, and otherwise remaining present. "It was his voice or even words," Liz explains. "I'd say something, and I knew it came from David, not me. I would tell Lily something, and it was David passing things along to her."

This was in keeping with Liz's Jewish faith, which dictates a seven-

day period of intense mourning, followed by thirty days without frivol-
ity and, finally, after a full year, the freeing of your loved one's soul to
ascend to a higher place. Liz followed these teachings and felt heartened that, as she mourned David, he remained a very real part of her
life. Being able to "hear his voice" meant her prayer had come true: in
her heart of hearts, she still felt David's might, and had only relinquished the joy of his physical presence.

But after almost precisely one year, Liz stopped hearing his voice.

"That was the weirdest thing," she says. "That sense of absolute proximity and connection went away. It made me think of a Chagall painting where a bride floats above her husband and he reaches out to touch
his dead wife, but she's just out of reach. That's how I felt and I had to
accept it. He's not within reach anymore."

Yet he was.

Liz first noticed that her connection to David had only changed —
and not ended — on what would have been his sixtieth birthday, July 14,
2014. It was a sad day for her, and she missed David even more than
usual — until, in the late afternoon, she reached into the pocket of a coat
she hadn't worn in some time and pulled out a fifty-dollar bill. She had
no idea when she'd left it there, or why she chose that coat that day, yet
the serendipity of the surprising gift lifted her heart. "And then almost
without thinking about it, I knew the money had come from David,"
Liz says. "It was just like him to get me a present on *his* birthday."

She could hear David's words in her head: "Go across the street and
buy something beautiful, and know that the gift is from me."

On David's next birthday, Liz received an unexpected royalty check.
On another, she was sent a contract for a literary project that had been
delayed for six months. One year, she found a precious ring she'd lost
years earlier. "After about the fifth time it happened, year after year,
you start to think, *Okay, this isn't just cool, this is weird*," Liz says. "The
gift was always something totally unexpected that brought me happiness and made me think of David."

Ten years have now passed since David's crossing, and, Liz says, "he
hasn't missed a single birthday yet."

.   .   .

Not long ago, Liz faced a difficult task made harder by David's passing—it was time to move out of the beautiful old house they had lived in together for nearly thirty years.

"We were only moving eight blocks away, but it meant going through everything in the old house and packing it up," says Liz. "It felt like a kind of big, heavy goodbye."

With help from friends and family—including her now-teenage daughter, Lily—Liz boxed up their possessions and thoroughly cleaned the house before the movers arrived. For some reason, just before t was time to leave, Liz sat back down at the large desk David had used for his work. "I'd already completely emptied it out," she says. "Papers and envelopes and letters and stamps, a million things, and I boxed them all up. I mean, I got every last paper clip."

Though she knew the desk was empty, Liz opened the top center drawer and peered inside, not knowing what she expected to see.

There was nothing in the drawer.

Then she reached into the back of the drawer, as you do when you're trying to scoop out everything that has gathered there over the years. Again, she found nothing—until her finger reached the farthest corner of the drawer. There, she felt something and pulled it out.

It was a coin. A lightweight coin that somehow got overlooked in her first thorough cleaning.

Liz held the coin in her hand, trying to figure out what it was. She had never seen it before. It was flattened and had a hole in the center, like one of those souvenir pennies you get at a carnival or an amusement park. Then she saw a small and smudged but legible inscription:

Always and from the start.

The phrase on Liz's wedding ring—David had etched it on this silly carnival coin he kept in his top drawer. And now Liz had nearly left the coin in the desk, forever consigning it to a storage locker, until something compelled her to reach into the drawer again.

"I just sat there and looked at this coin, and I thought I was dreaming," she says. "It was so clearly a message from David. I mean, I was so sure the desk was empty, and then, last of all, out comes this beautiful coin. It was like a magician's trick."

And what was the message David was so clearly sending her?

"It was like he was saying, 'Okay, you've packed up and you're leaving this place that we shared, and you're leaving all these memories behind and in a way leaving our life together behind, but guess what—it doesn't work that way. You can't get rid of me that easily. You never could. It's what I told you all those years ago: *Always and from the start.*'"

So go their lives together, Liz and David, always and from the start. Liz still hears his voice sometimes—she believes it was David who got into her head and persuaded her to tell their daughter, Lily, that she should visit the campus of Hofstra University before accepting an invitation to another school, resulting in Lily declaring, the moment she stepped on the Hofstra campus, "Okay, this is where I want to go."

The connection between Liz and David is different from what it once was; she still misses his big, bearlike presence, his physical warmth, his expansiveness with other people. But she no longer feels that David is out of reach. Instead, she knows he is right there with her—that there has been no severing of their love. Both Liz and David are Light Workers, and together they lived an illuminated life—sharing their love and life and wisdom with others, honoring their interconnected place in the Universe, manifesting their goodness in the world. Today, together still, they are lighting a path for others to follow.

"If there is only one thing in existence that is universal, I believe it is love," Liz says. "If you believe that, then you know you can never be separated from the people that you love and who love you. In the teachings of Judaism, when a parent dies, their ability to protect their child does not decrease but actually increases. Their influence still exists in the Universe. That is true for all of us—our love is eternal. Maybe I can't see David anymore. But that doesn't mean he's not there. He is there, right there with me. That will never change."

At any moment, you have a
choice that either leads you closer
to your spirit or further away.

THICH NHAT HANH

14

Those Who Guide
and Change Us

Perhaps you're curious about how I came across Liz and David's beautiful story of love and connection. If so, I'd like to share something that is sacred to me and rooted deep in my heart. I had the privilege of knowing David, whom I called Professor Bosnick, during a pivotal time in my life—a time when I was seeking and searching for my own path. David, in short, illuminated the way.

He was one of those key people who, if you are lucky enough to encounter one in your life, point you in the right direction and help you become a better version of yourself. They help you see the light of your own being. They guide you. You become changed for having known them. David did that for me. I've come to understand that such connections are not accidental, nor are they coincidences on our paths. I have come to know that the Universe guides certain magical people into our paths at pivotal times.

On a crisp fall day during my sophomore year at Binghamton University in upstate New York, I took my seat in the classroom of the Detective Fiction course I'd signed up for. I was a literature and rhetoric major who was also pre-law. The title of the course intrigued me. I expected the first day of class to go as all the others had: the professor would politely introduce him- or herself, hand out a syllabus, go over the expectations, and discuss the scope of the course. My peers and I sat a bit impatiently as we noticed no professor had yet arrived at the front of the classroom.

Suddenly, the door to the classroom flew open. A rather burly man, shoulders square, dark blond hair in curls spilling over his head, wearing a trench coat and carrying a hard, rectangular, burgundy-colored briefcase, burst into the room. Saying nothing, he slammed the briefcase down on the desk. While my peers and I tried to take in this sudden development, the door suddenly flew open a second time, and in rushed another man in a dark black coat. He quickly grabbed the briefcase that had been set down on the front desk and darted out with it.

It all happened in a flash, and the class didn't know how to react. Hushed giggles, whispers and exclamations of "What was that?" echoed around the classroom.

We all looked at each other, dumbfounded. Who was this man standing in front of us in a beige trench coat? Who was that other man? Why did he just steal that briefcase? What was going on?

The man in the front of the room took off his coat, placed it on the desk in front of him, cleared his throat, and said, "I'm Professor Bosnick. Welcome to Detective Fiction. Please take out a piece of paper and write down a description of the perpetrator and of what just happened."

Varying accounts ensued. The perpetrator was tall, short, brown-eyed, blue-eyed. He had on glasses, no glasses, sunglasses. He wore sneakers, dress shoes, boots. His hair? Brown, black, blond, light brown, red.

For real.

What we learned was that most of us would be horrible witnesses.

I was hooked. This unconventional—thrilling—teaching method lit me up!

But who was this Professor Bosnick?

Over the course of the semester I quickly learned the answer.

Professor Bosnick was an adjunct professor at Binghamton. His wife, Liz Rosenberg, was an English professor at Binghamton, equally beloved by the masses. (My friend Erica was in Liz's creative writing course and raved about both the course and its professor.) In addition, Professor Bosnick owned the local bookstore, The Bookbridge, in nearby Vestal Plaza. He and his wife had an adorable two-year-old son, Eli. Professor Bosnick's energy invited us all into his kaleidoscopic world. He was a seeker, a creative, a poet. A man of truth, honor, and intelligence, with a great sense of justice, an equally great sense of humor, and a twinkle in his eye. His love for his family was palpable. He would light up when talking about them. I looked forward to every class he taught, and to going to poetry readings at his bookstore. Liz was a published poet, and I fell in love with her writing, particularly her poem "My Husband Takes a Photograph of Me," from her collection *Children of Paradise* (the husband, of course, was David). I found them to be the ideal family. Full of goodness and kindness and light— vibrantly engaged in life and learning and community.

It is said that to earn the respect of those you admire is one of the most powerful and meaningful things we can experience. And that proved true for me. At the end of the course, Professor Bosnick invited me to be a teaching assistant (TA) for him the following semester, for a course he would be teaching called Literature and the Law. I was bursting with joy. It was such an honor to be asked, especially by someone I admired and respected so profoundly. Most important, I was excited to continue to be around his effervescent, inspiring energy, and to continue to learn and be mentored by him.

My semester as a TA was one of the most meaningful of my life. By placing me in this role, Professor Bosnick had shifted how I viewed myself. Here I was, teaching a discussion section of my own, grading the papers (which often included those of some of my senior sorority sisters). Being a TA also had an unexpected result on me. I fell in love—with teaching. There were three other TAs besides me, all of whom were seniors, and it was wonderful to be part of a collaborative group. I felt that I was being guided into seeing something about myself that I hadn't recognized before: how passionate I felt about teaching. One of my very favorite parts of being a TA was our weekly meetings, where Professor Bosnick and the four of us would discuss curriculum, as well as our paths ahead of us. I'd already shared I was pre-law and planned to become an attorney.

"The world is full of lawyers, Laura. TEACH! Create! Bring about change! Dive into ideas!" Professor Bosnick would declare to me loudly, unapologetically, and enthusiastically, with joy in his voice.

Little did he or I know how profoundly the experience of being a TA would change my path. For his words stuck with me, and the opportunity he gave me revealed my true passion for teaching. Neither of us knew it then, but right after I graduated college, I would turn down my admission to law school at the last minute and I would instead about-face and sign up for graduate school to become a teacher, beginning in the fall.

At our last meeting at the end of the semester, Professor Bosnick changed the usual meeting place from The Bookbridge and instead took all four of us out to dinner at Number 5, which was the fanciest, most expensive restaurant in Binghamton at the time. At dinner, he thanked us and gave us each a card and an envelope. In the envelope, he explained, was an equal portion of the salary that he got paid for teaching the course. He had split it between us all. He wanted to honor our hard work and dedication, he told us. He wanted to honor our role as teachers. That is the type of person Professor Bosnick was. He'd see the light in you and raise it. In the card he wrote to me was a simple inscription: *Like Dorothy said to the Scarecrow, I think I'll miss you most of all. Remember, our job is to be the flame.*

It's odd how you carry the energy of people who have guided you with you on your path. That was true about how I felt about David Bosnick. Years later, in April 2013, now a seasoned teacher myself, I looked him up on Facebook and sent him a message. I told him I'd become a teacher (not a lawyer) in great part thanks to him, and I let him know what a wonderful and powerful influence he had been on me and my life journey. He not only changed the course of my life but also changed how I felt about myself. I thanked him for inspiring me and helping direct the wind in my sails. He wrote me an incredibly kind message back, stating, "All I can think of is how lucky your students are to have a teacher with your many gifts, compassionate nature, and sense of humor. I wish my daughter were to be in your class." That was Professor Bosnick—always refocusing the light on others, finding a way to catch the facets of them, and make them light up and shine. Giving compliments and kindness that would go straight to your heart and make you feel you could do anything. He also wrote about Liz's new novel, *The Laws of Gravity*, which he was so excited was about to come into the world. That was Professor Bosnick, too: celebrating and cheering on all those he loved. He was a model teacher, father, husband, and human being.

As you know from the previous chapter, he would cross to the Other Side less than a year later.

I will always be glad I sent that message to him a few months before he crossed. And I want to tell you there is one thing I'd love for you to do right now: Reach out and send a message to someone who impacted you positively, someone who guided you and lit the way for you. Don't just think about doing it—*actually do it*. It will spark that light and cord of connection within you. You will be better for it; trust me on this.

I will always find it a bit unfair that only a few of us got to experience the light of who David was while he was here on earth, but my hope is that, through this chapter, you get a glimpse of his light. For what is true for me is true for you, too. You have purpose and meaning here— and there is an illuminated path laid before you. Our Teams of Light will find all different ways to guide us to it. Sometimes it is connecting us to Light Workers on the ground—special key people divinely placed in our path who inspire us, change us, and help us become better versions of ourselves. They help us shine brighter and see the truth of our own light. David is one of those key people who helped me find my path.

I'd like to share a final gift from David. It is a poem David wrote only a few months before his death. The timing of it, and the subject matter—well, there are no coincidences. When I corresponded with

Liz about her and David being part of this book, she shared it with me and told me I could share it with all of you. She wrote, "It just occurred to me that shortly before he died, he wrote a poem that he sent to his older sister. He did not show it to me. I think he must have known it would have scared me. But I think it shows how connected he was to a higher source, and that he knew what was coming. I'm not sure if the title was meant to be 'First Poem in a While' or 'What Do You Say o Me.' I always call it 'First Poem in a While,' but I think that's because it emphasizes the odd timing of it, that the poem came to him at a time when he wasn't really writing poems." Here now is that poem:

First Poem in a While

What Do You Say to Me in Your Sleep at Night

Someday I will wrap my arms around you
For the last time. I will be gone or going,
You will be already gone or not coming back.

The room we have yet to enter has many doors.

But on the other side, across the patch of sky,
river, snow, glare of light—
We, thee, you, me are waiting,
Leaning against, sitting on, or standing next to
All those loves who have gone before
Holding steady, marking our place.

In our own familiar shadow we are waiting for those
Who even now are gathering on the risers behind us
Dropping like flakes of snow back to earth
In a rounding chorus of love, the sky shaken
Into faith with stars.

David Bosnick

Now, as David would say, get out there and light the world!

Your heart knows the way.
Run in that direction.

RUMI

15

The Phone in the River

The spectacular Chippewa Falls are alongside the Trans-Canada Highway—a route that runs from the Atlantic to the Pacific—and during the winter melt the waters are high and cascading. Found thirty-five miles north of Sault Ste. Marie in Ontario's rugged Algoma District, the falls and the surrounding raw country are a paradise for hikers and campers and paddlers, and the fishing—steelhead, smallmouth bass, Chinook salmon—is excellent.

It was there, in the clear, cold waters of Chippewa Falls, that a woman named Jordan Miezlaiskis lost her cell phone—and caught an amazing glimpse of the Other Side.

So much of Jordan's story, and life, takes place outdoors. Jordan and her brothers, Kyle and Jesse, grew up in the Great Lakes region, in the small town of Cobourg, east of Toronto, and she spent most of her childhood out and about, camping, climbing trees, playing ice hockey. She and her brothers were an inseparable trio—Jordan made sure of it. "I was the little sister who tagged along," she says. "I was always by their side, and we did everything together. My best memories are of our summers together, canoeing and fishing and wading out to a rock on the lake and diving and swimming. It was all so perfect."

Only the passage of time could separate Jordan from her brothers, and when they grew older they went their separate ways. Kyle stayed in Cobourg and started a family, Jesse moved to Sault Ste. Marie, and Jordan went south to Florida. In 2020, just before the Covid pandemic struck, Jordan married Scott Kjelson (not surprisingly, an avid out-doorsman) in a ceremony in Florida's Redlands, close to the Keys. The wedding reunited Jordan and her brothers, who picked up right where they'd left off.

"By then Jesse had traveled a lot on his own, but I remember he said, 'There is nothing like being on vacation with your family,'" Jordan recalls. "He even said, 'After this, I don't want to travel alone any-more.'"

To Jordan, her brother Jesse was one of those inexplicably magical people—good at everything, loved by all, the family's center of gravity. "If he had a passion for something, he would be great at it," she says. "He had the funniest, most outgoing personality, the jokester, the goof-ball, but he also gave selflessly to other people without even thinking about it. I can't remember him ever complaining or crying about any-thing. My mom always said, 'Jesse is different. He's the special one. He has the biggest heart of us all.'"

And yet, after an early heartbreak in his life, Jesse spent much of his time alone. He bought a home on the Goulais River in southern Canada, a ten-hour drive from family, and he built a beautiful, nature-filled life there, surrounded by everything he loved most—except his family.

In July 2020, Jordan and Scott, who by then were living in Asheville, North Carolina, visited Jesse at his home to celebrate his birthday. Jesse and Jordan's parents were there, too. The brother and sister spent three glorious weeks together, enjoying all the outdoorsy things they grew up with. One morning, Jordan, Jesse, and Scott went fishing on Chippewa Falls, twenty minutes from Jesse's place. They picked a deep spot, hoping the fish were biting. Before she cast her reel, Jordan placed her cell phone on what looked to her to be a flat stone near the riverbank.

And then the phone began to slip off the rock, toward the river. Everyone watched as, in an instant, the phone disappeared into the sun-sprinkled water.

"Don't worry, Jordan," Jesse said. "I have this powerful magnet that can pull it up. I'll get it back for you."

The next day they returned to the spot with Jesse's magnet. Jordan could clearly see her phone at the bottom of the river, some twelve feet down, in its shiny pink protective case. But after several attempts with the magnet, they simply couldn't pull it up—the water was too fast and deep. "We had a few laughs trying to get it," Jordan says, "but by then I was pretty sure the phone was already destroyed. After a few hours Jesse said, 'Don't worry about it, Jord. I'll try again another day.'"

That was the trip's low point (Jordan had to buy a new phone). The high point for Jordan was getting to be with Jesse. "We'd never really spent that much time just the two of us, but on that trip we had so much one-on-one time, just sitting and talking about everything," she says. "He was so proud of what he had created up there." Every day they would go fishing or hike a trail or just sit and gaze out at a shimmering lake, and their conversations about life and love and anything and everything were more intimate, more leisurely, more meaningful than ever.

"Jesse never wanted it to end," Jordan says. "We sat at the top of a mountain one day for a couple of hours and he said, 'I love spending time with you, let's stay a little longer.'"

Two months later, Jordan was fast asleep in the early morning when her cell phone sounded. She didn't hear it, but her husband heard his phone ringing and answered it. Jordan woke up and recognized her father's voice coming through her husband's phone.

"My heart dropped," she says. "I knew immediately. I didn't know who—maybe my grandmother? But I knew it was bad."

In fact, it was unthinkable—her beloved brother Jesse was gone.

In the previous months, Jesse had been happier than ever. His parents had bought a piece of land just a mile away from his house, and he was over the moon that he would get to see his family more often. Sometimes Jesse took his beloved all-terrain vehicle to his parents' property and rode around, enjoying the view.

Jordan remembers that when he got the ATV she immediately texted him: *Have fun, but you need to be safe on that. Don't drive fast.*

Oh, I know, Jesse texted back. *Don't worry about me.*

One spectacular evening, Jesse rode up to the property to take a picture of the sunset. He took pictures of every sunset to send to his parents, to show them what they could expect to see once they built their new home. Jesse wore a helmet that night, as he always did, and there was no evidence he was driving excessively fast. No one had any doubt that Jesse was a conscientious motorist.

But something went terribly wrong. There was an accident, and Jesse passed away. Piecing together what happened has been difficult, but the best guess is that the sunset temporarily blinded Jesse, who drove his ATV into the rope that was cordoning off the property. The rope caused a fatal injury. It was a terrible and tragic accident.

"That's what really hurts us," Jordan says quietly, thinking back on that time. "He knew where the rope was; he'd put it up himself. We can only conclude he was blinded. It happened so quickly that he was gone before he even knew what happened."

Once she learned of her brother's passing Jordan sprang into action while at the same time not quite accepting what had happened. "It just seemed impossible that Jesse wasn't with us anymore," she says. Within six hours, she and Scott had flown up to Canada and arrived at Jesse's Ontario home on the Goulais River, deep in the dense woods. "There was a book sitting on Jesse's table—he loved to read, he was a true historian—and I sat there in shock and absently opened it," Jordan recalls. "It was a little journal he kept, a little brown leather journal. And right there on the first page was a list of things he reminded himself to do every week."

At the very top of Jesse's to-do list:

Always call my grandma on Sundays.

That was Jesse—he would do anything to stay connected to the people he loved most, his family.

In the weeks after his passing, Jesse's family learned something surprising about him. Despite Jordan's fears that he was too isolated and spent too much time alone, Jesse, it turned out, was part of a thriving, close-knit community—his neighbors and other friends on the river. "Our family spent two weeks at Jesse's house just trying to deal with things, and we met about forty people who loved him and were a big part of his life," says Jordan. "They rallied around us and they just kept showing up and we could tell the whole town was devastated, just like we were. We consider them family now. They showed us Jesse wasn't alone at all."

One of Jesse's obituaries said, "His thirty-three years of life gave hundreds of years of love and comfort to so many people he touched and encountered."

After a small service at the local funeral home, everyone gathered at Jesse's house, and neighbors and friends filled the place with food and love and positive energy. They played music they knew Jesse loved—Merle Haggard, Neil Young, some other old-time folk and country singers—and Jesse's friends and family shared stories about his special magic. "He was such a good person, it was really hard for us to comprehend that he was gone," Jordan says. "It was like all of us had this very strong feeling that Jesse was still here."

Of course, in a very meaningful way, he still was.

Not long after her brother's passing, Jordan had a particularly rough day, during which she missed him desperately. So she decided to have a conversation with him out loud, staring out at the river.

"Jesse," she said, "I need some crazy sign from you that you're still around."

The very next day, as Jordan sat talking with her mother on a big rock, remembering Jesse, a magnificent American bald eagle suddenly appeared and swept right over their heads.

"Since then," Jordan says, "Jesse sends us eagles all the time. Last year at a barbecue in his honor, an eagle circled leisurely overhead for thirty seconds, just letting us know he was there."

Batman, the superhero, became another sign (Jesse loved the TV series when he was young). After Jordan became pregnant with her first child, she was driving with her husband when suddenly she wished aloud that Jesse knew he would soon have a nephew. Just then, they parked next to a motorcycle, on which, prominently displayed, a colorful sticker depicted Batman, heroically gazing back at them.

"Jesse always gives us special moments like that," Jordan says.

Even so, something irreplaceable connected to Jesse had been lost—the very last photos taken of him with his family. They were snapped on the family's joint vacation at Jesse's home, and they were on the phone that sank to the bottom of the Chippewa. It was only after Jesse's passing that Jordan realized how devastating it was that the photos were irretrievably gone.

"*Everything* was on there," she says. "Photos going back weeks, months, all of us together happy and smiling. The last photo I ever took of Jesse. All these beautiful images, and they just disappeared."

One year after Jesse's passing, Jordan, her parents, her husband, and her brother Kyle all planned a return to Jesse's home in the woods to mark what would have been his thirty-fourth birthday. Everything would be the same as the year before—lots of great hiking, fishing, eating, and storytelling—except Jesse himself would not be there.

Or so everyone thought.

Just before Jordan and Scott set out for the long drive to Jesse's home, Jordan checked her Facebook messages and saw a mysterious note from a total stranger:

> Sorry if this message is really out of the blue, but my brother
> and I were diving on the Chippewa River the other day and
> my brother found your phone.

The stranger explained he knew it was Jordan's phone because it had a little pouch with her ID attached to the back. He said he tried to turn it on, but it didn't work. Then he asked her if she'd lost it recently.

"I had to tell him I'd lost it one year earlier!" she says. "It had been at the bottom of the river for fifty-two weeks, and the river had frozen over for the winter and thawed. But it was still there, right where it slid off. I wrote back and told the guy he had no idea how meaningful it was for me to get the phone back. It was a sign from Jesse."

But there was more.

Jordan told the stranger she would be in the area soon, and he offered to bring the phone to her at Jesse's house. When he showed up on Jesse's birthday, he immediately reminded Jordan of her brother. "His mannerisms, how kind he was, everything," she says. "It was eerie. I offered him some money for coming all the way up to return the phone, and the last thing he said was, 'You don't have to give me anything. God works in mysterious ways.' I could almost hear Jesse saying that."

Everyone gathered around the dinner table and looked at the phone as if it were a sacred relic. Finally, as a lark, Jordan said she would plug it in—she'd already been told it no longer worked. But just one second after she plugged it in, something remarkable happened.

"The phone came on!" Jordan recalls. "I couldn't believe it. And I went straight to my photos, and, incredibly, there they were—all the photos of Jesse and us! The phone had been twelve feet underwater for twelve months, and there's no way it should have worked, but it did! My mother said, 'That's your brother. He's telling us he is here.'"

Jordan thought back to the day she watched the phone slip off the rock and into the river. She remembered what Jesse said to her that day—"Don't worry, I'll get it back for you."

And now, a year later, against nearly impossible odds, he had done just that.

"It was like Jesse coordinated the whole thing," she says. "Putting these guys there who knew how to dive. Finding guys who were good, kind, honest people like him. And having the phone delivered right into my hands. Anything could have happened to that phone, and yet, somehow, it wound up back with me. That *had* to be Jesse."

As Jordan was already starting to realize even before her phone turned up—and turned on—her brother Jesse had not simply disappeared after his passing. He was, in very real and meaningful ways, still there.

Still connected to his family, as he always wished to be.

In my experience, this is precisely how the Other Side works. Because we are all connected to one another and to the Universe, no one is ever cut off from existence—there is always an avenue for connection.

Think about the Chippewa Falls, and about water in general.

Water is everywhere on this planet, and it does not stand still—*it moves and connects.* All of the earth's waters course continually in a massive swirl of heat and wind, leaves and groundwater, rain and hail and sleet and snow, ice crystals and surface runoff, swamp water and permafrost, clouds and currents and channels and tides and basins and glaciers, little springs connecting to gentle lakes, rolling rivers to heaving oceans, and all the oceans bound to one another in an endless impossible ballet known as the global water cycle.

The tiniest drop of dew and the mightiest ocean wave—they are all part of the very same beautiful, interconnected story.

And this is true of people, too. Just as universal forces guide water toward more water, the Universe tries to guide us to more people— people we need, people we love, people who are supposed to cross our paths. When I talk about being guided, this is what I mean—we need to acknowledge that we are all part of a great cycle of humanity, none of us living our own separate lives but all part of the same wonderful story.

The story of all existence.

Jordan Miezlaiskis is a great example of someone who honors her interconnectedness in the world. She's now a mother with a beautiful young son and a fluffy white dog. She's an executive with *Disrupting*

Grief, a podcast that tries to normalize conversations about grieving and mental health. She created an Instagram community called The Heart of Grief to help others feel less alone in their own grief journeys. And she remains intensely open to connections of all kinds—to living an illuminated life.

"I've always believed there is something bigger than us here on earth," she says. "My father was a skeptic, and I used to tell him, 'Dad, be open to the signs!' and he would grumble. But after the phone thing happened, he started to believe. Now when I call him, he says, 'I can't talk, I'm watching a psychic on YouTube.'"

Jordan keeps some of Jesse's ashes in a small, engraved velvet satchel and brings them with her whenever she travels—especially on vacations. "Basically, Jesse comes with me everywhere I go," she says. "I don't believe that when we pass, we are gone. I feel Jesse's presence all the time. There is no way that Jesse is *not* here."

Not all of us will get a sign as powerful and persuasive as Jordan's once-lost, then-reclaimed cell phone and photos. But all of us can receive signs from our loved ones who have crossed, as long as we stay open to these signs and allow ourselves to be guided toward them. "I always tell people, 'Grief exists where love exists,' and if you love someone and they pass, you will grieve," Jordan says. "But that does not mean they are gone. If grief is what it takes to remind me that Jesse is still here, I'll take the grief. It's all part of this shared journey that we're all on."

Out of suffering have emerged the strongest souls; the most massive characters are seared with scars.

KAHLIL GIBRAN

16

Releasing the Darkness

The Universe tries to help us grasp our way out of the darkness of trauma. Not only that, but the path out of the darkness illuminated by the Universe always leads us to a *higher* path — a place of healing and growth. As humans, we are constantly growing, and one of the keys to that growth is moving through trauma rather than harboring it inside us.

We can only grow if we release the darkness.

This is not just something I've learned from the Other Side. More and more scientific evidence is emerging of the importance of releasing trauma — not just to the health and happiness of those of us here now, but to future generations as well.

Studies have shown that stored or unprocessed trauma — keeping the darkness inside rather than releasing it — can, over time, alter our brain chemistry and even our cellular structure. According to a 2021 article posted by the behavioral health provider Wellmore, citing a study by a research scientist with the Harvard T. H. Chan School of Public Health, "Research shows that [traumatic] events can trigger emotional and even physical reactions that can make you more prone to a number of different health conditions, including heart attack, stroke, obesity, diabetes and cancer." Just as a virus can affect the workings of your computer, trauma can dysregulate the wiring in your brain. And unless you deal with the virus/trauma, your computer/brain will not function properly.

What's more, studies also show that trauma can be handed down generationally. "Some research suggests that trauma can affect a person's DNA and potentially influence the health of future generation far removed from the traumatic event," wrote Rachel Zimmerman in a 2023 article in *The Washington Post*. This *intergenerational trauma* can derive from behavior that is passed down, from changes in our biology, or even "from the collective experiences of a group."

The study of this phenomenon, called epigenetics, is "an emerging area of scientific research that shows how environmental influences—children's experiences—actually affect the expression of their genes," according to Harvard University's Center on the Developing Child. The epigenome is a collection of chemical marks on our DNA "that determine how much or how little of the gene is expressed." Accumulated trauma does not change our DNA, but it can affect the behavioral instructions generated by our DNA.

Put simply, stress and trauma we don't confront and eventually release are types of negative energy stored inside us, and that energy works against us in our pursuits of an illuminated life.

Scientists are also devoting themselves to the study of post-traumatic growth (PTG), which is defined by the D'Amore Mental Health Treatment Center in Costa Mesa, California, as "the positive psychological change that some individuals experience after a life crisis or traumatic event. Post-Traumatic Growth doesn't deny deep distress, but rather posits that adversity can unintentionally yield changes in understanding oneself, others, and the world." The psychologists who identified PTG in the 1990s offered five areas of potential growth: embracing new opportunities, forging stronger relationships with loved ones, cultivating inner strength through knowledge, gaining a deeper appreciation for life, and evolving a relationship to religion and spirituality. It might not seem that any of these positive changes are possible when you're stuck in the dark, but scientific evidence—and what I've learned from the Other Side in my readings—shows that they are.

Another emerging area of scientific study is retrocausal quantum physics, which suggests that influences can travel not only from the past to the future but also from the future to the past. Experimenters measuring a particle determined that the experimenters' choice of measurement settings "can influence the properties of that particle in the past, even before the experimenter made their choice," reported the website Phys.org. "In other words, a decision made in the present can influence something in the past."

This theory, like so many other emerging fields of scientific study, undermines the conventional physical, or materialistic, view of existence, which doesn't allow for any logic-defying phenomena and depends entirely on what the physical world shows us. Today, science itself is closing the gap between what is evident and what is possible. But it's still up to us to challenge the materialistic paradigm by questioning conventional thinking. Is this really the way life works? How do we know it's true? Isn't there another possible explanation? The scientific community tends to bury groundbreaking research that doesn't align with conventional models, and important discoveries in the fields of energy and trauma rarely reach the mainstream. I wish that popular websites and magazines like *People* ran weekly sections on new scientific research and developments in the study of psychic phenomena. We need to understand that our belief in paranormal experiences and events is often thoroughly backed up by science.

However, I find evidence of this all around us. For example, I came across a story on the remarkable site called *Humans of New York*, which features short interviews with thousands of random New Yorkers stopped on the street, that illustrated this. This story was about a young woman with a complicated relationship with her often distant, unaffectionate mother. One of the few ways they were able to connect was by watching the TV show *Law & Order* together. This young woman always remembered a particular episode in which the main character called his friend a "hoe," which became the pet name the woman and her mother laughingly called each other. But beyond that, there was precious little bonding, even though the young woman would practically beg her mother to bring her along on her outings.

"It's lonely being the one who always initiates," the young woman admitted. "People would say, 'Your mom loves you so much,' but I never felt that way."

Things between them were just starting to improve when the young woman's mother passed away. The young woman was devastated, and their relationship remained unresolved. An aunt told the woman that every time she saw a butterfly, that was her mother saying hi. "But that made no sense," the woman said. "My mother would never choose to be a butterfly." The woman started seeing a therapist to discuss her fractured relationship with her mother, and during one session she talked about how, having rejected the butterfly idea, the woman felt all lines of communication with her mother had been shut down.

"The whole time, I'm staring at this magnetic letter board with the word *hope* written on it," the young woman recalled. "And just as I was talking about missing my mom, the *P* falls off the board."

The word that remained?

Hoe.

"My therapist must have noticed my reaction," the young woman wrote, "because she laughed and said, 'Does that mean anything to you?'"

In fact, it meant the *world* to her.

Physicalism would insist that the appearance of the one word that connected the woman to her mother was a simple coincidence. But was it? Or was it the Universe lighting a path for the woman out of the darkness and into a place of love and healing and growth? As you read the chapters in this section, you will find vivid examples of people in the midst of crises finding ways to release the darkness through forgiveness, through confronting trauma, through love—and all with the gentle guidance and illumination offered us from beyond.

The more I think it over, the more
I feel that there is nothing more
truly artistic than to love people.

VINCENT VAN GOGH

17

Manifesting Those We Love

Every now and then, if you're lucky, you cross paths with someone whose energy and centeredness are so extraordinary you can't help but feel dazzled by them. I was lucky enough to meet someone like that when an artist named Pam Smilow attended one of my workshops and later emailed and asked if I'd like to visit her at her studio.

Once again, I sensed the Universe sprinkling breadcrumbs for me, so I followed them to Pam's incredible multi-floor studio—which doubles as her apartment—in New York City. It was instantly clear that Pam is a beautifully intuitive and expressive painter who honors all her connections to both the here and now, and to the Other Side.

"When I make a painting," she has said of her work, "I seek to create a little piece of beauty and a refuge from our busy and chaotic lives, an inspiration to reach above our daily existence and contribute some piece of wonder to the Universe. I see each piece of my work as one step on a continuum, each painting not precious unto itself, but as an ongoing journey."

The way Pam views her art and her life is one of the keys to living an illuminated life. Put simply, Pam *embraces* the journey. Some people react to adversity by treating it as something unfair that hapɔened *to* them, which can lead to becoming immersed in grief and ɔitterness.

But Pam doesn't see it that way. She believes that everything that ɥappens in her life, the tragedies as well as the beautiful work she creɑtes, are all part of her singular, multilayered adventure in this world, ɑnd as such should be not only experienced but embraced.

And the way she embraces it all is through her art.

"Art in all of its forms for me is about surrounding yourself with joy ɑnd bringing inspiration and light into your life," Pam says. "Someɥhing visual, written words, music, whatever it is—art is what lifts us ɔut of the daily doldrums of life. It's a way of leaving a positive mark on ɥhe world." Pam also believes art can play a big part in the healing ɔrocess, in some surprising ways. Or as she puts it: "Art can be a way we ɛan manifest our loved ones outside of ourselves."

Pam creates both small-scale paintings and collages, and large ɱixed-media paintings. She doesn't so much draw an image as she *layers* it, painting colors over other colors and creating textured, dimenɛional work. Her subject matter draws heavily from childhood memoɼies and playful images—fanciful trees and gentle birds, green fish and ɯhite lilies, stars and crescent moons. Her paintings impact you first ɥhrough the vibrancy of their colors, and then through their exhilaratɨng creativity. Her large-scale painting *The Planets*, for instance, shows ɥs an array of moons and planets and orbital patterns set against a deep ɛpace that is not pitch black, but rather a lush and layered crimson. The effect is inviting and whimsical, shrinking the Universe into a ɬind of celestial playground.

A big part of Pam's career has been her decades-long collaboration ɯith her husband, the renowned Danish artist Gert Mathiesen. They ɛhared the same studio and worked together on several pieces, nourishɨng each other's creativity. "From day one, Gert and I inspired each ɒther and approached our careers in unconventional ways," Pam says. "We thought out of the box out of necessity. In the beginning, we ɛouldn't afford canvas stretchers, so we would just pushpin our raw ɛanvases to the wall and paint them that way." Together they flew back and forth to Europe quite often, and they traveled with their work in rolls, stretching and framing a piece only after they sold it. Rather than concentrating exclusively on gallery and museum exhibitions, as some artists do, Pam and Gert also conducted home salons, showing their work in intimate, personal settings, much like a musician might give a house concert.

Sadly, their journey together took a sudden and unexpected turn in 2013, when Gert died of an aneurysm with no warning while on a trip back home to his native Denmark. It was a tragedy Pam never saw coming—but within her deeply human response to the passing of her great love, there are many inspiring lessons for living an illuminated life.

Pam grew up immersed in art. Her father, Mel Smilow, was an award-winning modern furniture designer known for, as one critic put it, "the clean lines and beautiful proportions" of his pieces. Pam's mother, Edith, "did all of these amazing crafts and taught us how to make our own gifts using household items like sponges and dishwashing soap bottles," Pam recalls. Her family literally lived *inside* art—in a beautifully designed home in the planned Frank Lloyd Wright community of Usonia, an hour north of New York City.

"I was told to look at this, look at that all the time," Pam has written of her childhood. "And I did. From a young age I was always comfortable using a visual vocabulary." Her earliest creations were paintings, sculptures, woodcut prints, and pottery pieces she threw on her family's pottery wheel. It was a childhood in which art, home, and life all merged together, and as a result she places great value in her environment. "It really matters to me," she says. "I think architecture, design, and art have a profound effect on most people, but they don't always realize it. My father was all about using natural wood and creating light, uncluttered environments. The architecture I grew up with was all about building into the land, not obstructing it. For all of us, art was about harmony."

Pam met the dashing Gert Mathiesen in the mid-1980s, when Gert had his own ceramics studio in Somers, New York. They got married and moved their shared studio to nearby Croton Falls (while living in New York City and reverse-commuting). Their daughter, Morgan, was born in 1993, and Pam and Gert settled into a richly artistic life filled with collaborative gallery shows, art exhibitions throughout the United States and Europe, and a thriving business selling their work directly to clients.

"People agonize over decisions about their carpets and window treatments, but it's art that has the loudest voice in the room," Pam says. "Since environment was so important to me, I started seeing architecture and interior design as an extension of my palette. Gert and I visited clients' homes and looked at the art in the place it would hang, which helped them choose the right art for their space."

Pam and Gert wanted "to create a cohesive, harmonious environment that emphasized the well-being of the inhabitants." But getting to know her clients was also fun for Pam, who understood that studio work can be a very solitary experience. "Getting out in the world and seeing how people lived, seeing their homes, seeing the walls, which sometimes also led to creating commissioned works—that was all very exciting to me. It's all about connections, and the thing I feel most rich about in my life are the long-lasting friendships and relationships I've cultivated over the years."

Pam worked with one client who commissioned a piece to commemorate her beloved father, who had passed. "In a way it was like re-creating her loved one," Pam says. "Immortalizing them in the art. The client sent me pieces of her father's ties and other things that reminded her of her dad, and I wound up using them in the portrait. This is what I mean by manifesting a loved one outside of yourself."

The commission steered Pam in a new direction—portraits in which she featured personal items and strove to evoke the physical presence of someone who had crossed. She used bits of fabric or pieces of dresses, old letters and wedding invitations, and any other small mementos that helped summon vivid memories of the subject.

"Since I used elements of collage anyway, I began offering clients the chance to use these objects to commemorate their loved ones, or to suggest images themselves," Pam says. "And whenever I did that, I found that it was healing for me *and* the client. It kept our loved ones present in our lives."

After losing Gert, Pam had a series of vivid dreams about him. "He would come and pick me up and drive me around and then drop me off back home," she says. "The second time I had that dream, I woke up feeling like Gert had been lying right beside me on the bed."

The dreams weren't like any Pam had ever had before, and she began to ask questions about what she was experiencing. "It felt like it wasn't just a dream, but if it wasn't, then what was it? It was kind of unexplainable. I've always been an inquisitive person and I started to ask myself, 'What is a dream? What is death? Where do people go? Where did Gert go?' It felt like I was searching and growing and expanding my mind."

Pam's mind has always been open when it comes to the unexplainable. Her father, she remembers, had ESP experiences, including one in which he sensed his own father had died, even though he wasn't with him when it happened. On another occasion, Pam's father was playing tennis with a friend, and the friend stopped to tie his shoe. At that moment her father had an overwhelming sense of darkness come over him and he knew his friend was very sick. Days later, his friend found out he had an inoperable brain tumor.

"I have always found that kind of stuff very intriguing," Pam says. "ESP, paranormal stuff, the Bermuda Triangle, reincarnation. When I was a kid, I was afraid of exactly three things: tidal waves, tornadoes, and coming back as someone I didn't like."

After Gert's passing, a friend gave Pam a book about death and grief and the afterlife, "which kind of gave me permission to go see a medium," she says. "I basically thought, 'It can't hurt.' I was really struggling with my husband's death, asking all these questions, reading about how other cultures handle death and whether elephants grieve. It was like I went on an eight-year crash course on death and dying."

. . .

Gert's passing was followed a few years later by another devastating loss—the death of Pam's sister, Judy, from ALS in 2018. Not long after Judy passed, Pam had a vivid dream about her. "The minute I woke up from the dream I knew what I had to do," she says. "I was going to paint a painting of my sister and have her wearing this jacket I gave her that she loved so much."

The painting, Pam decided, would not be a modest little portrait.

"I decided I was going to make it seven feet tall," she says.

When she finished the painting, its power surprised even her. "It was right when Covid started, and I'd given up my apartment and moved into my art studio," she says. "And when I woke up in the middle of the night one night, I looked up and there was my sister on the wall, all seven feet of her. It kind of took my breath away. Because I couldn't go outside much, having my sister there with me in the studio was *huge*."

Forced indoors by the pandemic, Pam made another decision. "In my solitude," she says, "I decided I was going to manifest and surround myself with *all* the people I love."

Her husband, Gert, was next. Pam made him seven feet tall, too, but otherwise depicted him as realistically as she could. "I hung the painting on the wall I see every morning from my bed when I get up," she says. "The first week it was up, it would startle me to see him there. It really felt like Gert was in the room with me."

By the time she finished her project, Pam had painted twenty portraits of loved ones. Some were portraits of people who had passed; others were of people who were still alive, of people she admired. One was of her and Gert's daughter, Morgan, when she was three. "It was amazing," says Pam. "For two years I was mostly by myself and yet I felt surrounded by all these people I love."

As Pam said, art is about bringing joy and light and color into our lives and allowing the energy of creativity to infuse and envelop and elevate us. Whenever I walk through a museum I am overwhelmed by the vibrant, swirling energy of so much creativity, and swept away by all the blazing colors and brilliant ideas. What I'm seeing is the *manifestation of someone's thoughts and feelings*—the way artists over the centuries have tried to transfer the powerful energy of their thoughts, feelings, and ideas to the canvas, or to the blank page, or through a musical instrument.

Manifesting is treating our thoughts like energy.

This is what Pam Smilow did in her New York City studio: She manifested her loved ones who had passed by transferring their still vibrant and present and living soul energy to the canvas.

Her powerful portrait of her husband may not have completely answered her question "Where did Gert go?" But it did at least provide an answer—he didn't go anywhere. His presence, his energy, the love they shared between them was all still there, in their studio, all the time.

Another way Pam manifests Gert is by continuing their earthly collaboration even though Gert has passed.

"All of a sudden, when he died, this infinite, endless fountain of his art became finite," Pam says. "What remained was just so precious, and I couldn't bring myself to sell it. Gert left us his art, or basically his soul—he left it on this planet for me and his kids to have. Most people get shoes or jackets; we got his art. And that gave us *so much* of him."

Yet even though at first she refused to part with any of the dozens of original works Gert left behind, Pam found a way for them to continue the collaborative process that so defined who they are as artists.

Rather than sell her husband's pieces, Pam made high-quality giclee prints of them. Then—she painted on *top* of the prints, essentially using them as canvases, so that the result would be a blend of both of their ideas and artistry. "It was just another way for me to celebrate Gert and celebrate what we shared," Pam explains. Even so, early on, the collaboration was a slow process because Pam was reluctant to paint over any of Gert's imagery. "I was cautious about changing his work," she says.

It took hearing Gert's voice in her head for that to change.

"He would say, 'Are you kidding? Just change it. Stop worrying and do it.' Even though it was out of reverence that I didn't want to do it, I came to realize that Gert would have wanted that continued collaboration and connection between us."

Pam painting on top of Gert's images echoes the way that Gert often left little love notes for Pam on the gesso canvases he prepared for her, which Pam would then paint on top of. The love notes may have been obscured, but they did not disappear. They were still there, beneath layers of colors, an invisible dimension of the finished work.

Pam's art, like her life, is all about these many layers of meaning and experience blended into a single, continuing journey through existence, and still touched by those who have passed to the Other Side. These days she often begins the first layer of a painting by writing an inspirational quote on the canvas that she later paints over. She sees this as a subliminal inspirational message to the viewer.

In this way Pam and Gert keep on with their beautiful collaboration, with Pam not only creating new work with his imagery but also making sure his legacy endures through exhibitions and museum placements, and with Gert watching to see what they will create next, and whispering to his wife, "Stop worrying, nothing is so precious, just do it and don't be afraid."

This is a brilliant example of how the love we share in our time on this planet continues to connect us well beyond our earthly limits, and how the energy of our loved ones who have passed does not disappear but rather endures, there for us to harness and absorb.

One of the many unique things about Pam is that, unlike most artists, she does not require complete silence or solitude to work.

"In fact, I can paint and have a full conversation at the same time," she says. "It's like I'm using a completely separate muscle."

Pam has a term for what she does—*unselfconscious art.*

"Watch a child create a painting," she says. "They don't need quiet or solitude, they just let their ideas spill out on the page. All they're doing is expressing themselves, and it's a beautiful thing to see. They're not self-conscious, and they're not judging themselves—they're just creating something because they feel compelled to do it. Only later, when we turn seven or eight, do we begin to judge ourselves, and that's when that unselfconscious creativity can go away."

What Pam realized was that she was able to connect directly to her inspiration without having it pass through any negative filter. "I realized my intuition was crucial to my work," she says. "For instance, I use a lot of different colors that most people might consider a clash—a red next to an orange, for example. But to me, these colors just vibrate with each other and they end up being a family of colors. My interest lies in intuitive art."

Pam's message is that *any* of us can connect with our intuition and tap into the precious energy inside ourselves, which then allows us to do magical things like manifest a loved one whose energy has passed.

"You don't have to *try* to be artistic," Pam says. "Not everyone necessarily considers themselves artistic, but every child can sit down and draw things and just express themselves. I have people come through my studio and ask if they can work alongside me on a project. I love doing this, and I even gave it a name: jump-start your creativity. I consider it important work to get people going in this direction and learning how to trust their intuition to discover their creative voice. But in the end, they really don't need me to do that. They just need the jump start."

Okay, but how? Haven't we all been wildly frustrated by our inability to transform some brilliant idea in our brain to an actual creation? Haven't we all stared at the blank canvas, or the blank page, or the guitar we've been promising to learn to play, and thought, *Nope, I got nothing. I don't even know where to start.*

Pam believes those crippling negative thoughts are the product of what she calls "the curse of self-consciousness and self-judgment."

"That is the biggest battle we face when we want to create something—judging ourselves," she says. "We have to learn to leave our judgment at the door, just like children do. Don't think about technique. Don't think about the result. Just let the art come out of you."

Just let the art come out. What an incredibly freeing approach to being creative! Tapping into our creativity is not about being perfect or being proficient or even being *good*. It is about somehow bringing joy and light and color into our lives. It is about bypassing the negative filters that our fears and previous mistakes have put in place and directly accessing that which inspires us and fills us with energy and passion.

"When people tell me they're afraid to get started, I always ask, 'What are you afraid of?'" says Pam. "'What is fear?' I use acrylic paint, so what's the worst that can happen if I mess up? Nothing, I just paint over it. Do not be afraid, and do not be judgmental. *Just get it out.*"

As Pam explained, she grew up with parents who were very environmentally aware and taught her to be keenly observant of her surroundings. Ever since then, Pam has remained rooted in the importance of place and space and the effect our environment can have on our lives. When she and Gert went shopping for a school for their young daughter, for instance, one of the key factors in their decision was the appearance of the classrooms. "Gert and I talked about how we really liked the Scandinavian look, which is very environmentally pure and uncluttered," she says. "That's what we were looking for."

This openness to your surroundings, a heightened awareness of the world around you, is one of the things that allows you to receive messages from the Universe and from your loved ones on the Other Side. It's the difference between having your antennae positioned and poised to receive transmissions and pointing them down at the ground. Pam, for one, is *highly* open to the many signs, messages, and signals that swirl around us, something she says has enriched her life.

"It has allowed me to stay connected to Gert and Judy and my father, Mel, and other loved ones" who have passed, she says.

To illustrate this point, Pam told me the amazing story of a recent trip she took to Maine.

Pam has a strong connection to the state: When she was young her parents had friends who owned a lovely home built on a cliff adjacent to the rugged coastal rocks jutting out into the Atlantic. The house had a daybed surrounded by windows that offered a 180-degree view of the shimmering diamond-like waters. "It was such a beautiful spot, and we all loved going up there so much," Pam recalls. "The hosts were so relaxed and they let everyone do whatever they wanted, and we all made so many great memories there. It is still my favorite spot on earth."

In fact, Pam scattered the ashes of her parents, her sister, and Gert into the ocean from those rugged rocks.

Many years later, during the Covid pandemic, Pam spent the month of August in a rented cottage not far from that special home with her stepson, her daughter, and her two grandchildren. They had such a good time that Pam decided to return by herself that October. The first rental home she stayed in was terrible, she says: "I was up all night thinking there were mice scuttering all around me." But then she found a listing for another rental sandwiched between an inlet and the ocean, and from which she could see her parents' friends' house.

"So I drove up to check it out, and as I was coming around the corner, this Dylan song came on the radio," Pam recalls. "It was 'Tangled Up in Blue'—the song Gert and I played *all* the time when we had our studio in Croton Falls. That was Gert telling me, 'We're in the right spot.'"

The next day Pam made plans to have a friend over for lunch. While sitting out on the deck, she noticed a couple walk by with a little dog and thought, *They look interesting.* An hour later they walked by again, and Pam struck up a conversation with them. She learned they'd owned a house in the area for twenty years, and she told them about the house she used to visit when she was younger. Pam also mentioned having stayed at a local place called Echo Farm Cottages.

"I never knew anyone who stayed at Echo Farms except for this one wild Danish guy," the woman remarked. "My mother was Danish and she was so happy to be able to talk with this Danish guest. I remember he and I had a long conversation about how in Denmark you have to pick your children's name from a list, because they think it's cruel to punish your kid with a weird name, and . . ."

The woman went on and on about the crazy Danish guy, and somewhere in the middle of it all Pam realized the Danish guy she was talking about was Gert.

"She was telling me these stories about my own husband!" Pam says now. "My jaw dropped out of my mouth! I sat there in shock and thought, *This is amazing. She is manifesting Gert by remembering these conversations from eight years ago.*"

That very evening, the manifesting continued. Pam went to dinner at a place on Round Pond called Muscongus Bay Lobster—a place she'd been going to with her family since she was a teenager. "It started as this little shack where you'd hand them a stick of butter and they'd melt it for you for your lobster," Pam remembers. "It's changed and grown, but it's still a pretty simple place."

Pam was dining with friends from New York City and shared her many fond memories of Muscongus Bay.

"I can still see my dad standing at that window in his tennis hat with his two friends, ordering lobster," Pam told them.

Just then—*just then*—a name came over the loudspeaker.

"Mel, your order is ready. *Mel! Please pick up.*"

Once again, Pam was shocked.

"Mel was my father's name," she says. "There were only a handful of people there at the time, and yet I heard the name Mel booming out."

Just three days later, Pam was out on her deck again when a woman walked by, stopped in her tracks, craned her neck to get a better look at Pam, and finally said, "Judy?"

"Judy was my sister's name," Pam says. "She didn't think I was my sister, but she thought I was someone else, a friend of hers named Judy. Once again, my sister was manifest while I was sitting right on the body of water where her ashes and my family's ashes were scattered."

Four different times over the course of four days, three of Pam's loved ones who had passed were manifested—through a song, a conversation, a fulfilled lobster order, and a case of mistaken identity—and all on the beautiful body of water that is their symbolic resting place *and* the spot Pam calls her favorite place on earth.

And in each case, these manifestations could have been easily missed had Pam not been entirely present in her environment, noticing the people passing, the sounds in the air, the memories evoked, the very energy of her cherished surroundings.

"It is about being *observant*," Pam says. "Observant and connected to your environment."

Living a guided life—one that leads you down the path to illumination—starts with you. It starts by opening your mind and heart to seeing all the ways that love surrounds you: by seeing the ways your loved ones who have crossed, your Team of Light, reveal themselves to you. It starts by recognizing that you are never alone on your path. And it grows brighter when you not only recognize but also celebrate the truth of that connection. Say thank you to your Team of Light in your thoughts. Tell others the stories of connection you have experienced—of the signs, of the love. And invite others to share their stories with you.

When I accepted Pam's offer to visit her at her New York City studio, I found that I loved her energy and I loved the energy in her workspace. I did a reading for her there, and she gave me two beautiful paintings in return—something she felt called to do when we first met at the conference. "You were talking about art and the importance of art, and that really resonated with me," Pam says. "It felt like you were giving me a gift, and I felt like I wanted to return a gift to you with a piece of art."

Pam had one other thought that I would describe as a download from the Universe. I say that because I had the same download.

"I would like to work with you sometime," Pam said.

"It will happen," I assured her.

I envision a workshop about art and creativity, and manifesting, and staying connected to your environment—and all the wonderful qualities that Pam personifies in her illuminated life.

"I feel like I've grown and learned so much in the last ten years," Pam says. "There's so much about the Universe we don't understand and we have to stay open to all the possibilities. We can connect with and manifest our loved ones and incorporate them in our lives. That is the healing power of art—we can all find a way to summon and celebrate the people we love in some way."

Those we have physically lost are energetically still with us. We can bring our loved ones who have crossed along with us on our journey through life. They want us to live vibrant, engaged lives. All they ask of us is that we stay open to their continuing presence, guidance, and love.

All goes onward and outward, nothing collapses
And to die is different from what any one
supposed, and luckier.

WALT WHITMAN

18

ILY

Christine Dimmick has always been a "feeler." She has, for as long as she can remember, *felt* things, often intensely. Not just her own emotions but also those of others around her—she experiences other people's anger, sadness, confusion, or fear almost as if she were feeling those things herself. No one explained this special sense to her, or came up with a name for it, or even told her if it was a blessing or a curse. For Christine, it's always just been the way she was. "It didn't feel like a gift," she says now. "It almost became a negative: 'Oh you're too sensitive, you feel too much.'"

It wasn't until Christine and I crossed paths—when I was a guest on her wonderful podcast *Be the Change*, which is about how positive life forces like love and resilience and gratitude can help solve the world's most intractable problems—that Christine first came to understand what it is to be a feeler, or, to use the term I gave her, an *empath*.

An empath is simply someone who is especially and sometimes exceptionally sensitive to the emotions of people around them—someone blessed with an abundance of empathy. Sometimes it can seem as if you have invisible feelers that pick up other people's vibrational energy. Being an empath, I told Christine, is *definitely* a gift, and a gift that she rightly intuited can change the world.

She wasn't just a feeler, I explained. She was also a healer.

"That was the first time someone described to me what I'd been experiencing all my life," she says. "I could tune in to people's emotions especially people I was connected to, in a very vivid way."

Even so, Christine did not fully open herself up to her gift until the Universe sent her the clearest sign yet that her connections to her loved ones and those around her were deeper and more powerful than she ever imagined.

That beautiful sign came to her in the form of two dreams, one pad of paper, and an eventful little stroll along the beach.

Christine was raised in the rural area around Bowling Green, Ohio, by parents who were fourth-generation farmers. Her ancestors were among the first settlers to come through, and local roads are still named for them. The fields Christine's great-grandfather tilled in the early twentieth century are still a farm, and still in the family.

Even after her parents divorced when she was two, and moved away from Ohio, Christine would return to the farm to spend the summers with her cousins. The time she spent there shaped her strong and enduring sense of home and community. "My grandparents' lives were hard but simple," she recalls. "When my mother was young, they had donkeys and Christmas trees and a farm stand, and every morning my grandfather got up early and worked all day, and on Sundays my grandmother was active in parties and christenings and potlucks. Everyone came by and spent time, and that was how it was—it was a real community."

Along the way, Christine experienced her occasional flashes of "feeling." Quite often she would run into friends and almost immediately ask them, "What's wrong?" Inevitably, there was some bothersome issue the friend needed to talk about. When she was older, Christine visited a friend and instantly knew she was pregnant, even though her friend wasn't showing. When she asked her about it, the friend confirmed it was true. "I didn't really want to tell anyone yet, but

I want to honor your intuitiveness," the friend said. Just a few years ago, Christine's mother, Pam—who was her best friend, and with whom she spoke on the phone several times a day—told her she believed Christine was psychic.

"I laughed it off, but my mother wasn't kidding," Christine says. "I think she may have even been a little scared of what I could do."

In 2019, Christine and her mother traveled together to Canyon Ranch in Lenox, Massachusetts, one of Pam's favorite getaway spots, for a quick vacation. There, Pam fell ill. She lost her appetite, felt fatigued, and developed a bad cough. They left Lenox early, and Pam felt better once she was home, but she remained wary of going on a longer scheduled trip to Antigua. Right around then, Christine had an unusually vivid dream.

In the dream she was with her grandmother, who had passed away two years earlier. "We were having lunch and pouring tea and laughing, and it was wonderful," Christine remembers. "Suddenly my grandmother got up and said, 'I have to go.' I asked her where she was going and she said, 'I have to go be with your mother.'"

Christine told her mother about the dream and how she believed it meant her grandmother would be with her in Antigua. "She will keep you safe!" Christine assured her. But not long after arriving in Antigua in the first week of January 2020, Pam fainted. Her blood oxygen levels were dangerously low, and she was medically evacuated to Mt. Sinai Hospital in New York City. Doctors ran several tests, including ones for cancer, but could not figure out why she was sick.

Pam spent weeks in the hospital without a proper diagnosis. By then, there were media reports about a strange new virus that had made its way to the United States from Europe. Christine knew her mother had spent time with a sick friend who'd returned from Europe just a week earlier, and she asked her mother's doctors if Pam might have this new coronavirus.

"We don't even know how to test for that," they told her.

After a week in the hospital, Pam lost her voice. To communicate, she had to send texts or scribble words on a pad of paper. On one of her first days without a speaking voice, Pam wrote three capital letters on the pad and passed it to Christine.

"She wrote *ILY*," Christine says. "*I love you*. And she put her hand on her heart to make sure I knew what she meant."

After a few more days, Pam didn't have the strength to get out of bed. Food tasted different, metallic, and her appetite dwindled. All she could tolerate was a few sips of homemade smoothies Christine brought in for her. Doctors from five different hospital departments ran more tests—"just about every test they had," Christine says—but still made no diagnosis. All they could say was that Pam's liver was being attacked by her mystery disease, causing jaundice. She was put on oxygen and given a catheter. Her body, essentially, was failing her.

"Here was this beautiful, glamorous woman who traveled the world and was always so elegant, and now she couldn't even go to the bathroom," Christine says. "Her life was being taken away bit by bit."

One day, Christine got a text from her mother. It read, simply, *I can see all the birds*. Pam had a window in her hospital room, and at first Christine thought she was literally seeing birds in flight. But soon another text followed.

I can see all the angels, Pam wrote.

One of Christine's friends, her Tibetan sound bowl teacher, urged her to try to keep her mother grounded—to keep her on earth, in other words, and not let her slip away. But by then, Christine knew her mother was beginning to surrender the fight. She also knew Pam had everything to live for; she adored her grandson, Christine's young son, Rome, and cherished the time she got to spend with him. But Pam did not want Rome to see her in the hospital because she feared her condition would frighten him. Everything pointed to the inevitable, and Pam seemed perfectly fine with it. "If she had been in pain she would have complained, but instead she was completely at peace during that entire time," Christine says. "No pain, no complaints, just calm. To me, she was already on her way."

· · ·

Several years earlier, Christine had her own brush with death. At the age of forty-five she was diagnosed with non-hereditary breast cancer. She had friends in their forties who were diagnosed with breast cancer, and many of them had lost their battles, leaving young children behind. Christine thought of her son, Rome, and the cancer diagnosis nearly paralyzed her with fear.

Luckily, a mammogram had caught the cancer early, and she was prescribed six weeks of radiation treatment. Her highly regarded oncologist suggested she supplement that treatment with sound therapy—the use of music and other soothing vibrations to release tension and anxiety. Christine contacted Katherine Hamer, a certified practitioner in the use of Tibetan sound bowls who suggested several bowls that Christine slowly learned how to play. "The bowls were heavy and stubborn, and at first I couldn't get them to play," she says. Eventually, she says, "the bowls became my healers."

The radiation and sound therapy worked, and Christine was cancer-free just six weeks after her diagnosis.

It was Katherine Hamer who gifted a sound bowl to Christine's mother. "It was a dolphin bowl," Christine says. "When you play it with water and tilt your wrist, it makes a sound like a dolphin."

Pam loved the deeply soothing sounds, and her eyes widened whenever Christine asked her if she wanted to listen to the bowl.

"I played it for her two or three times a day," Christine says, "lulling her to sleep."

When Pam's condition worsened, her dearest friends arrived from Los Angeles to sit with her. In time, she was moved to the intensive care unit. Around then, Christine had another vivid dream in which she was distinctly shown the number 12. "Not only did I see the number 12, but I was shown it twelve different times," she recalls. "It was like I was kind of taken out of the dream to be shown it. Once it was circled. Then it was white on black. I saw it twelve different ways."

Christine researched the number 12 but could not figure out what the dream was trying to tell her.

One day in the ICU, Christine played the dolphin bowl and danced and sang for her mother, while Pam's best friend sat by her bed and held her hand. The friend assured Pam that she would always take care of Christine and Rome, and make sure they were okay.

At precisely 11:11 P.M., a single tear fell from Pam's eye, just before she crossed over. She passed away on February 12.

In the next few months, the world shut down around Christine as the Covid pandemic officially began. The lockdowns cruelly kept Christine trapped at home with her overwhelming grief, and most nights she felt like the only person she wanted to talk to was the person she had just lost. "My safety net was gone," she says.

During that time, in the absence of the usual human interaction, Christine experienced what she says was an abundance of signs and premonitions, almost as if the normal day-to-day chatter of life was replaced by deepened spiritual connections. She felt a strong pull to explore her healing powers, and she played a sound therapy bowl for a friend who'd been hospitalized with necrosis on her shin.

The very next day, her friend's condition began to improve, and she was soon released from the hospital.

Then there were the signs—unlikely happenings that seemed to Christine to be communiqués from her mother. Several months earlier, before her mother's illness, Christine had been on a walk with Pam in upstate New York when Pam bent down and picked up a lone blue jay feather and handed it to her, knowing Christine loved blue jays.

"I thought you might like it," Pam said.

After her mother's passing, Christine was on a business trip to New York City when she found herself walking idly along the city's sidewalks, reflecting on her mother's crossing. Just then, she noticed something remarkable on the ground.

It was a bright and beautiful blue jay feather, right there in the middle of the concrete city. On that walk, Christine found *four more blue jay feathers* on the city sidewalks, for a total of five.

"I knew," she says. "It was Mom saying hello."

Just one week after Pam's crossing, Christine took a walk by herself n the sand along the water's edge at Rockaway Beach in New York. She'd always been drawn to water and found it healing. That day, as her thoughts again turned to her mother, Christine noticed something white lying atop the sand. At first, she thought it was a seashell, but when she picked it up, she saw it was a shard of pottery.

Christine turned it over to look at its underside. There, she saw something had been printed on the pottery—letters in a font she recognized as Helvetica. Not an entire word; the fragment was too small. Instead, all Christine could make out were three consecutive letters: *ILY*.

Christine passed her fingers in wonder across the letters on the shard of pottery. *ILY*—the very three letters her mother wrote for her on her pad in the hospital, shorthand for *I love you*. What were the chances? What were the odds? Could it be just a coincidence?

Christine did not need to ask herself these questions. She knew exactly how she'd been guided to that one particular piece of pottery along the endless sands of a seven-mile-long stretch of beach.

"It was a sign from my mom," she says. "Since she passed, I've often asked her to send me signs and so she did, in a place she knew was meaningful to me. ILY—what more could I have asked for?"

In fact, Christine's mother was far from done. Besides the feathers, there were hearts: stones on the ground shaped like hearts, a heart-shaped piece of fruit tossed in the sink, coffee grounds at the bottom of a cup, swirled and swished and finally settled into a tiny heart. Hearts everywhere. "Sometimes it happens after I have an argument with someone, and I look down and there is a heart," Christine says. "It's my mother letting me know, *I'll always be with you.*"

Still, it was that simple piece of pottery, lettered with *ILY*, that Christine cherished most of all. Months after her mother's passing, she bought a home on a Caribbean island and went for a walk along the beach, curious about what she might find this time. There was no pottery in the sand, but there was coral. Lots and lots of pieces of coral in all different shapes. One of the first pieces she found was, not surprisingly, shaped like a heart.

But that wasn't all. Christine kept walking and found a piece of coral that looked like the letter *E*. Her mother's maiden name began with an *E*. Christine picked up the coral and said, "Okay, Mom, I see you."

Then there was another piece in the shape of an *L*. Then a piece with a hole in the middle that looked like an *O*. Christine kept scooping up coral that looked like letters until she had a collection of about fifteen pieces. Out of those, she was able to fashion a full sentence.

I LOVE YOU.

"I still have that coral spelling out *I LOVE YOU* on a table right in my living room," Christine says. "It's like an artifact that I really treasure, because my mother brought it to me."

Christine has managed to take all the profound influences and experiences of her life and turn them into a remarkable career as what I would call a professional healer. She founded the Good Home Company, a wellness-oriented business that makes and sells home goods that are free of toxins, a philosophy she wrote about in her groundbreaking book, *Detox Your Home: A Guide to Removing Toxins from Your Life and Bringing Health into Your Home.*

She is also an inspirational speaker and an educator who teaches groups how to live sustainably and toxin-free, and she is a certified Tibetan sound bowl and Reiki practitioner who is "available for sound baths for wellness and healing." Personally, I find her social media posts on Instagram and elsewhere to be singularly beautiful and inspirational—joyous depictions of a rich, celebratory existence.

She is, quite simply, the embodiment of what I mean when I refer to living a guided, illuminated life.

"I've accepted that part of me that feels other people's emotions, that feels the collective emotion of the world around me," Christine says, "and I just want to help people live lives of wellness and beauty."

While she does just that, Christine continues to receive magnificent signs from her mother, letting her know that she is close, ever guiding her. Sometimes the connection is so powerful, it takes her breath away.

"Recently, I booked a massage with a student at the Swedish Institute of Massage in New York City," she says. "I didn't know the masseuse; it was just a random appointment. But at the end of the massage, for some reason, the student held my hand for a while, and as I lay there, I felt that I was holding hands with my mother. It was so powerful and so surreal, and since then I've felt my mother's hands resting on my shoulders or on my back. It happens all the time. It's because she never really left me. She's still right there by my side every day."

Sleep is the best meditation.

THE DALAI LAMA

Even a soul submerged in sleep is hard at work
and helps us make something of the world.

HERACLITUS

Man is a genius when he is dreaming.

AKIRA KUROSAWA

19

The Power of Dreaming

One of the ways the Universe helps illuminate our paths is through dreams.

The physicalism model of existence rules out the possibility that we can receive information in our dreams that originates anywhere other than in our brains. Neurobiological theory subscribes to the "activation-synthesis hypothesis" of dream imagery and messaging, which holds that dreams are meaningless hodgepodges of thoughts and images from our memories scrambled together by electrical brain impulses. Dreams are simply our mind unwinding.

But are they? History is littered with powerful examples of original, revolutionary ideas appearing first in dreams. Abraham Lincoln's friend and former law partner described how Lincoln, just a few days before his death, shared a dream he had of seeing a covered corpse in the East Room of the White House and being told it was the president, killed by an assassin. Lincoln also told others he foresaw maneuvers and outcomes of Civil War battles in his dreams.

Samuel Clemens, better known by his pen name, Mark Twain, related a dream he had about being aboard the riverboat *Pennsylvania* with his brother Henry, and seeing Henry as a corpse in a metal casket, wearing one of Twain's suits and with a bouquet of white roses, and one red rose, placed on his chest. Not long after, Twain and Henry were together on the riverboat *Pennsylvania*, Twain as an apprentice, Henry as a mud clerk, before a squabble between Twain and the pilot led to him being transferred to another riverboat. Shortly after his dream of his brother in the casket, Twain learned the *Pennsylvania's* boiler had exploded. Twain hurried to Memphis and found his wounded brother, but Henry died the next day. When Twain went to a so-called "death room" in Memphis to see his brother's remains, he was shaken to see him in a metal casket and in a suit he'd borrowed from Twain—just like in his dream. The only thing missing from the real experience that had been in Twain's dream was the bouquet of white roses with a single red rose in the middle.

But then, just as Twain was standing by the casket, a woman came in and placed a bouquet of flowers on Henry's chest: all white roses, except for a single red rose in the middle.

There are so many more incredible examples of dreams containing more than just a rehash of memories. The Canadian pharmacologist and orthopedist Frederick Banting dreamed of treating a dog with diabetes by tying up its pancreatic duct. Once he was awake, Banting arranged to try the dream procedure for real, leading to his discovery of insulin, which won Banting the Nobel Prize and saved many tens of millions of lives. And the chemist Dmitri Mendeleev saw a fully formed and arranged table of elements in a dream, and then created the periodic table of elements we all know today.

Creative artists routinely find powerful inspiration in their dreams. Paul McCartney had a dream in which he heard a familiar tune. When he awoke, he went up to his Beatles bandmate John Lennon and asked, "What's this song that's been bugging me? I dreamed it last night." John said he'd never heard it before. Paul then went to his producer, George Martin, who didn't know the tune either. "It didn't exist, except in my head," Paul later explained. "And so, I claimed it. It was like finding it in the street." That tune? It became the classic hit "Yesterday." The Rolling Stones' guitarist, Keith Richards, similarly came up with one of the most famous guitar hooks in rock history in a dream.

He bolted awake early one morning, grabbed his guitar and turned on a tape recorder, played the hook, and went back to sleep. On the tape, said Richards, "there's this, maybe, 30 seconds of 'Satisfaction' . . . and then there's like 45 minutes of snoring."

Dreams can fit several different categories: *inspiration dreams* (like the examples above, all of which led to huge advances in science and medicine); *visitation dreams* (in which we get to spend time with loved ones who have passed); *lucid dreaming* (the experience of having a conscious awareness of your dream while you're having it); and *precognitive dreams* (which give us information about something about to happen in the future).

I've had dreams that were very unpleasant but that I later realized were energetic blueprints of an upcoming event. Lots of times we have frightening dreams that prepare us for something ahead, and even those terrible dreams come to us from a place of love. For it is our Teams of Light that are guiding us even then, preparing us so that we know we are supported and surrounded by love.

For instance, a recent scientific study had eighteen women with a known diagnosis of breast cancer complete a survey about what are called warning dreams—dreams that specifically allude to them getting breast cancer. The study concluded that "warning dreams of breast cancer were often reported to be life changing experiences that prompted medical attention leading directly to diagnosis."

Dreams can save our lives.

Dreams can also *enrich* our lives. The art project *Humans of New York* includes an interview with a woman who wanted desperately to study abroad in Italy but, even after scholarships, was $10,000 short on the tuition. The woman then recalled her grandmother, who had recently passed away at age eighty-nine. "Grandma was always on the lookout for numbers to play," she said. "Inspiration could come from anywhere: license plates, street numbers, radio stations. Then every night she'd watch the numbers roll out on Channel 8. But she hardly ever won. She used to split her winnings between her grandchildren, and it was never much. A couple bucks here and there. I remember getting $10 one time."

The woman never played the lottery herself—until one night, after attending a remembrance mass for her grandmother, she had a peculiar dream: "I was at a Cumberland Farms gas station near my house scratching off a lottery ticket, and suddenly I started laughing because I won a bunch of money. The next day I text my friends that we've go to buy a lottery ticket. We headed straight to Cumberland Farms and bought one lotto ticket for five dollars."

As Beyoncé's song "Halo" played over the radio, the woman scratched off her ticket. "When I get to the third row of numbers, *bam!*," the woman recalled. "I had a match for ten thousand dollars. Enough to cover one whole semester in Florence."

Dreams can be conduits for the loving guidance we receive from the Other Side. Dreams can deeply and meaningfully illuminate our lives. Whether you ask a loved one who has passed to visit you in a dream or ask to receive guidance on a particular issue in your dreams, or just think about how your dreams apply to your waking life, you can find powerful connection and guidance in your dreams, steering you toward your highest self.

The dream state is part of the path to an illuminated life. Dreams create that blank space that we need to explore and create. In our waking hours, our monkey minds tend to hop from branch to branch, or chore to chore, never slowing down or stopping anywhere long enough to find the blankness in which so many wonderful things can sprout.

But dreams—dreams give us that time and space. Although they take place in the dark, they are full of the light of guidance. And what happens in our dreams can wind up changing our lives.

I have loved the stars too fondly
to be fearful of the night.

SARAH WILLIAMS

20

Tasso

It came out of nowhere and seized her and wouldn't let go—a vague but urgent feeling of impending doom. Irene Tsako: tried to ignore it, but as the months passed the feeling not only persisted but intensified. Her husband, Anastasios—she called him Tasso—was in his fourteenth year as an officer with the New York City Police Department, and Irene had always worried about his safety, but suddenly her concern was turning into something like panic.

Then came the dream. In it, Irene was in her home and glanced toward the dining room, where she saw Tasso's late grandparents sitting at the table with several other people, sharing bread and drinking wine and acting excited about something. "I went over to them and told them Tasso was at work and that he'd be home soon," she recalls, "and I asked what could I get for them while they waited. And Tasso's grandfather looked at me in disbelief and said, 'What are you doing here?' It was clear I didn't belong there."

The dream and her feelings of doom pushed Irene to the point of nearly breaking down. "It got to where I'd sit in my car in the parking lot of my children's school bawling my eyes out," she says of that time in 2021. "I'd call my brother's wife and cry to her about it and tell her I was worried that something bad might happen. I started begging Tasso to quit his job. He was considerate about it, but he just kept saying, 'Don't worry, I'll be okay.'"

Then, around four in the morning on April 26, 2021—while Tasso was out on patrol working a graveyard shift in the borough of Queens—Irene was jolted out of sleep by another vivid dream.

In the dream, Irene saw Tasso sitting on a balcony with a woman named Zoey. Irene told Tasso to come down to her, but he didn't respond. She asked again, and he still wouldn't go with her, so she turned around to leave. But before she could, she heard Tasso singing to her—'S'agapó, S'agapó"—which means "I love you" in Greek. Irene woke up and felt alarmed, because she knew that the name Zoey comes from the Greek word meaning "life."

The dream was trying to tell her something.

She sent Tasso a text message: *Are you okay? I had a nightmare.*

Tasso texted back a sad face and told her he was fine and would be home soon. *It was just a dream,* he wrote. *Go back to sleep.*

Do me a favor, don't stop any cars tonight, Irene responded. *Just get home as soon as you can.*

Tasso's shift ended quietly, and he made it home safely.

The next day, April 27, 2021—at the very same hour Irene had been awakened by her dream the previous morning—she was awakened again, this time by a hard, incessant knocking on her front door.

The ancient Greeks believed that dreams were either prophecies of events in the real world or attempts by those on the Other Side to contact their loved ones on earth. There was even a Greek god of dreams named Morpheus. (His name was derived from the Greek word *morph*, meaning "shape" or "form"; think of the word *metamorphosis*, which means "a change of physical form.") Morpheus had the ability to shape the dreams of kings and common folk alike.

Irene Tsakos, who was born in Queens and moved with her family to her parents' native Greece when she was seven, understood as a child that dreams in her culture were not merely dreams. They carried meanings, messages, affirmations, or warnings. One of Irene's dreams, which she had when she was nineteen, was so powerful that "it became more like a spiritual experience than a dream."

She eventually attended college in the United States but returned to the city of Nafplio in Greece each summer to be with her mother and her father, who was a fisherman. Early one morning, her father left their home at 3:00 A.M. to go out on his fishing boat, and while he was gone Irene had a dream. In it, Irene walked into her home and saw her relatives packed inside. But while she could see her mother and brothers and cousins, she could not find her father.

"I was asking everyone, 'Have you seen my dad?' and they all shook their heads no," Irene says. "I checked upstairs and in all the bedrooms, but I just couldn't find him."

The next morning, Irene described the dream to her friend Victoria. Suddenly, Victoria's mother, who was listening, spoke up.

"Irene," she said gravely, "that is not a good dream at all."

The next day, Irene was on a boat headed to Crete with her cousin when she heard her name called over the ship's PA system. She was instructed to report to the captain's deck.

"As soon as I heard my name, I turned to my cousin and said, 'Something happened to my father,'" she remembers. "My cousin said, 'Oh, come on, you don't know that.' But I knew."

In the captain's quarters Irene was told her father was in the hospital, and she was needed back home right away. Irene asked to call her mother. Irene's aunt answered the phone and told Irene her mother was too busy to come to the phone.

"Tell me the truth," Irene insisted. "My dad died, didn't he?"

After a pause, her aunt said softly, "Yes, Irene, he died."

The boat continued to Crete, where she would take a flight home. For the rest of the boat trip, Irene sat off by herself in the fetal position in a quiet corner of the boat and cried. "And all of a sudden," she says, "I felt a hand brush across my cheek." She looked up, but no one was there. "There was no question that a hand brushed my cheek, and I fully expected to see my cousin or someone else there, but I was alone," she says. "I knew that it was my father trying to comfort me."

Back in Nafplio, Irene walked into her parents' home and saw her dream realized—all her relatives gathered in grief, with only her father missing. She learned he'd been found dead on his drifting boat, likely from a heart attack, doctors said. The night after his funeral, Irene had another powerful dream. In this dream, Irene's father *was* there.

"He was sitting on a wooden chair in our kitchen. He was wearing a white, short-sleeved button-down shirt and brown pants, like he would wear to church. And his green eyes were very bright, almost like light was pouring out of them, coming out of his whole body. I was so surprised and so happy to see him, and I said, 'Baba!' And my father looked at me and said something to me without moving his lips."

"Είμαι καλά, άσε με να φύγ," he said in Greek. Which means, "I am well, let me go."

"And then I woke up, and I was so happy, and I told my mother I'd seen my father and he looked so good, so radiant," Irene says. "I had no words for it, I couldn't explain it, but I truly and deeply felt like I had been with my father. Like I had actually been with him. Not in a dream—like I had been with him in my heart."

Irene's entire life, it turns out, has been filled with surreal occurrences. When she was nine, she choked on a piece of candy and felt herself pass out and leave her body, only to be greeted by her late grandmother Angela, whom she had never met. "She was stroking my hair and saying, 'I love you, but you can't stay, you have to go,'" Irene recalls. "I was so confused. I didn't understand what had happened. But the encounter was so vivid, and I can still see it clearly."

At another point in her childhood, Irene saw an unknown woman standing peacefully outside her bedroom every night. "I asked everyone if they could see her, but no one could. But I had no doubt she was there."

During an especially hard time in her life—when she had to drop out of school and work double shifts to help her family financially— she went to bed one night feeling lower than she ever had. "I remember praying that I wouldn't wake up," Irene says. "I felt like such a disappointment to everyone and to myself."

That night, her prayer was answered in an unexpected way.

She had a vivid dream in which she was bathed with a bright peach-colored light and shown a giant dome filled with light beings singing and playing music. "I tried to make out their faces, but I couldn't," she says. "But it didn't matter because the music was so beautiful that I felt my jaw drop and my eyes fill with tears, and I was just utterly overwhelmed by love and beauty. And a presence behind me said, 'They are playing for you.'"

Irene awoke with an unfamiliar but powerful feeling of lightness and joy. "I felt like I was just so *loved*," she says. "It was like someone somewhere knew what I needed and just filled me with these joyful feelings. I believe we all have these kinds of powerful light beings that look out for us and care for us and guide us. And those were mine."

Irene met her future husband at a diner in Great Neck, Long Island. She was meeting a friend who brought Anastasios and other friends along. "It was a semi-setup," says Irene. "They were all crowded around these two tables, but as soon as I walked in the front door my eyes went straight to Tasso, and he was looking straight at me, too. And I remember thinking, *Wow, he is so, so handsome.*"

Meanwhile, Tasso, who was already working as a cop, had the same reaction and later told a friend, "I am going to marry that girl."

Their courtship, however, was long and uneven. Irene had recently returned from Greece, where she'd moved to be with her widowed mother, and because of the stock market crash, her finances were a disaster. Just about all she owned were the five outfits she carried around in a small suitcase. "I told Tasso I wasn't looking for a relationship," she says. "I had no job, no money, no apartment, nothing. I was totally starting over and I needed to get on my feet first."

Tasso took the news well. He told her he was happy just to be her friend—but he never let go of the idea that they belonged together. "He didn't want to lose me, and he refused to close that door," Irene recalls, "so we hung out and went to dinner as friends."

A few days before Christmas, Tasso asked Irene to spend some time with him; she said she couldn't because she had shopping to do.

"Fine," he said, "I'll come, too. I can help."

Together they drove to the John's Farm grocery store in Levittown. Irene picked through vegetables as Tasso happily followed along beside her, pushing the cart. "I was holding a lemon, and I turned around and looked at him and all of a sudden it dawned on me—*I love this guy*," Irene remembers. "I just couldn't imagine not having his support, and I realized all he wanted was to be there for me and be with me when I was happy or sad and help me get through life. Suddenly I understood that I was already in love with this man. It just happened."

When she got back in the car, Irene said nothing about her feelings. Then Tasso told her to close her eyes.

"Why?" Irene asked.

"I have these little presents for you."

The sight of the wrapped boxes made Irene burst into tears.

"What's wrong?" Tasso asked.

"I love you," Irene said.

Tasso flashed an enormous smile.

"He was ecstatic," Irene says. "He just said, 'I love you, too. I always loved you. I was waiting for you to catch up.'"

Not much later they were engaged, and they had their wedding in Greece. Tasso was a rock for Irene during two miscarriages, and he was a doting father to the two children they had, Jennie and Steve. They moved into a larger apartment in Flushing, Queens, and Irene stayed home to raise the children while Tasso took extra shifts to pay their expenses while studying to become a sergeant. It was a hard time, but together they were getting through.

"Tasso would tell me, 'All I want is to be near you and make sure you are all right and happy,'" Irene says. "But the truth was, he didn't need to do anything heroic to make me happy. All I needed was to be with him. His *presence* was enough."

On the night of April 26, 2021, Tasso went out on patrol for a grave-yard shift, and Irene had her dream about not being able to reach him on the balcony.

The next day, Tasso worked another early-morning shift.

Tasso's assignment was highway patrol. He was tasked with cruising, looking for speeding cars and drunk drivers. Many times, he had bravely pursued fleeing cars and criminals, and his record showed he'd made more than two hundred arrests (without calling in for a single sick day in ten years). He was a good, courageous, dedicated cop who never shied away from his duties.

Around two in the morning on April 27, 2021, Tasso responded to a call about a vehicle that had crashed into a wall and was in flames on an exit ramp on Long Island Expressway in Queens. (Sadly, the driver did not survive.) Tasso began closing the ramp and diverting traffic away from the scene while waiting for an ambulance to arrive.

Suddenly a 2013 Volkswagen, driven by a thirty-two-year-old woman, came speeding toward Tasso and did not slow down. The car struck Tasso and threw him in the air; the force was so strong that he was knocked out of his long police boots. He was rushed to a hospital but, tragically, did not survive his many horrific injuries. (Police say the driver admitted to drinking wine, vodka, and tequila, and doing drugs, before getting in her car, and her blood-alcohol level was allegedly .15, almost double the legal limit of .08; she was found guilty of aggravated manslaughter and other offenses in 2024.)

At the Tsakoses' home, loud knocking woke Irene at 4:15 A.M. She looked up and saw flashing red lights through the bedroom blinds. "As soon as I saw that, I knew something bad had happened," she says. "I tried not to think of the worst. Maybe he was just injured."

The police helped Irene take her two children—then six and three and a half—to her brother's house, then rushed her to the hospital. There, Irene kept asking, "Is he alive?" But no one would answer her. Finally, an NYPD official sat her down and told her the terrible truth.

Tasso was gone.

Irene demanded to see him. She was led into a room where Tasso lay on a table, covered by a white sheet. Irene walked to his side. She didn't lift the sheet, but she gently touched her husband's face through the thin white fabric.

"Where are you, Tasso?" she asked softly. *"Where are you?"*

When police officers drove Irene home, it was still sometime in the early hours of the morning. When she switched on the house lights, they dimmed and flickered and went on and off. "I knew it was Tasso," Irene says. "It was comforting, but I needed to know where he was. He promised me he'd never leave, but now he was gone. And I needed to know—*Where is he?*"

The funeral and burial for Anastasios Tsakos took place in Greenlawn, New York, under gray skies. Several hundred police officers in full dress attended, along with the mayor of New York City, Bill de Blasio. "He was the envy of his peers, the American Dream, an example of an extraordinary call to service," said Police Commissioner Dermot Shea, before giving Tasso a posthumous promotion to detective first grade and presenting Irene with his gold detective shield.

Then it was Irene's turn to speak.

"I wish we had more time to watch the kids grow, see them off to college, get married," she said. "I wish we could grow old together. That was the plan." Instead, "Our kids will grow up without their dad. I will make sure they know who he is. Every day they will see his face and learn about all the wonderful things he did, and what a hero he was."

What she would miss most of all, Irene said, "was his hugs."

The shock of losing a loved one can often include a disbelief that they are no longer physically present in our lives. We relate to each other in physical ways—shaking hands, dancing, hugging, nudging—and simply having a friend or a loved one near us, close enough to touch, can be an affirmation that all is right with the world. Conversely, losing those things can be disorienting and devastating.

For Irene, Tasso's physical presence made her feel safe from the moment they met. Even before they fell in love, Irene liked being with Tasso, going shopping with him, seeing a movie, whatever it was. And Tasso, too, did not push for anything other than Irene allowing him to be near her. Their love was born from their instant physical connection and was expressed through simply being *present* with each other.

And then, suddenly, shockingly, Tasso was gone. Disappeared, vanished. No longer there to see or hug or touch. The joy of his presence transformed now into the agony of his absence.

For Irene, this agony was especially acute and only worsened as the days dragged on. "I didn't just *want* to be with Tasso, I *needed* it," she says. "I would tell him all the time when he was alive, 'Wherever you are, *we* will be. I will be next to you.'"

Not having Tasso with her and the children was all but unbearable, and finally Irene pleaded with God. "I need to know where Tasso is," she said. "I need confirmation that he is all right."

Irene's plea did not fall on deaf ears.

First were the flickering house lights. Next came the phone calls, two of them, from someone whose number did not show up on caller ID, and both offering only endless static.

"I know it's you, Tasso," Irene said before hanging up.

One morning a small bird flew into the house and woke Irene. "It wasn't panicking or flying into things; it was gently soaring around the room," she says. "We opened the sliding door to the backyard, but the bird did not want to go. It flew three beautiful circles around the yard and then it finally flew away. This bird was so happy just soaring around the place, like it was saying, 'Look at me, this is my house.'"

Then the downstairs computer began turning itself on. "Three in the morning and it would suddenly play *Peppa Pig*, which is what Tasso used to play for the kids." Just weeks after Tasso's passing, Irene was in a minor car accident and drove to see a mechanic. "I was sitting at a red light bawling and crying, and I looked up and a store was right there."

The store was called Anastasios Supplies and Materials.

There was more. Irene noticed that every time she went to visit Tasso at the cemetery, the same song would come over the radio: "Every Breath You Take," by the Police. "Not just once," she says. "*Every* time." One day Irene turned off the radio to see if the sign would continue without the radio on. "I stepped out of my car in the parking lot, and another car was there with its door open, and the driver was taking out flower pots, and her car radio was playing 'Every Breath You Take'!" Irene says. "By a group called the Police. Of *course*, Tasso would use that song to announce his presence to me."

On the first Valentine's Day after his passing, Irene put a huge photo of Tasso in front of her bed. That night, she looked at the photo and cried because, for the first time in thirteen years, she would not be able to kiss her husband on Valentine's Day. Still crying, she drew the string on her pajama pants and saw that something small was stuck to the string. She picked it off and saw that it was tiny red foam heart—the kind you might glue onto a Valentine's Day card. Irene had no idea where it came from or how it had gotten affixed to her drawstring. "I even asked my kids, 'Is this yours?' But they didn't know where it came from, either." Only then was Irene sure of what it was.

"Tasso found a way to give me a Valentine's gift."

Ever since she was young, however, Irene's most powerful connection to the Other Side has been through dreams.

A few months after Tasso passed, Irene received a text from her cousin's friend Lisa. *Please call me,* it read. Lisa told her she'd had a dream about seeing Tasso in Irene's backyard.

"*Tell Irene I love her,*" he told Lisa in the dream. "*Tell her I am there with her and the kids, and I see her crying when she is out there watching them play. Tell her it's okay because I am there with them.*"

At first, Irene was in disbelief. "I *did* sit in the backyard every day with the kids, and while they played, I *did* sit there and cry, just like Tasso said," Irene says. "But how could he know that?"

Not much later, Irene had her own dream about Tasso.

In the dream, she was dropped into her own living room and opened her eyes to see Tasso standing there, just six feet away. "He was so *beautiful*," Irene remembers. "So healthy and bright and shining, just like my father had been when I dreamt of him." Irene wanted to go over and kiss him, but as soon as she took a step toward him, Tasso took a step backward. The more she approached, the more he moved away.

"He didn't say anything, he just slowly stepped backward," she says. "I understood that I wasn't supposed to touch him."

Then, in the dream, Irene realized there was nothing more Tasso needed to say that he hadn't already communicated to her. "What was he going to say? 'I love you'? 'I'm sorry for leaving'? 'Thank you for being the mother of my children'? What could he possibly say that would mean more to me than just being there with me?"

Tasso did not need to voice a message, because his presence in the dream *was* his message.

"It was always about his presence for me," Irene says. "I always loved seeing him and knowing he was there with me, and when I woke up, I truly felt like I *had* seen him and *had* been with him. I mean, I don't even think of it as a dream. It was Tasso finding a way to show me he will always be there with us."

The signs continued and continue still. When Irene has an especially sad day of missing Tasso, she'll open the mailbox and find a letter or a bill with his name on it. One day, she was driving and started to cry, and immediately saw a license plate in front of her that read LOVE LIGHT. Seconds later, another car pulled in front of her with a license plate that read CARRY ON. And today, when Irene drives by the overpass between the Long Island Expressway Exits 26 and 27, she will drive by what will forever be known as the Detective Anastasios Tsakos Memorial Bridge.

On earth, Tasso only wanted to be with Irene, his presence enough to make her feel safe and happy.

And now Tasso continues to want to make his presence felt, and has proven adept at communicating with Irene in different, vivid ways.

"I know he is around," Irene says. "I do believe that we endure beyond this life, that we go somewhere. I can't pretend to know exactly what happens, but I do know that we endure. There is no way we *don't* endure. I won't try to convince anyone else, but I know what I believe, and I know that we stay connected to our loved ones forever. Tasso has convinced me of that."

I will not allow my life's light to
be determined by the darkness
around me.

SOJOURNER TRUTH

21

Hide-and-Seek

The loss of any loved one affects us profoundly and indelibly, but there may not be any loss more excruciating than the loss of a child. According to a study of bereavement by the U.S. Institute of Medicine, many of the parents surveyed "felt the experience of losing a child is by far the worst [pain,] because it conflicts with our life-cycle expectations." Our children are supposed to outlive us, not the other way around.

The study also noted that children represent a future filled with hope and promise. "All parents have hopes and dreams about their children's futures," the study concludes. "When a child dies, the hopes and dreams die, too."

Sadly, I have spoken with, and read for, far too many parents who have lost children, and there's no doubt that such a trauma brings a uniquely devastating kind of pain. But my experience working with these parents, and receiving messages from their children who have crossed, makes me believe that children on the Other Side *continue to have a meaningful effect on the hopes and dreams of their parents.*

Everything changes when we lose a child.

But not everything ends.

. . .

Kristen was a twenty-eight-year-old elementary school teacher in Florida when her sister Mary Pat told her, "You've got to come and meet my kid's pediatrician." Mary Pat offered only one other bit of information about the doctor: "I don't see a ring on his left hand."

Kristen knew exactly what her sister was up to, since she'd tried to play matchmaker before. Still, she went with her sister one day to Alex Anton's office. "I just sat there, and the whole thing felt kind of ridiculous, and as soon as we left my sister said, 'You have to go back in there by yourself.'" Because Kristen was so sure nothing would come of it, she *did* return to the office and asked the friendly receptionist, Aida, if the doctor was single.

Aida smiled and answered, "Well, yes, he is."

Kristen didn't know what to do next, so Mary Pat took charge again. She called Dr. Anton herself and left him a message to phone Kristen. "He'd always told Aida, 'Don't give me anyone's phone number, they're all married moms with kids,'" Kristen remembers, "and Aida told him, 'Not this one, she's a mom's sister with no kids.' Next thing, he called and left me a voicemail asking me out."

Mary Pat's instincts were spot-on. Kristen and Alex had their first date in 2010, got married in 2012, and welcomed their first child, daughter Caroline, in 2013. Two years later their second child, son Nicholas, arrived. Nicholas, says Kristen, "was just pure joy. He was so happy all the time. He loved to make us laugh and play little tricks and he loved to dance and explore." Nicholas also adored his older sister and insisted on playing dress-up right along with her. "Everything she did, he wanted to do," Kristen says. "She loved Tinkerbell, and so he loved Tinkerbell to the point where he insisted on wearing the Tinkerbell shoes with the little white puffs on them. He and Caroline were inseparable."

Both children were obsessed with the animated movie *Trolls*. Not yet two years old, Nicholas would march downstairs after his nap chanting "Trolls, trolls, trolls," and Kristen would pull up the movie on the living room TV and fold the day's laundry while her kids propped themselves up on two big ottomans, cradled their faces in their hands, and watched a bunch of happy trolls get in all sorts of trouble and narrowly avoid being eaten by the grumpy Bergens at the end.

"The song that comes on when they don't get eaten is 'Can't Stop the Feeling.' The song from the movie is this joyful celebration of being alive, and when that came on the three of us would all jump up and dance all over the living room," remembers Kristen. "We just had so much fun watching that movie and dancing, it became our little thing. The kids would make fun of me because I'd cry at certain parts. It's one of my cherished memories."

Nicholas had just turned two when, one evening, he ran a little fever. The day before he'd been his usual happy-go-lucky self, and the family had gone to the beach, where Nicholas swam happily all day long. The next day, a Sunday, Kristen and Alex were happy to just have a restful day at home. Nicholas took a nap in the afternoon, and when he awoke Kristen noticed he had a small fever, but it didn't seem to bother him much at all. That evening Nicholas cuddled with his father in the living room, eating a fruit bowl and watching the movie *Dumbo* while Kristen put Caroline to bed.

Later that night, Kristen—who had fallen asleep in Caroline's bed— heard Nicholas calling for her from downstairs in the living room. "I went down and he ran over to me and I picked him up and brought him upstairs and rocked him to sleep," she says. "I sang songs to him for a very long time, longer than usual." Finally, when Nicholas was fast asleep, Kristen gently put her hands on Nicholas's cheeks and whispered, "Good night, my precious, precious boy. I love you."

The next morning, Kristen checked on Nicholas in his bedroom. He was still in his bed, and Kristen figured he needed extra sleep after the busy day on Saturday and the fever on Sunday. She went downstairs and occasionally checked on Nicholas through the baby monitor. Suddenly, after seeing in the monitor that he still wasn't moving, an awful feeling washed over her—a feeling that something was terribly wrong.

Kristen ran upstairs and into Nicholas's bedroom and instantly understood what had happened. Speaking softly, Kristen says, "I could see right away that his body . . . that he . . . that Nicholas was gone."

Kristen screamed, picked up her son, and ran him downstairs to the living room. She called 911, and a dispatcher told her to lay Nicholas down on the floor. Kristen laid him right beside the ottomans he and his sister used to curl up on. The dispatcher talked Kristen through administering CPR. "I just did what I was told," she says, "but even then I knew that Nicholas was not coming back."

Kristen gave Caroline an iPad and set her up in the front room, away from the chaos. The police arrived, and a female officer sat with Caroline while another tended to Kristen and Nicholas. "I kept saying, 'Can someone call my husband?' But no one did, so I just called him myself," Kristen recalls. The receptionist, Aida, picked up, and Kristen said, "You need to get Alex home right now. Nicholas isn't breathing." Alex jumped in his car and sped all the way home, angry horns blaring behind him. He arrived to find police and paramedics everywhere.

"There was nothing either Alex or I could have done," Kristen says. "It was every parent's nightmare. No one knew what was wrong."

Inexplicably, illogically, unthinkably, Nicholas was gone.

In the days that followed, medical examiners performed several tests, including a DNA test, but found no conclusive evidence of any illness or malady. They even tested Caroline over the course of the next year to try to find some reason for what happened to Nicholas. The best they could do was suggest that Nicholas may have been afflicted with the parainfluenza virus, which, according to the Centers for Disease Control, "commonly causes respiratory infections in young children, [though most] patients usually recover on their own." In very rare cases, however, the virus can cause a serious lower respiratory tract illness and prove fatal.

But even that diagnosis didn't make any sense to Kristen, because Nicholas had barely been sick at all. Still, she says, "that was the only diagnosis we had to hold on to. At least we had something that could put a stop to our searching for an answer."

Nicholas's funeral was somber, held on a day of dark clouds and heavy rain. Caroline, two weeks shy of turning four, was the only one in attendance not wearing black; she chose instead to wear a colorful dress that looked like it had been splattered by a rainbow. After the church service, Caroline joined other children in an activity while her parents took care of final details with the priest. When Kristen finally came out through the church front door, she was happily surprised to see that the gloom had lifted and the sun was shining brightly. Little Caroline ran over wearing a butterfly mask she'd just made and asked if it was okay for her to wear it to the cemetery. "I told her, 'Of course you can,'" Kristen recalls. "Actually, I wanted one, too. I wanted to hide behind a mask and disguise myself and be someone else for a moment—anyone but the mother who had to go and bury her child."

At the cemetery, the priest asked Alex, Kristen, and Caroline to kneel before the coffin. At the very moment the priest began his prayer, an enormous monarch butterfly—"the biggest, most beautiful one I've ever seen"—fluttered over the casket and floated there in the air. "It was just breathtaking for everyone there," Kristen says. "But then I looked over and saw Caroline kneeling and still wearing her butterfly mask, and it hit me—Nicholas, who always had to wear whatever Caroline wore and do whatever Caroline did—had 'dressed up' as a butterfly and showed up at the cemetery! In this moment of gut-wrenching sadness, the worst moment of my life, Nicholas was able to bring me peace."

Later, in the car, Caroline confirmed Kristen's interpretation of the butterfly. "You know, Mom," she said, "wherever I go, Nicholas comes with me." That hadn't changed. It was still true.

"We looked through the windshield, and there were literally these beautiful little rainbows everywhere," Kristen says. "I started getting texts from all these people saying, 'Look outside, there's a million rainbows!'" It was true—the Florida sky was filled with colorful rainbows, just like the one on Caroline's dress.

Just then—*just then*—the song that came over the car radio was "Can't Stop the Feeling," from *Trolls*.

Since then, Nicholas has continued to send his family a series of re-markable signs that have given Kristen "a true sense of knowing that he is here with us," she says. "I always think of Caroline saying, 'Wherever I go, he goes, too.' That's how I feel about it—that wherever we go as a family, Nicholas comes with us."

In particular, Nicholas has used the movie *Trolls*, and the two songs that appear in the movie at the end—"True Colors" and "Can't Stop the Feeling"—to keep the lines of communication open. "He has taken those two songs and woven them into our lives over the last six years in extremely meaningful ways," Kristen says. "We hear those songs playing *everywhere*, and they've become a really big sign for us"—particularly the happy, upbeat anthem "Can't Stop the Feeling."

Three months after Nicholas crossed, Kristen had the chance to run in a half-marathon. She hadn't been much of a runner, but after Nich-olas's passing, her brother and sister kept showing up at her house and insisting she join them for a run. Her brother even signed her up for the half-marathon two months ahead of time. "I said, 'Yeah, right, sure, I'll run it,'" says Kristen, not believing for a second that she could. But then her one-mile runs with her siblings turned into two miles, then three miles, then ten, then *thirteen*.

Three months earlier, simply getting out of bed in the morning had been nearly unthinkable for the grief-stricken mother, who trudged around her house "like I was walking through quicksand." But now, there was no turning back—Kristen was running a half-marathon.

At the four-mile mark, Kristen turned a corner and saw all of her girlfriends, who surprised her by showing up with signs cheering her on.

"They positioned themselves right by the DJ who was playing music during the race, and when I saw them the song the DJ was playing was 'Can't Stop the Feeling' from *Trolls*," says Kristen, who still can't quite believe that happened. "That song and my friends and family are what kept me going in that race."

To mark their tenth wedding anniversary, Kristen and Alex stayed at a fancy Ritz Hotel. "I walked out of the hotel bathroom," Kristen says, "and Alex was sitting on the bed with the TV on, and he said, 'Guess what's playing on NBC?'"

It was—you guessed it—*Trolls*.

"So of course, we just sat there and watched it from start to finish to celebrate our anniversary."

Nicholas has also used rainbows as a sign, harking back to his sister's rainbow dress and the multiple rainbows that appeared the day of his funeral. What's truly magical is that Nicholas has managed to make rainbows appear not only in the sky, but *in the very room where he crossed.*

It happened on March 22—fittingly, Kristen's birthday. By then, Kristen and her husband had a third child, whom they named Madelyn and called Maddie. March 22 began with rainbows outside, and the resplendent light outside beamed through Kristen's living room window, which somehow refracted in a way that created a thin rainbow streak that ran across the living room, *precisely over the spot where Kristen had laid Nicholas the day he crossed.*

"This was also right by the two ottomans where he and Carolyn used to watch TV," Kristen says. "I looked for this little rainbow over the years, and it comes and goes, and I have all these photos of Maddie sort of chasing it and playing with it. I have no doubt that this is Nicholas. He is literally showing us this light in the midst of darkness. He is telling us to have hope, to believe that he's still here."

When Kristen was pregnant with Maddie, "I told Alex I had a strong feeling that that should be her name," Kristen says. Her husband's reply: "Hmm, I don't know about that."

"Well, she could be Madison, and we'll call her Maddie."

"I don't know about Madison. How about Madelyn?"

"Perfect! As long as we get to call her Maddie."

Kristen never had that kind of certainty about a name with her other children, but this time, she just *knew* it had to be Maddie. "It felt to me that my daughter would be mad at me if she wasn't named that," Kristen says. "I really didn't know where it came from."

Until—

—one afternoon when Kristen was sitting in her car and idly flipping through family photos on her phone. She came across one that she'd seen before but that suddenly took on a breathtaking new meaning.

"There was this coffee shop that I used to bring Caroline and Nicholas to, and I took a photo of Nicholas standing in the children's play area, in front of a black chalkboard," Kristen remembers. She studied the photo and noticed, for the first time, that a name had been written on the board in purple chalk, in big block letters, just above where Nicholas was standing.

The name?

Maddie.

"There it was, in big purple letters," Kristen says. "I don't know why it was there, and I hadn't ever noticed it before. But now I believe it was Nicholas who put that name in my head. And it was Nicholas letting me know that he'd always been with Maddie, and that he would always be with her in the future."

There was more. In the weeks before he crossed, every time Kristen tucked him into bed at night, Nicholas would smile up at his mother and say, "Two, two."

Kristen knew what it meant. "He wanted me to put two blankets on him. One was a quilt, and the other was a hand-knit blanket my mother made for him. I'd pull them over and lay them on top of him and tuck him in, and then as I was leaving I'd always say, 'I love you,' and he'd always answer, 'Ayo.'"

Ayo was the sound Nicholas made for "I love you."

Fast-forward three years, to when Maddie was nearing the age of two. One night, as Kristen was tucking her into bed, Maddie looked up at her mother and smiled and out of nowhere uttered a familiar phrase.

"Two, two."

"It wasn't possible," Kristen said. "I mean, for her to say the exact same thing Nicholas used to say?"

By then Kristen had stored the blankets away, but she retrieved them and gently laid them over Maddie and tucked her in, just as she'd done with Nicholas.

When she was leaving the room, Kristen said, "I love you."

"And I swear, I *swear*, I heard Maddie say 'Ayo' back."

How could all this have happened? How could Maddie know that the brother she never met used to say "Two, two" and "Ayo"? How could her name have appeared on that chalkboard back when she hadn't yet been conceived? How could a beautiful sliver of a rainbow slowly stretch itself across the very spot on the rug where Nicholas had lain?

And why did "Can't Stop the Feeling" never stop playing?

The answer is not in any textbook that I know of. Much more likely, it's in the title of the very song that has become the most life-affirming sign Nicholas shares with his loved ones. The love that existed between him and his family when they were together on this earth *did not merely end when he crossed.* That love endures, for all of us, as a powerful connective force that, like the song says, cannot be stopped. It's always there, always radiating, always dancing in the air, just like "Can't Stop the Feeling" is always playing. And our loved ones on the Other Side work really hard to send us signs that allow us to believe in this enduring love, and to be open to it whenever we need to feel it the most.

Nicholas, it turns out, is exceptionally good at sending signs. But the signs are there for all of us, every day, all the time, guiding us to lead illuminated lives of love, vibrancy, and connection—as long as we are open to receiving them.

In this way, the hopes and dreams created when Nicholas was born did not vanish when he crossed. They did not end. Instead, they changed into something else, just as deep, just as meaningful, just as impactful on the Antons. After all, it was Nicholas who helped Kristen come up with a name for her third child. "It was like he was *involved* in this little bit of planning for our family," Kristen says. "I honestly and truly feel that way. Every time Nicholas sends me a sign, I can't quite believe it's happening, but over all these years of experiencing them, there's no question that the signs he sends have helped guide us and helped us heal."

One of the fun things Nicholas loved doing was playing hide-and-seek. "Like I said, he was a little trickster, and he loved making us laugh," Kristen says. "We'd be taking a walk and he'd put his little hands on his eyes and count, 'One, two, three,' like he was about to run off and hide. He was able to find the joy in every moment, every place, and that's still the message he sends us today—laugh, play games, have fun with your life."

And Kristen is always on the alert for more signs and guidance from Nicholas. "It's like I'm on a continuous treasure hunt to see the next message from Nicholas and what he's come up with now," she says. "Knowing that Nicholas is there feels like a swirling, powerful energy all around me, and it brings me so much joy. I feel like Nicholas and I are still playing hide-and-seek."

22

Staying Alive

Sometimes when I do a reading the message coming through from the Other Side can be a little muddy. I might be shown an image or a letter that is just a bit off, a bit unclear, and that can make deciphering its meaning more difficult. All readings are different and all souls communicate in different ways, and some are, for whatever reason, a bit better at it than others.

But sometimes the messages that come through are so strong and so precise, so *crystal clear*, that I know we are receiving a very special gift from the spirit, undiluted and powerful.

This is what happened in a reading I did for a woman named Nicole Sciacca. I began the reading as I usually do, by examining her bright aura, but almost immediately my attention was pulled away.

"I'm sorry, I just . . . There is someone *so* eager pushing through already," I told Nicole. "I'm going to have to come back to your aura."

Very quickly, it was clear that the soul coming through in the reading was the loved one Nicole had recently lost.

"Oh, wow, he's got jumping energy, like getting ready for a big game," I said. "I feel a soul mate connection immediately. He is telling me to 'grab some popcorn and snuggle up, 'cuz this is about to get good!'"

Our one-hour reading turned into two intense hours, and at the end of it I told Nicole that, though a mutual friend had reached out to me on her behalf, the reading had actually been orchestrated and made possible by the very strong presence on the Other Side, as a gift to her.

This is the story I want to share with you now—the story of a truly profound bond between two very special people.

As a child growing up in Birmingham, Alabama, Nicole understood she was different from her parents. Her father was a head and neck surgeon, and her mother ran their busy household. They were quiet, traditional, and conservative, while Nicole was, well, the opposite of that. "I was super sparky compared to them," she recalls. "Just always up and on and loud." Luckily, her parents did not try to stifle her energy. "They fed it and fueled it," she says. "They just let me be my own person and facilitated that side of me."

When she was two, Nicole poured her intense energy into dance. "I felt like dance chose *me*," she explains. "One day out of the blue I just started dancing and then I never stopped." Even when she developed other interests, dance was the only pursuit that really mattered to her. "I got to be good at swimming, and my dad told me, 'If you do this year-round, you can go to the Olympics.' And I said, 'Um, that's not happening, I've got ballet class at four.'"

After three years of college Nicole moved to Los Angeles, ready to begin a career she felt was preordained. A producer she knew set her up on an audition, and though she didn't book the job, she soon found work assisting popular choreographers like Chris Judd and Eddie Garcia. Just like that she was in the inner circle, the heart of the dance scene in Los Angeles, and her dreams seemed perfectly within reach.

Then she agreed to do a free job for a choreographer she'd never met, as a favor. The rehearsal was late at night, and the choreography was fast and complex. "I mean, it was *way* too fast, and as I was dancing, I thought, 'This is not good.' The next thing you know, it happened."

Nicole collapsed to the floor, writhing in pain. She had ruptured four discs in her spine. Somehow, she managed to drive herself home, and she scheduled an MRI that revealed the extent of the damage. Her doctor prescribed a month of bed rest and told her spinal surgery was likely in her future. The injury changed everything.

"After that my willingness to confidently get up and dance went away," she says. "I didn't want to perform anymore. I just felt different."

Still needing an output for her powerful energy, Nicole immersed herself in the healing process, learning physical therapy, network spinal analysis, and other wellness methods. Before long, she felt physically healed—and she felt a strong desire to help others heal in the same way. "Once I realized I could do all of these things I became so excited to share it with other people," she says. Nicole opened her own yoga and cycling studio in Venice, California, and focused all her energy on healing others.

"To be able to get people into their bodies and help them feel good was just so transformative for me," she says. "I feel like we're not meant to work nine to five and sit in a car on the 405 all day. I think people just forget there's so much more to experience in your own body. And when people begin to understand that and feel it, it's just such a blessing."

Nicole was twenty-one and in an acting class in North Hollywood when she met a fellow acting student named Matt. He was an exceptional athlete and a stuntman who, Nicole soon learned, shared her profound interest in what might be called the supernatural—near-death experiences, the afterlife, black holes, time and space. (One of the first books Nicole read when she was young was Stephen Hawking's *A Brief History of Time*.) "We sat down and we had this amazing conversation, and we completely found ourselves in that conversation," Nicole says, recalling the moment. "The minute I saw Matt—and I've never felt this about anyone, ever—I just knew we were connected. It was like we were bound by an invisible cord of energy. I can't explain it, but I just knew that we were meant to be together."

As memorable as their conversation was, they went their separate ways. Nicole married someone else, had a beautiful baby boy, and two years later was divorced. But even then, though they hadn't spoken in years, the connection between Matt and Nicole persisted.

"When I got pregnant, I decided to name my son Beau, which was the name of Matt's nephew," says Nicole. "I don't know why, I just loved the name. I didn't tell Matt about it, I just did it. So it was like the connection between us continued, unbeknownst to him and even to me."

And then, like clockwork, Matt reappeared in her life. Shortly before Nicole's divorce was finalized, Matt sent her a message on social media wishing her a happy Mother's Day.

"How are you?" he asked.

"I'm great," Nicole answered. "I'm getting a divorce."

"Let's have lunch."

Their reacquaintance get-together went on for five hours, and after that they were never apart again.

They didn't get married, but they were together for eight years and lived with each other for four of those years. Together they took care of Beau from the age of two. "Matt raised him as if he were his own boy," Nicole says. "He was one hundred percent present and devoted. He coached his baseball team and his football team, and he just showed up for Beau in every way that Beau needed. And they were just so alike. They had so many similarities. It was like they were also connected in some way we didn't fully understand."

The night of September 15, 2023, Matt woke himself up with his loud snoring and went to sleep in his office in their home so that Nicole, who had an early yoga class, could get her rest. The next morning, Nicole woke up and heard the alarm ringing in Matt's office. She knew he had to get up early, too, to coach Beau in a football game, and she assumed he was just grabbing a little extra sleep. Nicole took a quick shower and came out to the sound of Matt's alarm still ringing. She walked into his office and found him lying still in his bed.

"He was very clearly not there anymore," Nicole recalls. "He was gone. And I became hysterical with anger and confusion and disbelief because of how absurd it was to walk in and find your partner deceased. And I remember that I was crying and I said to Matt, 'You better be up there ready to send me some signs because I am going to need some *immediate* signs from you.'"

Matt's heart had given out. Although he had been uncommonly athletic and in peak condition, the autopsy revealed he had arterial sclerosis, a genetic hardening of the walls of the arteries. There had been no external signs that anything was wrong, and Matt, who Nicole calls a "hypochondriac," would have gone to the emergency room "that night if he had any idea his heart wasn't working right." The shock of his unexpected passing was overwhelming, yet Nicole found some solace in the hundreds of hours they had spent together talking about near-death experiences and otherworldly communications and the idea that our love and our energy live on. It was this shared awareness of our consciousness enduring that led Nicole to immediately continue talking to Matt in the moments after she found him.

"It was like our conversation never ended and just went on," she says. "It's been nonstop since we met."

This is why Nicole so quickly asked Matt to send her signs—because she believed he would find a way to keep the conversation going on his end. "I told him, 'Send me signs, signs, signs, and more signs,'" she says. "Like, 'From today on I need signs *every day*.' I felt like I could keep Matt's consciousness alive in these conversations with him. I knew he would guide me."

Sure enough, the signs came. The morning after Matt's passing, a whitish bird settled on the ledge of Nicole's living room window and calmly sat there, peering in through the glass. Nicole had never seen that type of bird before, so she called over her father—who with Nicole's mother and brother had come to stay with her—and asked him what kind of bird he thought it was.

"It's a mourning dove," her father said.

A *mourning* bird? Really? Showing up just then?

"No, Dad, I think it's an albino pigeon," Nicole said.

They looked it up. It was a mourning dove. And it just sat there on the window ledge, staying with Nicole.

That same day Nicole was in her bedroom when she heard her mother—who was in the kitchen making breakfast—cry out.

"Matt!" her mother screamed.

Nicole ran in to see what had happened.

Her mother had been scrambling eggs, and when she peppered the eggs, the top flew off the mill and pepper sprayed everywhere, including all over the eggs and the counter and floor.

"What's going on?" Nicole asked.

"Oh my gosh," her mother said. "This is crazy. A year ago, when Matt came to visit us in Alabama without you, he went to pepper the eggs I'd made him, and by mistake he flipped open the spoon side and he dumped pepper all over the eggs and the counter and the floor."

And now the scene had been magically re-created in Nicole's kitchen—an incident she'd never even heard about. That was why Nicole's mother had yelled out, "Matt!" He had sent her a clear message to let her know he was still there.

More signs followed. That very night, the electricity in Nicole's house went out for the first time in four years. "I was like, 'Okay, Matt, I know I asked you for a sign, but don't you think it's a little too early for the ghost stuff?' I guess I wasn't as ready for him as I thought."

At his funeral on Siesta Key Beach in Sarasota, Matt sent Nicole a special sign. One of several businesses Matt ran was called Rubber Tubbers, a company that made bathtub toys done up as college team mascots. On the way to the beach through the parking lot, Nicole walked straight up to a parked Jeep—Matt's favorite vehicle—with its dashboard absolutely *covered* with rubber ducks. "There were dozens and dozens of them," Nicole recalls. "Of course, it was Matt."

Yet all these signs didn't compare to the two most powerful messages Matt sent her—one through a song, the other through a rash.

·   ·   ·

Two months before Matt passed, Nicole had developed an odd rash on her chest. She'd never had any skin issues, and she had no idea what caused the irritation. "I thought maybe it was from all the sweating I do during yoga," she says. "But mostly I just ignored it."

The rash, however, did not go away and began to spread across her body. She scratched herself in her sleep so furiously that she'd bruise her skin and wake up black and blue. She saw a dermatologist and tried different diets and regimens, but nothing worked and the rash persisted. Even two biopsies came up inconclusive. No one knew what was wrong.

Then came September 16, when Nicole walked into Matt's office and found him there. The day was a blur of tears and grief, and it wasn't until later that night that Nicole realized something strange — the rash that had spread across her whole body was, suddenly, gone. "I am saying it literally disappeared," she explains. "It was a hundred percent gone. There was some discoloration, but the rash itself was gone. Even my family, when they arrived, said, 'Hey, what happened to your rash?' My skin suddenly felt like silk."

Medically, it made no sense, and Nicole understood that. But in her grief she didn't have the luxury of dwelling on her suddenly vanished rash, and she just let it go. Only weeks later, when Nicole and I had our reading, did the subject of her mysterious rash come up again.

Early in our reading, Matt came through and delivered a stark and clear message to Nicole: *You are healed.* At the same time, he told her, *You have to stop.* I understood what he was communicating — she needed to stop reliving the moment when she found him and stop wondering if there was something she could have done to save him.

Then Matt got even more specific.

"What's interesting," I said to Nicole, "is that you were having some sort of visceral reaction prior to him passing. Months prior, right?"

"Yes!" Nicole quickly responded.

"You both knew something was off, something very acute . . . Were you itching yourself? Did it get crazy bad at night?"

"Yes!"

Nicole shared the story of her rash, and of knowing that at midnight on the day Matt passed — his approximate time of death, it was later determined — she had been wide awake and scratching her skin just a few feet away. That she had been awake at that time haunted Nicole and filled her with guilt.

Now Matt was telling her she had to let go of it.

"Matt was letting me know there was nothing I could have done to save him, that I had been blocked from knowing about his condition and I had no reason to feel guilty about it," Nicole says now. "The rash, which had started across my heart, was my light body preparing me for the fact that Matt's soul was going to go. My logical, rational mind could not have known that, but my light body was getting me ready. And when his soul left, so did the rash."

The concept of the *light body* is part of several centuries-old teachings and traditions, and an awareness of it opens us up to a vast pool of resources and opportunities for personal and societal evolution. When I told Nicole about her "light body," I was referring to the understanding that we all have an existence beyond our physical bodies that is comprised not of skin and bones but of our spiritual, molecular energy — an energy that is so strong and powerful it transcends our physical existence. In the case of Matt and Nicole, they had, as Nicole noticed when they met, a profound and intense spiritual connection — a bond so strong it existed beyond the physical plane.

In other words, we are all spiritual light energy inside our physical bodies. While Nicole's logical mind did not know what was about to happen, her body *did* know and tried to prepare her.

Neither Matt nor Nicole could solve the mystery of her rash while he was alive, yet their deep soul connection presented her with physical evidence that something was amiss, specifically, that Matt was about to cross.

"My light body understood that his soul was preparing to leave, even as my rational mind could not possibly have known," Nicole says. "Matt was so empathetic and so deeply connected to me that my body developed this rash that disappeared when he passed. When I finally

realized that's what happened, I felt so at peace. It made sense to me—
it was consistent with the relationship we had. Matt had helped me
heal."

Nicole's son, Beau, was just ten when Matt crossed, and his passing left
the child gutted. "They had a very special bond, too, and Beau was just
shattered," Nicole says. "He always wanted to be with Matt and he
didn't understand why he didn't get to say goodbye. They were developing this really beautiful relationship."

One afternoon while Nicole was driving Beau to football practice,
she brought up Matt's passing.

"You know, you could ask Matt to send you a sign," she said. "He
sends us signs all the time. You could ask him to send one for you."

Beau thought about it for a moment, then said, "Okay, I'm gonna do
it. I want him to play a song for me in the next twenty-four hours."

"What song?" Nicole asked.

"'Stayin' Alive,'" Beau said, referring to the Bee Gees' well-known
disco-era song from the John Travolta movie *Saturday Night Fever*.
"'Stayin' Alive' was Matt's baseball walkout song when he played pro-
fessionally."

Not only had Beau asked for a very specific sign—the decades-old
song Matt had chosen to walk out on the field to—but he'd put a strict
timetable on its delivery: one single day. Matt's powers of empathy and
communication were about to be tested.

The rest of that day and the following morning passed with no word
from Beau about the sign. That afternoon, while driving Beau back
home from practice, Nicole noticed there were less than two hours left
for Matt to meet the deadline. She figured she ought to explain to her
son that not all signs arrive just when we'd like them to.

"I mean, it's not like we can demand signs from the Other Side,"
Nicole said. "It's about staying open and being ready, and who knows,
maybe Matt will send the message next week."

Beau quizzically looked up at his mother.

"It already happened, Mom."

"Wait, what?"

"Yeah, I was walking down the hall at school with Logan, and Logan stubbed his toe and that's when I got it."

The chorus of the song Beau asked for is iconic and distinctive: *Ah, ah, ah, ah, stayin' alive, stayin' alive*. Beau explained that when his friend Logan stubbed his toe he didn't just say "Ow."

Instead, he sang: *"Ow, ow, ow, ow, stayin' alive, stayin' alive."*

Just like that, Beau had his sign from Matt, right on schedule. "Beau was like, 'Yeah, it's all good, I got the sign, I'm all set,'" Nicole remembers. "He wasn't the least bit surprised. It was what he expected Matt would do all along. To him, it was no big deal."

One of the reasons Matt is so effective at sending messages and communicating with his family is that he and Nicole spent countless hours discussing the afterlife and what happens to us when we cross. It was an ongoing conversation born of their shared intellectual curiosity, and it synced them up on the same wavelength. They were open to each other *and* to the persistence of our existence beyond the physical realm, and so when Matt crossed, they didn't need to find new ways to connect; they merely continued the conversation they'd been having for years.

"We always talked with each other about this, and nothing really changed even after he passed," Nicole says. "I talk to Matt out loud every day in my car, and it truly feels like he's right there with me."

One of the things I would recommend to couples is that they have similar conversations about the afterlife and the persistence of consciousness. It's not an everyday topic for most couples, or even a once-every-ten-years topic for some, but discussing what we believe happens to us when we cross is a good way to strengthen the spiritual bond between us, and to become more and more open to each other.

This is what Matt and Nicole did while he was here on earth and it's what they've continued to do now that he has crossed. I can hardly think of a conversation that would be *more* worth having with a loved one than a talk, or series of talks, that could make it easier for us to stay connected to each other after someone crosses.

Today, the gateway between Matt and Nicole remains impressively open. Certainly during my reading with Nicole, Matt came through loud and clear, on matters both big and small. "One of his messages to me was that he apologized about the laundry," Nicole says with a chuckle. "Matt was supposed to be in charge of the laundry, and the day after he passed I got stuck with it and I yelled out, 'Great, now I gotta do all this laundry *and* all my other chores, too!' So Matt was saying he was sorry he left it for me to do."

During the reading Matt even settled a couple of long-running disagreements between them, telling Nicole that "Samsung is superior to Apple" and that "aliens are real" (both messages made her laugh out loud).

Outside of our reading, Matt has communicated with Nicole through some of her friends as well. "Days or weeks after we had our reading Matt would come to them in a dream or something and they would call me out of the blue and tell me what he wanted to say," Nicole explains. "Not just one or two of them, but all of them. And the message was always the same: Matt wanted me to make sure that Beau understands he is still with him, still there on the field with him, or in school, or in the car. That he will *always* be there with him, protecting him and guiding him. That's why every day I ask Beau, 'Hey, how's your heart? Have you heard from Matt today?' The communication between the three of us is a constant, everyday thing. And I think that's really beautiful."

I think so, too. Matt's energy is always there with them, loving and guiding them.

In my reading with Nicole, Matt was insistent that all aspects of our lives are intertwined once we cross, which meant that he would continue to be there for Nicole, propelling her to grow and grow in ways even she couldn't understand. Part of Matt's mission here on earth had been to love Nicole, deeply and unconditionally, and doing so helped him remain fully engaged in his own life. In this way they helped each other grow, which they continue to do today.

"Matt was telling me that it's not about my grief or guilt, it's about how I live my life from here on in, and how many people I can reach with this message of love and openness," Nicole says. "It's all about love and spirituality, and I'm lucky to be in a position to help a lot of people grow and heal and become more open to the world.

"Look, I still sometimes feel traumatized by what happened to Matt and by not fully understanding where he went when he crossed. It was abrupt and devastating. But knowing that I can still feel his consciousness around me, that we can both keep giving and getting love . . . well, that is everything to me."

PART THREE

OWNING THE LIGHT: ILLUMINATING YOUR LIFE

Many years ago, I came across an anthology of poetry called *A Book of Luminous Things*. It was assembled by the Nobel Prize–winning poet and prose writer Czesław Miłosz. I was drawn to it and leafed through it and was immediately taken with the poems I read. I felt a little spark go off in my mind, and a clear message emerged: *This book will matter to you later on. There is an idea here that needs to be explored—the idea that* this is what we're here for.

So the book stayed with me, in my mind and energy, for years and years, until I realized that "later on" is right now.

As soon as I was ready to write this book, I pulled out my copy of *A Book of Luminous Things* and waited to see what would jump out at me. The first thing that did was a short passage right at the start of the book, in which Czesław talks about the meaning of the word *epiphany*:

> Epiphany is an unveiling of a reality. What in Greek was called *epiphaneia* meant the appearance, the arrival, of a divinity among mortals or its recognition under a familiar shape of a man or woman. Epiphany thus interrupts the everyday flow of time and enters as one privileged moment when we intuitively grasp a deeper, more essential reality hidden in things or persons.

In a way, every poem in Czesław's anthology is a beautiful epiphany— a moment in which time is interrupted and a deeper reality is revealed. Every experience we have, every person we meet, is a kind of epiphany, giving us the opportunity to learn something new about our reality and existence. This book is really a collection of stories about remarkable people who, through these pages, have crossed your path and whose experiences are meant to help you intuitively grasp the deeper, more hidden reality in all persons and things.

This is what I mean by *owning the light*. Once we see the light and explore the light, we can begin to *own* the light, which means always being open to the rich and dazzling array of art and ideas and creativity all around us, adopting a new way of thinking about the world, and ultimately being able to shift our energy to tap into the greater power of the Universe. We begin to see that the little sparks of energy that ignite our passions and heal our wounds are *exactly* the secret, guiding light we've been talking about in this book.

Seeing and feeling moments of epiphany can lead you to a truly illuminated life.

I hope the next chapters will light more sparks in you, and help you see and embrace, and ultimately *own*, the light that is guiding you to and illuminating your path through life.

Eventually, you will come to
understand that love heals everything,
and love is all there is.

GARY ZUKAV

23

10,000 Grandmothers

Clint Ober has never forgotten what happened when a childhood friend's sister fell ill with scarlet fever.

The stricken girl's Native American family took her to see doctors, who told them there wasn't much they could do. "A lot of people were dying of scarlet fever back then," says Clint, who grew up on a sprawling cattle farm in Montana in the 1940s. "This girl had a very high fever and was really sick. It didn't look good."

Clint watched as some elders in the girl's family dug a shallow pit in the earth, a foot deep and five feet long. They placed some straw in the pit and laid the sick girl in it, then built a small fire nearby and settled in. "Her grandfather sat with her day after day after day," Clint recalls. "After a few days the girl suddenly got out of the pit and started running around like nothing was wrong. I didn't know what to think."

Today, many decades later, Clint understands exactly what it was that he witnessed as a boy.

"The earth," he says, "healed the girl."

Since then, Clint Ober has almost single-handedly pioneered the modern development of an ancient healing practice known as earthing, or grounding. Put simply, *earthing* means increasing our direct contact with the natural ground below us—for instance, walking barefoot in the grass. Something as simple as that, Clint believes, can fundamentally change our lives in a positive way, making us healthier, happier, sounder human beings. "There is something innate in us that goes back hundreds of thousands of years that drives us to live in harmony with nature," Clint says. "We have always known that the earth can heal us."

It is only in the last century or so that civilization has moved away from the natural earthing practices that existed through much of history—walking barefoot or in leather shoes, working in nature rather than in offices, connecting constantly to the ground. Thanks to the creation of synthetic polymers, which made rubber-soled shoes possible, we have essentially insulated ourselves from extended or even occasional direct contact with the ground. And, since the invention of the television, our lives have moved even more from outdoors to indoors. We have literally distanced ourselves from the earth.

Ironically, one of the men who played a big part in this societal insulating from the earth is Clint Ober himself.

I am excited to share Clint's story with you, for many reasons, not the least of which is that he has been on a truly unique spiritual journey that illustrates what it means to live a guided life.

"I've always felt I am on a mission that is being guided, not by me but by the Universe," says Clint. "It wasn't me behind everything that happened—I'm just a cowboy from Montana. But I've always been open to new people and new ideas, and the right people always seemed to show up at the right time."

Back in the 1970s and '80s, Clint forged a hugely successful career in the cable TV industry, first as the national director of marketing for what grew to become the largest cable television company in the United States, and then on his own running a business that developed cable TV systems. Clint was basically at the forefront of all the discoveries and inventions in the communications industry—satellites, microwave properties, in-home cable installation—that paved the way for national broadcast networks like CNN, ESPN, and HBO. "Once I understood how it all worked," Clint says, "my goal became more television signals, more cable, more programming, wider reach, as well as creating the demand for this wave of new in-home entertainment systems."

The industry exploded in a way even Clint couldn't have foreseen, and before long, cable TV became as American as hot dogs. By the 1990s, nearly 99 percent of American homes had at least one TV in them, most of them wired with cable. "In old days people would congregate outside," Clint says. "People would meet around the fire. Now we gather around the TV. Before we knew it, we all got addicted to television."

With that came the gradual but relentless move from outdoors to indoors. Not all that long ago "we couldn't get away from the earth even if we wanted to," Clint says. "We lived in the mud and the dirt. That all changed in the 1950s, and I'm afraid I played a part in it." Today, the average U.S. citizen spends 86.9 percent of their life indoors. And even when we *do* go outdoors, we most likely remain highly insulated from the earth. "A hundred years ago most people still went either barefoot or in leather shoes," Clint says. "Today, probably 95 percent of all footwear is synthetic [which blocks conductivity between us and the natural ground]. We created built-in buffers between us and the earth."

Always uncommonly good at seeing the big picture, Clint decided he'd had enough of the cable industry after thirty years and retired at the age of fifty. "I didn't know what I wanted to do," he says, "but I knew I didn't want to keep doing what I was doing." Then Clint faced a critical health crisis: an infection that started during a root canal procedure and traveled to his liver, causing so much damage that doctors told him to go home and get his affairs in order. Luckily, one young surgeon from the Swedish Medical Center in Colorado proposed an experimental operation that involved taking out nearly four-fifths of his liver. With nothing to lose, Clint had the procedure and slowly recovered his health.

One day during his six-month rehabilitation, Clint looked up at one of his favorite paintings on the wall of his home: a depiction of some Native Americans by the well-known Navajo artist R. C. Gorman. (Clint owned a large collection of Gorman's work.) "I'd always loved this painting, but suddenly I wondered what would have happened to it if I had died?" he says. "What would happen to all my possessions? Suddenly I felt really bad that my whole life had been about money."

The next morning, he looked out his window and was unexpectedly astounded by the raw beauty of the countryside. "Everything looked brighter, more alive, more filled with energy," he says. "I thought it might be one of the drugs I was taking, but it wasn't. It was just that I was appreciating how truly beautiful nature is."

Shortly after that, Clint sold everything he owned, including his house, leaving himself only two and a half suitcases and a small RV. He spent the next four years driving around the country, staying mainly in national and state parks and spending most of his time outdoors. After a youth spent tending to his family's farm and being outside nearly every waking hour, Clint the adult returned to nature. "It felt so comfortable," he says. "It made me think of being a kid on the farm, where every day I'd roam around and find old fossil bones and rocks. Sometimes when you pick up a rock and just hold it in your hands, it'll talk to you. It'll share a feeling. And it will fill you with energy."

Still, something didn't feel right. One day, "I was outside watching the sunset, and I had this sensation come over me. I felt the earth was talking to me, telling me I had to go back to work, do something good. And the words that kept coming into my mind were *Become an opposite charge.*"

For thirty years Clint Ober's expertise at grounding cable systems had driven people to spend more time indoors. But now he was going to get them back outside.

Clint headed west, settling in Sedona, Arizona, still unsure of how he was going to make up for his past career. The answer came to him while he was sitting on a bench across from a creek, and a bus full of tourists disembarked nearby. "I watched them get off the bus, and for some reason I noticed their shoes," he says. "They all had these big white Nike-type tennis shoes on with the big rubber soles."

A spark went off in his brain and produced a pointed question: *Is there a consequence to humans for no longer being naturally grounded to the earth?*

Clint raced home and took out his electrometer, a device that measures electrical charges. He grounded one probe and attached the other to his foot, then walked around his carpeted bedroom. "I got these high readings, indicating that there were electrical charges all over my body, mostly from static electricity and all these other environmental electrical fields in our homes," Clint says. He hurried to the hardware store, bought a roll of three-inch-wide aluminum foil tape (used mainly for sealing joints and seams in heating and ventilation systems) and also a stretch of copper wire. Back in his bedroom, he laid the aluminum tape across his bed, attached the wire to it, threaded the wire out his window, and stuck the other end in the ground. Then he lay on his bed, the aluminum tape beneath him, his electrometer in his hand.

"I took the meter and looked for the voltage and electrical charges on my body," he says. "As soon as I lay across the tape, the meter shot down to zero. I'd grounded my body and eliminated all these charges. I'd spent thirty years grounding cable and electrical equipment, and I never even thought about whether we could ground the human body. Well, we can."

Yet this wasn't even the most significant part of the experiment.

As he lay in bed and marveled at the zero reading, Clint nodded off. Ten hours later he awoke and saw it was morning. "Normally, for me to fall asleep, I need to watch TV and take Advil and put on a white noise and all this stuff," says Clint, whose years of skiing and horseback riding had left him with a host of aches and pains. "But that night, I hardly moved a bone or a muscle all night long. I woke up with the meter lying on the bed beside my hand. I thought, *Holy cow, what is this? This is incredible.*"

Clint immediately pored through search engines and scientific collections for any research into grounding the human body, and the relationship between grounding and bodily pain.

He found nothing. No experiments, no studies. Zippo.

"I mean, there were old stories about people wrapping copper wire around their beds and sleeping peacefully, but there was no academic research at all," he says. "So all in one, it struck me that this was the best day and the worst day in my life. The best because I'd rediscovered this miraculous cure for pain. And the worst because no one anywhere knew anything about this, and if I was going to educate people about it, I was going to have to do it one person at a time."

Sure enough, when Clint took his findings to university labs and science departments, he was pretty much laughed off campus. This was the 1990s, and "people weren't even talking about inflammation as being related to pain," he says. "These scientists all looked at me like I was out of my mind. The only people who were even willing to talk to me were the guys in the sleep labs, and even they ended up laughing. They were like, 'You expect us to believe that somebody's gonna tie a wire to their toe and stick the wire in the earth and that's gonna make them sleep better?' Nobody ever really thought about the body being electrical."

Finally, two university students happened upon Clint's experiment and offered to help him conduct a study. The problem: Most university studies cost $5 million and take five years or so. Clint's "grounding" experiment was going to have to be done on the cheap.

Which meant that Clint had to find sixty elderly participants.

"I was getting my hair cut one day at a local salon and I heard one of the beauticians talking about the pain she had," Clint remembers. "I went over to the salon owner and said I was conducting a study and did she know any people who had pain and couldn't sleep?"

"How many you need?" the owner said with a laugh.

Within two months Clint had his sixty participants, thirty of whom would be grounded while they slept and thirty of whom would have a dummy wire that wasn't grounded. Eight weeks later, a nurse hired by

Clint went to the homes of all the participants and had them answer a series of detailed questions about their pain. The thirty participants who were grounded confirmed that their chronic pain had significantly improved: 93 percent said the quality of their sleep was better; 85 percent said it took them less time to fall asleep; 100 percent said they woke up feeling better rested than usual. Static electricity readings in the homes of the grounded participants further confirmed Clint's premise—that the earth itself can heal us.

Clint wrote up his findings and published his study in the *ESD Journal* in 2000. "From the beginning of time, except for the past few generations, humans lived their entire lives primarily in direct physical contact with the earth," Clint wrote. Losing that connection has caused a variety of physical maladies that "all relate to excess stimulation of the nervous system and/or interference of the bio-electrical communications between cells." His conclusion:

> The human body when grounded is naturally protected from static electricity and the weak electric currents created in the body by radiated electric fields. The benefits of grounding the body are: sleep significantly improves, muscles relax, chronic back and joint pain subsides and general health improves.

And yet—the more mainstream medical and scientific journals declined to publish Clint's findings. He was still, it seemed, ahead of his time. Clint never stopped pushing his findings and developing new earthing technology, and, slowly, the world caught up with him.

In 2012, several scientists published a study called "Earthing: Health Implications of Reconnecting the Human Body to the Earth's Surface Electrons," in which they wrote:

> Emerging scientific research has revealed a surprisingly positive and overlooked environmental factor on health: direct physical contact with the vast supply of electrons on the

surface of the Earth. Modern lifestyle separates humans from such contact. The research suggests that this disconnect may be a major contributor to physiological dysfunction and unwellness. Reconnection with the Earth's electrons has been found to promote intriguing physiological changes and subjective reports of well-being.

The study rightfully noted that all research into this phenomenon began with "experiments initiated independently by Clint Ober."

In August 2023, *The Wall Street Journal* ran an article about the rise in athletes and other people taking up the practice of earthing, titled "Stand Outside Barefoot for Better Health? 'I Feel Like an Oddball, But If It Works, It Works.'" The article cited one recent TikTok video about grounding that was watched by nearly 700 million people.

Says Clint, "It took thirty years, but it's happening."

So what, exactly, is grounding, and why does it work?

It all starts with the sun, Clint explains. The sun radiates and warms the earth, which is covered with water, which creates a lot of electrical activity, like lightning. The earth becomes subtly electrified.

When we stand barefoot on the ground, we absorb free electrons from the earth, and the electricity in our bodies syncs up with the earth's electricity. This balance allows our bodies to naturally dispense something called reactive oxygen species molecules, which are capable of stealing an electron from pathogens roaming our bodies, thus destroying them. That is how our immune system works.

But as we gradually become more and more insulated from the earth, and greatly diminish our contact with the ground, we begin to run short of free electrons, making it harder for our bodies to combat the free radical molecules that contribute to chronic inflammation and cause several severe chronic diseases. "The immune system is trying to do what it's supposed to do, but now there's a disorder in the system," Clint says. "We've lost the protective shield that the earth builds for us."

The solution, Clint says, is as simple as spending more time connected to the earth. "All of a sudden the body starts sucking up electrons, and now there's an abundance of electrons, and these electrons put out the fire," he explains. "Your circulation improves and brings down the inflammation, and that's what stops the pain. We are putting the body back into its most natural state."

When I first encountered Clint many years ago and began looking into the concept of earthing, I was amazed by the simplicity of his premise—and yet also a bit unsure about how I could incorporate it into my life. I mean, it's not like I could pick up and move to the wilderness and never wear shoes again. I had three kids in various stages of their schooling, after all, and having them show up for class barefoot just wasn't going to work.

When I asked Clint how city-bound people, for instance, could get started in the practice of earthing, his answer was encouragingly simple. "The way you start is by doing your own research, and the best way to do that is by going outside, finding a place to sit on the grass, taking your shoes off and spending fifteen or thirty minutes examining how you feel," he says. "Do you feel that you are breathing a bit easier? Can you feel your body equalizing with the earth? Can you feel your blood thinning and absorbing electrons and reducing inflammation? Or just forget about the science of it and focus on how your body feels."

Imagine that—all we have to do to experience a potentially life-changing recuperative property is to carve out thirty minutes and find a park or a meadow and sit barefoot in the grass for a while! No doctors, no prescriptions, no pills or needles—just us and the beautiful planet.

And then if we find, in our own brief and low-tech experiments with earthing, that there really is something to it, we can dig in a little deeper, do further research, find other ways we can go about grounding our bodies and reconnecting with the earth. Clint, along with two colleagues, has produced a perspective-shifting book called *Earthing: The Most Important Health Discovery Ever?*, for example, as well as an array of earthing products he has spent years and years fine-tuning, all in the hopes of helping people change their lives for the better.

"Sometimes it feels like my penance for wiring every home for cable TV," he says. "But like I said, mostly it's been a guided mission."

It's not hard to see why Clint believes his journey through life has been infused with a universal energy. It all traces back to his youth on that Montana farm, to his exposure to and respect for Native American cultures, to his intense daily communion with nature, to his awareness of the vibrancy and health of the land around him; and to the ancient rocks that spoke to him when he picked them up. Clint has forged two distinct careers defined by top-level expertise, uncanny vision, relentless devotion, and an equally relentless pioneering curiosity about all that the earth has to offer him.

He is one of the most accomplished and spiritual humans I have ever met, and yet he remains, in his heart, the young boy who kicked off his shoes when school ended in June and didn't put them on again until school resumed in the fall. "I spent my life being open to all these little things that came across my path," Clint says, "and the thing I learned, more important than anything else, is that we should endeavor to be true and on purpose. Don't try to make life something you think it should be. Just let it be what it is. And be sure that along the way your eyes and your heart are open."

Long ago, Clint's grandfather told him, "All knowledge already exists within." Clint puzzled over the expression, but over the years he came to appreciate its wisdom.

"There is knowledge in our body that has been developed over the course of centuries and generations, a kind of genetic memory, an innate intelligence," he explains. "I call it my ten thousand grandmothers. Genetically speaking, we all have at least ten thousand grandmothers who existed and now exist within our genes. They are where we came from and what got us here. It took all ten thousand of them in a long unbroken chain to get me here, and I wouldn't exist without them. And I've learned to respect the beautiful knowledge and wisdom that they left behind for me."

Clint's search for answers and his understanding of unseen energy and how it affects us make him a perfect example of someone who is guided on a secret path to an illuminated life: someone who *owns* his light. What's more, his journey of discovery led him on a path that not only made his life brighter and more meaningful but also positively impacted others in beautiful ways. His gift of discovery became a gift for us all. All because he was willing to trust his inner knowings and the guidance he was receiving that was telling him, that was insisting, that there was something deeper, something more—something that could change us all for the better. If only we own our light.

24

We Are Each a Universe

ho·lis·tic

/hōˈlistik/

adjective

1. characterized by the belief that the parts of something are interconnected and can be explained only by reference to the whole.

2. MEDICINE characterized by the treatment of the whole person, taking into account mental and social factors, rather than just the symptoms of an illness.

When some people hear the word *holistic* they might tune out the discussion that follows, anticipating a bunch of mystical concepts and ideas. But the word *holistic* simply refers to a basic truism of our existence: *Just as we are all vitally connected to everyone and everything in the greater Universe, so, too, does everything in our minds and bodies work together in the service of our overall wellness, happiness, and vibrance.*

What foods you eat, how much you sleep, the amount you exercise, how stressful your job is, where you live, your closeness to nature, the company you keep, and the doctors you see and how often you see them—all of these and many other factors are interconnected parts of your overall mind and body health. No factor is isolated from any other, though it might sometimes seem that certain symptoms point to very specific deficits or maladies. In fact, your mind and body are a complex system that functions much like an automobile—if one small part isn't working or is out of balance, the whole car might just shut down.

When I talk about honoring the mind and body, this is what I'm talking about—the understanding and adoption of a *systemic approach* to our physical, mental, and spiritual wellness.

Consider, for instance, the toothache.

When we get a toothache, it's common for us to think about it as an isolated problem: My tooth hurts, so I will go see a dentist and get it fixed. But the more I research the many components of overall wellness, the better I understand that the health of a single tooth can play an outsize role in the quality of our lives. Why? Because a tooth is part of a mouth, and a mouth is part of a head, and a head is part of a body, and what happens in any part of that body can affect any other part.

"In dentistry there is a tendency to be emergency-focused," says Dr. Alan Farber, a longtime periodontist who is a past president of the Northeastern Society of Periodontists and a frequent lecturer on overall dental health. "We tend to bore in on the problem at hand, a chipped tooth or nerve pain. But oral health has a lot to do with whole body and mental health. When I treat patients with periodontal disease they often come back and say, 'You know, not only does my mouth feel better but I just feel healthier. *Everything* feels better.'"

Farber has been my periodontist for several years, and he is an incredibly knowing and accomplished professional, as well as kind enough to share his insights into the many ways dental health affects overall wellness. Dentistry, in particular, is a good discipline for us to focus on because it is generally isolated from the whole and seen as outside the more urgent field of general body health. Even insurance companies treat dental health like an afterthought, separating it from medical insurance and often offering only meager benefits. Patients, too, can fall into the trap of viewing dental health as basically brushing their teeth at night and seeing a dentist once or twice a year.

"The dental industry can seem as if it's geared to the single-tooth problem," Farber says. "We think about medical issues as our main priority, and so dental insurance is just an add-on, as if the mouth isn't really a part of the body. But there is no shut-off valve between the neck and the rest of the body. In other words, bacteria in the mouth can travel throughout the body. Periodontal problems can be linked to cardiovascular disease, diabetes, respiratory problems, and even serious depression. Our motto is 'Healthy mouth, healthy life.'"

Born in the Bronx and raised mainly in Queens, New York, Farber is the child of two Holocaust survivors—his Polish father spent the war in a German work camp, while his mother, also born in Poland, escaped to Siberia (they met in Canada and married when he was twenty-one and she seventeen). Farber grew up wanting to work with his hands like his father, a self-taught tailor, and studied dentistry in Texas and Pennsylvania before setting up a practice on Long Island, specializing in the gums and everything below—the mouth's foundation. In thirty-six years of practice, he has seen how closely related dental health is to our overall health.

"Our social lives can revolve around eating, especially with older people, and tooth problems can seriously impact our quality of life," he says. "I've seen people who've lost most of their teeth get new implants and bridges and literally cry from happiness when they see them. It is a *total* transformation from when they walked in and it's very emotional for them when their friends come up and tell them, 'Gee, you look great!' It changes the quality of their lives in a dramatic way."

One 2016 scientific study found that people who lived to be one hundred had in their earlier years, between ages sixty-five and seventy-four, "a lower rate of edentulism [whole or partial tooth loss] than did younger members of their birth year cohorts. . . . Oral health was consistent with compression of morbidity toward the end of life." In other words, caring for your teeth can lengthen your life. The study explored "the hypothesis that factors associated with oral disease and noncommunicable diseases may increase the risk of tooth loss and lead to diminished longevity as a result of multifactorial interactions"—maladies that are caused by a number of interconnected factors.

Similarly, another author on oral health has noted: "Oral health is much more than just healthy teeth; it also includes the health of many other anatomical structures such as the gums, bones, ligaments, muscles, glands, and nerves. It affects some of our most basic human functions, thereby shaping an individual's self-image and sense of well-being."

Farber recalls a patient referred to him by a holistic physician. The patient had very serious chronic hip pain, and several doctors had not been able to pinpoint the cause. The holistic physician knew the patient had a problematic endodontically treated tooth—a tooth that has undergone a root canal—and asked Farber to take a look.

"We ended up treating the tooth, and the patient reported that the hip pain she'd been suffering for years went away," Farber says. "It just disappeared. We don't always understand the precise connection between a dental issue and a separate body problem, but from what I've experienced that connection is very, very real."

Farber points to the concept of meridian pathways.

A *meridian* is literally a road weaving through the body and transporting energy. The concept of tooth meridian lines, which is based on the ancient wisdom of Eastern medicine and acupuncture, holds that different teeth connect through meridians to different parts of the body both above and below. A tooth meridian chart is a visual representation of the premise of this chapter—that all parts of our body are interconnected and are thus factors in our overall wellness.

As an example, the four incisors in the center of the upper row of teeth are said to be connected to the kidneys and (in men) the prostate. The lower-left canine tooth is connected to the liver and the eyes. An infection in any one tooth can lead to serious problems in the corresponding organs and glands. This insight can be helpful to all medical professionals. During an exam, for instance, a periodontist who is aware of a separate body issue might check the corresponding tooth for signs of an infection or other problem.

"Inflammatory proteins from the mouth can travel through the bloodstream to other organs, including your heart," Farber explains. "There is research that shows better oral hygiene corresponds to a lower rate of heart disease, the leading cause of death for men and women."

We don't need to become experts in meridian pathways or tooth structure to live better, healthier lives—we just need to be more aware of the interconnectedness of everything in our bodies.

There is also a connection between oral health and how we handle stress in our lives. "I've seen patients with healthy gums come in and suddenly their gums don't look well at all," Farber says. "I'll ask, 'What's going on?' and I usually hear, 'Well, I've been under a lot of stress lately.' If you don't have healthy ways to deal with stress, it can affect your teeth and gums, just like it can affect your heart."

We all face different levels of stress in our lives as the pressures of our careers and relationships pile up. Sometimes we'll prioritize work or personal issues over something as seemingly dispensable as a dental checkup. But as Farber notes, neglecting our oral health can have a detrimental effect on our immune system. "Think of it as your body having an army to defend itself against sickness and disease," he says. "If your army is busy fighting off an infection in your mouth, you've depleted the forces that do battle against more significant diseases such as cancer and heart disease. You've made yourself more vulnerable."

This is why a systemic or holistic approach to our overall well-being is so important. Throughout my books I've urged readers to carve out a little time and space to meditate every day, as one way to relieve stress and achieve more balance in life. Of course, I know how hard it can be to find a free fifteen minutes (or even a free *five* minutes some days), but it is essential that we not sacrifice too much of our physical and mental self-caregiving to the more immediate pressures we face. Living a truly illuminated life means developing a more inclusive, holistic approach to wellness, which in turn means maintaining a balance between *all* aspects and factors of our physical and mental health.

I'm not suggesting that you start obsessing nonstop about the condition of your teeth and gums. What matters is that we take small, manageable steps toward integrating oral health into your overall wellness routines. For Farber, that means visiting your dentist three or four times a year instead of once or twice (or not at all), as well as taking advantage of simple new tools that can improve oral health (he is keen on interproximal brushes, which help clean *between* our teeth). "In this country, unfortunately, we spend much more time on treating diseases than on finding ways to prevent them," he says. "But there are steps each of us can take to be more preventative and avoid dental issues that can cause larger problems elsewhere."

Years ago, I got a download from my guides on the Other Side. They showed me that both our gut and our gums are incredibly important to our overall health. They are the superhighways to health and wellness, and to illness and disease. And when the Other Side talks, I listen. That was when I initially sought out Farber, who had excellent and well-deserved reviews online. I am so grateful I reached out to him, and I urge you all—pay attention to your gums. Don't just occasionally visit a dentist; consider also seeing a periodontist twice a year. As for gut health, look into taking a probiotic and eating some fermented foods (think sourdough, sauerkraut, and kimchi).

As with any other discipline or action I include in this book, I am mentioning meridian pathways here to *introduce* them to you and hopefully pique your curiosity. The next step is for you to do more research and, in the case of your oral health, talk to your personal dentist about the mouth-body connection.

In other words, develop a more holistic approach to wellness.

"We are each a whole universe," says Farber. "Mind, body, spirit—it's all connected. Making a little repair anywhere will make you healthier everywhere. And your whole being will thank you."

We are all connected. To each other,
biologically. To the earth, chemically.
To the rest of the universe, atomically.

NEIL DEGRASSE TYSON

25

Honoring the Body

We are all eternal fields of energy temporarily housed in our physical bodies.

Ancient philosophers like Plato and Aristotle wrestled with the notion of body and soul: Do body and soul form a single entity? Or are body and soul separate? In fact, the soul-body relationship is one of the first recorded topics of philosophical debate. Throughout history, though, the idea that the body houses the soul has been consistent. To honor and nurture your soul, you must honor and nurture your physical body.

Unfortunately, the reality of existence today tends to work against the maintenance of ideal bodily health. Stress and anxiety wear us down; lack of sleep affects our metabolism; junk food saps our strength. A hundred other factors affect our energy and health. But to live a truly illuminated life is to find daily ways to honor the body.

Let's start with what we eat. The act of putting food in our bodies is the most intimate thing we do. The food we choose can either help or harm our bodies, and that is a choice we make several times every day. If you don't already, pay attention to the health benefits of what you eat, and choose to eat smarter and better. Organic food, for instance, has been shown to be richer in nutrients and less exposed to nitrates and pesticide residues than regular packaged food. Organic products also "reduce public health risks to farm workers, their families, and consumers by minimizing their exposure to toxic and persistent chemicals," says the Organic Trade Association—showing once again how the choices we make can have a ripple effect on others around the world.

Avoiding highly processed junk food is another smart move. We can all be tempted by appetizing roadside snacks and meals, and the occasional fast-food burger likely won't hurt us. But research from the 2020 European and International Conference on Obesity suggests that "people who eat a lot of industrially processed junk food are more likely to exhibit a change in their chromosomes linked to aging," and earlier studies "have shown a strong correlation between ultra-processed foods and hypertension, obesity, depression, type 2 diabetes and cancer." Junk food is so bad for us that it can literally alter our chromosomes and lessen our lifespan.

You might also want to look into the prevalence of microplastics in our food supply. Tiny fragments of plastics have been found in many foods and "enter food through packaging, such as plastic wrap on vegetables or tea bags that melt into hot drinks," the Harvard Medical School reported. Harmful microplastics have been detected in human blood, saliva, livers, kidneys, and placentas, and can even infiltrate our bodies on a cellular level. You don't hear all that much about the microplastics in our food supply, but the dangers are very real, and they are another example of what to watch out for when choosing the food you eat. I don't mean that we have to become obsessive label readers or absolute food purists. I just mean that as we make daily choices about what to consume, we need to be aware of whether what we put in our bodies helps or harms us.

We also get to choose—for the most part—how many hours we sleep. Obviously, life often gets in the way of a full, restful night of sleep, and society as a whole appears to value sleep less and less. In 1998, 35 percent of American adults got a healthy eight hours of sleep a night. Today, that is down to 25 percent. A massive research project called the

Nurses' Health Study followed sixty-eight thousand middle-aged American women for sixteen years and determined that, "compared to women who slept seven hours a night, women who slept five hours or less were fifteen percent more likely to become obese." And obesity can lead to a host of diseases. We've all heard the saying "You are what you eat," but it should come with the companion saying "You are how many hours you sleep." There is little question that not getting enough regular, quality sleep can lead to various diseases and disorders, which is why we must all be aware of the life-changing restorative power of sleep. Rather than being simple downtime, sleep is when "the brain totally changes function," says the University of Rochester sleep expert Dr. Maiken Nedergaard. "It becomes almost like a kidney, removing waste from the system."

And let's not forget how sleep also allows us to connect with something so much greater than ourselves, outside this physical realm, as we know from chapter 19, about the power of dreaming.

We can't always choose how much sleep we get, but we *can* establish a sleeping pattern that is consistent, healthy, and restorative. Keep that in mind as you schedule your usually hectic, overstuffed days. Sleep needs to move up a few spaces on our list of priorities.

There are many other decisions we make that affect our health and well-being, and all of them are worth considering and researching. Stress and anxiety, for instance, can have an immense impact on our energy, health, and overall balance. Are you aware of your stress level, and are you taking any steps to reduce the stress in your life? Simple meditation or yoga or any exercise, really, are great stress relievers.

What about your energy? Numerous studies have shown that we all possess a biofield, or a field of energy that surrounds and permeates us. In fact, the Soviet scientist Semyon Kirlian developed a photographic technique for capturing images of this energy field, comprised, he said, of electrical coronal discharges. A Kirlian image will show a bright aura around your body—literally your body's energy, or life force. There are also several biofield therapies—such as Reiki, acupuncture, and therapeutic touch—that are used to restore energy fields and overall health. A number of healing energy techniques—including infra-red sauna, aura cleansing, chakra balancing, and crystal healing—are fascinating and very much worth exploring. There are so many, many ways to restore health and honor the body.

So be aware that the energy inside you needs to be nurtured and cared for just like any other part of you.

What I've been taught by the Other Side is that our bodies are electric energy fields managed by different body processes that are connected all the way down to the cellular level. I've also seen that the Other Side is always trying to guide us to pay more attention to our bodies, and to recognize that they are indeed home to our souls. None of the guidance sent to us requires making drastic changes in our lives. They all point to the reality that small shifts in thinking and action can have wide-ranging positive effects. We can begin by asking ourselves these simple questions:

- Do we feel that our lives are in balance?

- Do we think we are honoring our physical bodies?

- Is there some small shift I can make—less junk food, more sleep—that will make a difference?

Simply asking and answering these questions is the beginning of our health journeys—and the start of a shift toward honoring our bodies and living illuminated lives.

We are not human beings having a
spiritual experience. We are spiritual
beings having a human experience.

PIERRE TEILHARD DE CHARDIN

26

Head, Heart, and Hands

There are many ways you can be a Light Worker in life.

A Light Worker is someone who honors the unique gifts they came here with and shares them with others. A Light Worker is someone who does not try to have power over others, but finds true power in helping others rise. In this way, Light Workers live illuminated lives and shine the path for others to live illuminated lives as well. Guidance, you see, can come from each other, as well as from our Teams of Light.

Becoming a Light Worker doesn't require a mountain of effort—a simple fix or two, a subtle shift in perspective, can lead to monumental benefits. Something as small in scale as finding an extra ten minutes of quiet, reflective time every day, for instance, can illuminate something inside of you that inspires you to be a Light Worker for others.

Some ways can be larger in scale—organizing a food drive, mentoring at-risk youth—so that your efforts as a Light Worker influence not just yourself and the people in your circle but *also* your larger community.

Still others involve major endeavors that impact entire cities or states or countries. Some people even set out to change the world.

And then there's Jeffrey Walker.

Jeff is a Light Worker on a *very* large scale. His list of accomplishments could fill three legal pads. For twenty-five years he was the CEO and co-founder of JPMorgan Partners, a hugely successful, $12 billion global private equity investment firm, as well as vice chairman of JPMorgan Chase. In that capacity he was one of the most forward-thinking and influential investors in the business, a singularly driven high achiever. Then, in 2007, at the age of fifty-two, he retired—or rather, he radically shifted his focus. Always philanthropic by nature, he began to use his considerable skills to do more than just generate money, devoting 90 percent of his life to what could be called venture philanthropy—an uncommonly effective method of helping others on a global scale.

"I have a spiritual belief system that is tied to reducing suffering and enhancing joy," Jeff has said. "If I can figure out the best way to do that, and be impactful by partnering with others to achieve that goal, then it makes me happy."

In other words, Jeff has become a Light Worker *for the world.*

Jeff Walker is a great example of someone who honors his mind—he is a critical thinker and lifelong learner who brings an open mind and heart to everything he does. He has a very cerebral and selfless approach that is based less on anyone's ego and more on doing whatever it takes to achieve good things.

"After twenty-five years of doing deals, I realized that just making more money didn't necessarily add a lot of value to the world," says Jeff. "I wanted to do something else and give back to the world. So I did a lot of research and tried to answer the question *How do you come up with social change that works?*"

Jeff's intense curiosity about how things work came to him when he was young and growing up in Daytona Beach, Florida. His father worked on computer systems for General Electric during the Apollo project, and Jeff got to watch rockets launching people into space, lighting a fire in his own imagination that still hasn't gone out. "That's when I became interested in the *what-ifs* of the world, the limits of possibility, but there was also a spiritual component to it," he remembers "Since then, I've always been a spiritual searcher."

In the seventh grade, Jeff walked into the band room at his school "I was tall, but I wasn't into sports, so I figured this might be the place for me," he says. "The band director looked me over and said, 'Wel , you're big and you have braces, and we have something that is big and has a big mouthpiece. Why don't you play that?'"

Jeff was handed a sousaphone, a huge marching-band version of the tuba. He took to the instrument, but more important, he took to the concept of playing with others in an orchestra—"the synthesizing of talents that creates something greater than any one person could alone," he explains. This formed the cornerstone of Jeff's future approach to finance and philanthropy: the criticality of collaboration in creating sustainable change.

"You put together all these different stakeholders for a common cause, and you can accomplish something no individual stakeholder could," Jeff explains. "The key is not just having some great innovaive idea, but rather having a problem that you go after with others with similar goals and passions, all in a unified way."

After college, Jeff rose quickly through the ranks of the finance world, graduating from Harvard Business School, interning at Chemical Bank, working as the chief of staff for the head of a new investment bank, and eventually becoming a venture capitalist engineering multimillion-dollar deals. Then he became a venture philanthropist.

Along the way he focused on investments that were not only profitable but also had a strong social upside. He was chairman of New Profit, a social change investment fund that backs access- and opportunity-expanding projects, and chairman of Millennium Promise, an Africa-focused incubator geared to eliminating extreme poverty; he co-founded Npower, which provides technology services to nonprofits; he tackled tropical diseases (by advising the END Func) and championed democracy (the Leadership Project); and he funded and joined the board of Giving Tuesday, which "reimagines a world built upon shared humanity and radical generosity," and which in 2023 alone raised $3.1 billion for charitable giving.

Jeff also worked with fellow philanthropist and humanitarian Ray Chambers to launch Millennium Villages, which raised money to improve healthcare, education, agriculture, and infrastructure in one hundred villages across Africa. The effort eventually focused on community health and on eliminating deaths from malaria, and through the United Nations Millennial Development Goals project succeeded in reducing malaria fatalities in Africa by more than *one million* a year.

It is not an exaggeration to say that Jeff Walker's philanthropic endeavors have saved millions of lives and positively affected many tens of millions more. Few people have ever had such a profoundly compassionate impact on the world.

Jeff is a Light Worker on the largest possible scale.

Yet there is something else — beyond his financial prowess and fierce determination — that sets him apart.

Jeff has taken a uniquely spiritual, holistic approach to the world of high-stakes investment financing. To the realm of capital markets and risk management and leveraged buyouts, Jeff has introduced a profound mindfulness geared toward helping people flourish and improve their well-being.

Through an investment group called Bridge Builders, Jeff has helped launch several wellness-oriented apps and programs, including Headspace, a meditation app; Wisdo, which tackles the loneliness epidemic; and Insight Timer, which provides "transformative programs to help awaken your full potential."

Jeff's commitment to wellness, however, goes deeper than business ventures: on a personal level, Jeff is a spiritual adventurer. He is a proponent of regular meditation, is practiced in tai chi, and is a student of holotropic breathwork, a relatively new form of self-exploration and psychotherapy. "It's a breathing exercise that you do for forty minutes, and it is transporting," Jeff says. "It can take you to another place, almost psychedelic." Jeff is also well-studied in the field of controlled psychedelic drug experiences and their potential for overall wellness recently, he spoke out in a podcast on "the emerging knowledge o psychedelics and energy work in the healthcare field."

"I've worked with a number of scientists and practitioners on how to start bringing these and other ideas and tools into our healthcare system," he says. "Tools that have been around and been proven to work for thousands of years: mindfulness, subtle energy, chanting, yoga. Its already a billion-dollar industry, but how do we convince people of the science behind it, and of the positive impact these tools can have?"

Jeff was still a student at the University of Virginia when his spiritual adventure began. He was minoring in psychology and had a profound curiosity about its different social applications, and along the way he read about meditation and decided to try it. One evening, he sat on the grass in a field near the center of the university, closed his eyes, and said, "Okay, let's meditate." He may or may not have brought a beer with him, he can't quite recall. The field was quiet and the stars were out, and Jeff felt himself slip into a deeply relaxed state.

"I remember thinking there was something very unique about he experience of being quiet with yourself, kind of managing your thoughts and trying to quiet the rest of your body so that you could be released a bit from all the commotion," he says. After that first time he was hooked, and he continued to research and experiment with different forms of meditation for the next fifty years and counting—while working with many others to bring it into the mainstream.

Jeff even became the chairman of the Contemplative Science Center at his old university and pushed to have a new building for the center constructed on campus. "When the architect came in, he said, 'Okay, we're going to put the building here, this is the best place for it,'" Jeff recalls. "And it was *exactly* on the spot where I first meditated. The center went up exactly on top of that grassy spot where I sat all those years earlier. Things like that have happened to me all the time. After a while you begin to notice these synchronicities that happen, where the Universe kind of validates your gut feeling." All those years ago, it seems, Jeff was already being guided into his role as a Light Worker.

Jeff likens his approach to wellness and philanthropy to something called the Head, Heart, and Hands (3H) model, developed in the eighteenth century by a Swiss educational reformer named Johann Heinrich Pestalozzi.

Put simply, to achieve and accelerate meaningful change, we must integrate all facets of the 3H model. The head represents the tools we bring to tackling an issue, such as decision-making, problem-solving, direction-setting, business acumen, or whatever our singular intellectual talents might be. The heart represents the love for others and the inner energy we bring to the situation—our personal, emotional devotion to the cause. The hands are what put everything into action and achieve real results.

Put even more simply, the head is what we know, the heart is who we care about, and the hands are what we do.

Many leaders are adept at the head and hands part, but Light Workers like Jeff are good at integrating the heart as well. "If a project makes me feel pulled in the direction of compassion for others, and also pulled to act, then I know I'm on the right path and the project is something I want to do," Jeff says. "Basically, it's wisdom, compassion, and action, and that is my personal test—does a project engage all three? If it does, then I know I'm okay."

This compassionate approach to achievement—born of Jeff's natural curiosity, decades of business experience, and continual spiritual exploration—has allowed Jeff to function at the highest level by *honoring his connection to the Universe and to his community of fellow achievers*. Jeff's special talent is assembling the right people for the right job, then motivating them to solve seemingly intractable problems—the synthesizing of talents to create something greater than any one person could. "I've said that my personal pronoun is *we*," Jeff says. "What I love is seeing these great entrepreneurs come to me with different business plans and all of us working together to create new ideas on how to make the world a better place. I have a lot of fun doing that."

.   .   .

Jeff Walker embodies many of the lessons in this book—honoring the body, honoring the mind, honoring the soul. He values our interconnectedness as well as our ability to access a greater source of energy around us to achieve remarkable things. He has spent his life nurturing a very bright light inside of him that has illuminated the path of countless human beings near and far. As I said, he is a Light Worker on the largest possible scale.

Yet the true lesson we can draw from Jeff's story is the capacity we *all* have to use our head, heart, and hands to achieve and spread wellness and happiness at *any* scale. We can all achieve remarkable things in our lives that make us Light Workers for others. Our impact may be personal, local, or even global, but the changes we make to our daily routines will always start within us, at the *smallest* possible level.

I'll give you an example that I've drawn from yet another project funded and encouraged by Jeff Walker.

It began in 2010, when two college friends, T. Morgan Dixon and Vanessa Garrison, began taking walks together near their homes in Los Angeles, California, for exercise and just to talk. Over time, more and more people joined them on their walks, and Dixon and Garrison organized a ten-week walking challenge. Eventually, they took it upon themselves to motivate as many people as they could to walk with them, inspired by a simple truism of black history: "When women walked and talked together," Dixon explained, "that's when everything changed."

Jeff was chairman of the organization New Profit, which philanthropically funded the start-up that grew out of these walks: GirlTrek. Just ten years after they started walking, Dixon and Garrison motivated a woman named Shameka Cornelius to join GirlTrek and walk with them.

Shameka was the *one millionth member* to join the walk.

Today, nearly 1.4 million women have signed up for the walks (fully 7 percent of the total population of African American women), some of which honor black history by retracing Harriet Tubman's hundred-mile journey, the fifty-four-mile civil rights walk from Selma to Montgomery, and the routes trodden by black students during the bus boycotts of the 1950s. The health benefits of the walks have been astonishing: some 90 percent of participants cited fewer symptoms of depression, while 60 percent have lost weight and continue to walk daily.

"When they walk, they talk, and when they talk, they organize, and so they get more active in their communities *and* get healthier," Jeff says. "Suddenly they have a real voice and they can get things done. It's a really great story, and it all started with two women walking."

Imagine that. Two friends taking a walk. The scale could hardly have been smaller. But the achievement has been exponentially greater and promises to get greater still. Where two women walked, now walk hundreds of thousands. Where Jeff Walker first meditated, with a can of beer, now stands a gleaming building devoted to contemplation. This is the power of an illuminated life.

We *all* have it within us to be Light Workers for each other. And, sometimes, for the world.

An old Cherokee is teaching his grandson about life. "A fight is going on inside me," he said to the boy. "It is a terrible fight and it is between two wolves. One is evil—he is anger, envy, sorrow, regret, greed, arrogance, self-pity, guilt, resentment, inferiority, lies, false pride, superiority, and ego."

He continued, "The other is good—he is joy, peace, love, hope, serenity, humility, kindness, benevolence, empathy, generosity, truth, compassion, and faith. The same fight is going on inside you—and inside every other person, too."

The grandson thought about it for a minute and then asked his grandfather, "Which wolf will win?"

The old man simply replied, "The one you feed."

NATIVE AMERICAN PARABLE

27

The Idealism Model

My background is not in science. I just wanted to put that out there. I mean, I took an Advanced Placement biology class in high school and I loved it, but that was about it. I studied literature and rhetoric at Binghamton University in New York and Shakespeare at Oxford University in England. Before I devoted myself to my abilities, I taught high school English. But I have always loved books and reading, and today I read a lot of science-based books and academic studies, just because I love learning so much. But, no, I'm not an expert.

I have, however, participated in many scientific tests and studies related to my abilities. I've had electroencephalograms (EEGs) that measured the electrical activity in my brain while I performed psychic and mediumship activities, and I took and passed a quintuple-blind reading administered by a noted scientist, Dr. Julie Beischel, to become a Certified Windbridge Research Medium. I'm a board member of the Rhine Research Center in Durham, North Carolina, an organization dedicated to psi research and education since the 1930s. (I highly suggest you look into this organization, as they offer online classes; go to www.rhineonline.org.) I've tried to keep up with the scientific literature about psychic abilities and other phenomena, and in my books I've always included scientific evidence that supports what I do.

Why?

Because while I know all the events described in this book—signs from the Other Side, uncanny visions, the endurance of consciousness after death, guidance from our Teams of Light—are very, very real, the scientific community isn't so convinced.

Yet there are some brilliant, forward-thinking scientists who are not afraid to explore unseen energy. One such scientist is a man I mentioned earlier in the book: Dr. Edward Kelly.

Ed is a professor at the Division of Perceptual Studies (DOPS) at the University of Virginia. He and others at DOPS are, as their mission statement declares, "devoted to the rigorous evaluation of empirical evidence for extraordinary human experiences and capacities." After earning a PhD in psycholinguistics and cognitive science from Harvard, Ed spent most of the next fifteen years involved in the field of parapsychology—the study of paranormal psychological phenomena—and his interest in developing scientific evidence to support these phenomena has never waned. I had the privilege of working with Ed when I was one of five participants in a study he designed on the physiology of mediumship, and I have followed his work ever since. I admire his academic rigor, natural curiosity, and sheer intellect.

"My interest in the paranormal was kindled mainly by Mrs. Piper," Ed says, referring to Leonora Piper, a well-known trance medium in the early twentieth century whose thoroughly investigated séance sittings convinced many researchers she had supernatural abilities. "She would sometimes write to one sitter with her right hand and another with her left and talk to a third sitter while writing. She would slump over and go into a state that would be very difficult to arouse her from. Someone even held a bottle of ammonia under her nose, but she had no reaction."

Ed is a student of the work of the psychologist William James (brother of the novelist Henry James and the father of the study of psychology) and the scientist Frederic W. H. Myers, two eminent nineteenth-century scholars who marshaled scientific evidence for a model of consciousness that did not reject paranormal experiences. Their philosophy is now known as the Myers-James model of consciousness. "They both fought to show that our everyday consciousness is embedded in a much larger consciousness that allows us to have all kinds of abilities we don't normally access," says Ed, describing a universal consciousness. "They got us to a terrific point about a century ago, but they've been mostly neglected since, and I think it's time to start over where they left off."

In the hundred years since James and Myers shook up the field, mainstream scientific opinion about human consciousness has shifted back to the belief that it is a purely physical process generated by the brain. If that is true, it would mean that the endurance of consciousness after death is not possible, because there is no realm beyond the physical from which it could arise. As noted in chapter 5, this science-based school of thought is generally referred to as materialism or physicalism, and it holds that any seemingly paranormal activities can be debunked and logically explained. "There are some people who are so convinced of the rightness of physicalism that they believe the possibility of there being any paranormal activity is zero," Ed says. "And because they believe it's zero, any counterhypothesis, no matter how loopy or improbable, has to be accepted."

In other words, logical explanations of psychic phenomena don't have to be elegant or even make sense. The explanations are deemed true because they *must* be true. Ed cites the example of one psychic who could identify the symbols on cards that were hidden from him. Skeptics insisted he was doing it with mirrors that he had somehow smuggled into the experiment room and managed to mount without detection. When the skeptics tried to re-create the experiment using mirrors, "they failed completely," Ed says. "One well-known skeptic actually wrote in his book that because we know that psychic phenomena cannot happen, any other explanation will do. Sometimes they even make stuff up."

Ed is currently writing a book about the Myers-James model of consciousness. Earlier, he was the lead writer of an influential book titled *Irreducible Mind: Toward a Psychology for the 21st Century*, which rigorously assembled scientific evidence for psychic phenomena that cannot be explained away by the physicalism model of consciousness. "The point of the book is that there are a whole bunch of events and research that should give physicalists heartburn," Ed explains. "I think evidence has already accumulated well past the point where it ought to convince people who take the trouble to study it. And I think we're on the verge of being able to display a kind of theory that would allow for psychic phenomena to occur and not be incompatible with what we know about physics today."

I am greatly heartened by Ed's belief that society, and perhaps even the world of academia, is on the verge of accepting a broader theory of consciousness. The stories I tell in this book and my other books are, I believe, very strong anecdotal evidence of the existence of psychic phenomena. But I understand that to convince the skeptics, we need equally strong scientific evidence, gained from rigorous scientific studies. That is where people like Ed Kelly come in. Ed has devoted his career to proving what some think is unprovable, despite the reality that bucking the materialistic trend in the scientific field "can be exceedingly damaging to one's career," Ed says. "For a lot of people, physicalism is a kind of secular faith."

Nevertheless, Ed has persevered in his research. One of his areas of study is extrasensory perception (ESP). He tells the story of a test subject, Bill, a remarkable man who showed a dazzling ability to perceive what was hidden from him. "We went to the local laundromat once, and at a certain point he said, 'Ed, you need to get a Coke, and if you put your quarter in the machine, you'll get a 1964 nickel in change,'" Ed recalled in a recent interview posted on YouTube. "I wasn't thirsty, but I put my quarter in the machine and got the Coke and the 1964 nickel. I said, 'Well, if I do this again, will I get another 1964 nickel?' He said yes, and sure enough I got another 1964 nickel."

Another time Ed asked Bill if he could somehow perceive the number of Cheerios he'd poured into a big bowl. Bill answered, "Four hundred sixty-four." Ed counted the Cheerios and came up with exactly that number. A different time, one of Ed's Harvard colleagues asked Bill to tell him what number between 1 and 100 he was thinking about. Bill nailed it. The colleague asked him to do it again. Again, Bill got the right number.

The statistical odds of that happening are small, yet Bill picked the right number three or four times before he got bored with the hallway experiment. "We published a bunch of papers about him," Ed said. "He erased any residual uncertainty I had about the reality of the basic phenomena of ESP."

Current ESP research, Ed says, "has the best, most convincing body of evidence behind it." But ESP is just one of many fields gaining credibility. For instance, "there's plenty of evidence to support the validity of psychokinesis," Ed says, referring to the ability to move objects using only the mind, or "thought energy." Near-death experiences (NDEs) are also supported by considerable scientific research. "For one thing, there's millions of people worldwide who have certainly had them, many under extreme physiological conditions such as deep general anesthesia and/or cardiac arrest," Ed said. "People who are having not only conscious experiences but the most intense and transformative conscious experiences of their entire lives." These NDEs imply the survival of consciousness even after the functioning of the brain is disrupted. "Science today thinks that any talk of the survival of consciousness is just nonsense," Ed told me. "But I come down on the side of survival." More research is needed, but the evidence that these experiences are real is just too plentiful to ignore.

Ed has also researched cases of apparitions, levitation, and mind reading, among other paranormal phenomena. In each field, there is powerful anecdotal evidence supporting the validity of these phenomena, but the science still needs to catch up. The good news is that in the last forty years, Ed says, "there has been this tremendous renaissance in consciousness research within mainstream science."

More and more highly learned, impressively credentialed scientists like Ed Kelly are venturing into the study of an alternative to the materialistic model of existence. In one hundred years, Ed says, "Sociologists and historians of science are going to make a good living trying to figure out why it took so long for the scientific community to catch up to this stuff, which is just hiding in plain sight. But whatever the reason, we're still fighting these battles."

As you read the stories in this book, keep in mind that the system we have for determining truths about the Universe—science and scientific experimentation—is slowly but surely tilting toward a much broader understanding of existence than the materialistic model allows. Eventually, all the events that occur in these stories—signs from lost loved ones, dream visitations, universal intervention in our lives—will no longer be seen by the scientific community as truth-stretching, fairy-tale occurrences, but rather as a normal part of the human experience. And that time, for Ed Kelly, cannot come too soon.

"I think there is a huge spiritual vacuum at the center of our civilization, and I think physicalism plays a big role in that," Ed says. "We need to fill that void with something that people can really take seriously, which means making the spiritual dimension of life justifiable in scientific terms. If we can do that, I think it would go a long way to helping us avoid killing ourselves as a species."

For now, Ed's message to us is that our conscious minds are not disconnected from the world, but rather "embedded in a much larger consciousness that allows us to have all kinds of abilities we don't normally access"—a kind of universal consciousness. Think of it as a powerfully flowing river just above us that we can all reach up and dip into from time to time, even when we're not aware we're doing so. And imagine that when we pass, we join this massive energy field, reconnecting us to everyone and everything in the Universe.

I saw the angel in the marble and
carved until I set it free.

MICHELANGELO

28

Honoring the Mind

What are thoughts?

Enormous amounts of research have gone into answering this line of questioning. Are thoughts, as a 2023 article in *Psychology Today* suggested, "maps representing and corresponding to things that our brains have either perceived with our senses, felt with our emotions, or formed as an action plan"? Are thoughts electrochemically mediated processes that involve neurons, impulses, and reactions? Do thoughts have mass, like physical things? If you consider driving a car to be a thought process, then thoughts produce actions that *do* have measurable mass—the turning of the car, fuel distribution, and so on. So what, exactly, is a thought?

One thing most scientists and researchers seem to agree on is that thoughts are energy. Some call thoughts a form of electromagnetic energy—brain-emitted electric signals that can be measured by an EEG. Some believe that since everything in the world is comprised of energy, so, too, are thoughts. What I've learned from the Other Side is that thoughts contain a powerful energy that can not only significantly change our lives but also impact the Universe.

One of the keys to seeking and finding the secret path to an illuminated life is acknowledging that our thoughts are energy, and that *all* energy matters. It is our minds that steer the ship of our souls, and it's our thoughts that can magically change our lives through meditation, energy-shifting, or just plain positive thinking. We have free will to implement whichever thoughts we choose. We decide how to make both small and monumental decisions—life choices like careers, marriage, children, divorce. This is what I mean by *honoring the mind*—we must recognize that our thoughts are the energy that powers our lives and defines our path through existence.

As you read the following chapters, and as you conduct your daily life, keep all of this in mind:

- There is great value in being a lifelong learner and critical thinker—of being curious and questioning.

- The power of intention is one of the key components to living an illuminated life; in short, our thoughts are energy and they matter, guiding and influencing unseen cords of connection all around us.

- Don't self-edit—you're not going to be perfect all the time, so let yourself explore and experience.

- Be cognizant of your free-will decisions and the power they hold to shape your path through life.

- There's no one-size-fits-all model of life, so embrace your journey of self-awareness and self-discovery.

- Always look for the wonder in life, and stay in that state of wonder as long as you can.

In honoring the mind, we strive to tend our thoughts more carefully and vibrantly, and we move further along the path to an illuminated life.

29

Henri and Teddy

A few years ago, the respected magazine *Psychology Today* addressed a question I've been asked more than once: Are dogs psychic?

The article cited some examples — a dog that appeared in the kitchen *only* when her owner reached into the fridge for her favorite food, cheese; a dog that always ran to the window precisely one minute before its owner arrived; and a dog who jumped and barked excitedly whenever his owner merely *thought* the word *Frisbee*.

As supernatural as our beloved pets can sometimes seem to us, the researchers decided that they could not scientifically conclude that these animals were psychic. But they also concluded that the sensory world of dogs extends well beyond our own, particularly when it comes to their strong sense of smell. "Dogs can also hear sounds that we cannot hear and will pick up on different visual information than we do," the article stated. In other words, they *could* conclude that dogs can be far more *perceptive* of human emotions and feelings than even we humans are.

If you were to ask me about the seemingly supernatural perceptive ability of dogs, I would go a little further than that.

In my experience, I have found not only that dogs and other animals are exceptionally good at picking up on, and responding to, their owners' emotions while here but also that they are also still deeply connected to us after they cross.

In fact, dogs are really good at sending signs from the Other Side.

Let me give you two examples, featuring a couple of magical little fellas named Henri and Teddy.

Samantha Childs grew up in Southern California alongside a series of pets—dogs, cats, and a bird, among others. Remarkably, she dearly loved them all *despite* being allergic to pets. "It wasn't always easy, but I'd wash my hands and face and change my clothes a lot, just so I could be around them," she recalls. There was little question, then, that she would have a pet of her own when she grew up, though at first she wasn't sure what kind of pet that would be.

Then she irrationally fell in love with French bulldogs.

"I used to go to Frenchie Meetup groups, and I was the only one there who didn't own one," Samantha says, laughing. "I just thought they were the cutest things." Then she moved to New York City to get an MFA in nonfiction writing. "I'd see a lot of Frenchies being walked on the street, and every time I'd run after them and, when I got closer, pretend to be casually walking toward them just so I could stop and say hello and pet them. I'd be all out of breath trying to play it cool, when actually I'd chased after this Frenchie for blocks."

Finally, Samantha decided she was ready. For her thirtieth birthday her parents bought her a Frenchie, whom she picked up and instantly fell in love with.

"It was like he immediately knew that he was mine, and I was his," she says. "In the back of the cab on the way home he just climbed into my lap and fell asleep. It was a crazy, crazy feeling, but I just knew we were meant for each other." Even better, Samantha wasn't at all allergic to this Frenchie. "It was kind of miraculous," she says. "He was just perfect for me in every way."

The French bulldog had a smooth reddish-brown coat, huge ears, a sassy little snout, and a unique howl that was "somewhere between a baby crying and a cat screaming," Samantha says. He also snorted, and Samantha would snort back at him—a little secret language of their own. In their first days together, the bond between them only tightened. "You know how in *The Grinch* his heart suddenly grows and grows?" she says. "That's how he made me feel, like my heart was expanding. Like I was filled with love that went beyond the borders of my heart."

She named her new nine-pound friend Henri, pronounced like Henry but with the French spelling.

Together they eventually moved back west to Solana Beach, in the northern part of San Diego, and Henri became a beach dog ("though he was always a little bit scared of the water"). As a way to procrastinate from working on her MFA thesis, Samantha created an Instagram account called *@henrilefrenchie*, on which she shared the many wonderful moments and adventures of her constant companion.

Eventually the photos and videos of Henri proved so irresistible that his Instagram page drew more than seventy-six thousand fans. "People just kept asking for more pictures, more pictures, and we became this little community connected by the love of Henri," says Samantha. "One man wrote to me and said he had debilitating epilepsy, and the only thing that helped him get through each day was seeing new photos and videos of Henri. Another woman whose daughter was in the hospital asked me to post more videos, which were her daughter's favorites, so her daughter could watch them from her hospital bed. So not only did all these people love Henri, but he was making a difference in a lot of their lives. It was mind-blowing. He was just pure joy."

Samantha even started writing a children's book about Henri to help kids deal with bullying (she'd been bullied as a child herself) and to encourage them to love themselves and others. It would be titled *Henri and the Magnificent Snort*, and she planned to take Henri to readings at schools and libraries and share even more of his joy.

Then the unthinkable happened.

After a few days of treatment for pneumonia at a specialty vet, Henri passed away. He was only eight years old. Samantha had been with Henri that morning, sitting on the floor of the exam room with him in her arms, holding him close to her. She'd thought he was going to be just fine, and she made plans to return to see him later that day. Then she got a phone call telling her to return to the vet's office immediately.

The vet told her Henri had died because he'd had a stroke. Later, Samantha learned from a necropsy (an animal autopsy) performed by an outside vet that Henri had actually died from pneumothorax, caused by a puncture wound from a misplaced nasal feeding tube—a tube she was told had never been used and for which she was never charged.

News of Henri's passing triggered an outpouring of love, grief, and consolation from his tens of thousands of Instagram followers, all of which gave Samantha some solace, but only a little. The sense of loss she felt was profound and inescapable. "Henri had this sweet innocence and goofiness and silliness to him, and he would look at me and I could just feel the love coming out of his eyes, and it would make me teary," she remembers. "He made me feel so special and he did all of these goofy, sweet, amazing things and he was just the most special spirit I'd ever encountered, and then, just like that, he was gone."

Those of us who have lost pets can empathize with the searing pain Samantha experienced. Just as there isn't anything quite like the unconditional love that dogs feel for us, and us for them, there isn't anything quite like the bottomless sorrow and helplessness we feel after losing a canine friend. I've done readings for dozens of people who have lost beloved pets, and I've seen the mixture of agony and guilt that overwhelms them and sometimes leaves them emotionally in shreds.

And in these readings, I've learned that dogs are very good at communicating from the Other Side, specifically to assure their owners that they shouldn't feel any guilt about their passing, and that their owners gave them the most wonderful lives imaginable. I've also clearly picked up on the reasons why some dogs leave us and cross: Sometimes it's because they've taught the life lesson they were brought into our lives to teach; sometimes it's to clear the path for another dog that is meant to enter our lives. I try my best to assure dog owners that, although the crippling loss they feel will likely endure for some time, they should not feel bad for the dogs they lost, because these animals are fulfilled and happy on the Other Side—and because the vast love they brought into our lives *is meant to endure beyond their crossing.*

Such was the case with Henri le Frenchie.

After Henri passed, Samantha felt only loneliness and despair, partly because she grew up an atheist and did not believe in the continuation of consciousness after death. But when Covid disrupted everyone's lives in 2020, Samantha began searching for a deeper meaning to existence. She spent a lot of time alone and in nature, read many books about spirituality, and found that she was gradually feeling more at peace with the world. "It was like all these crazy, magical little things started happening that made me feel more connected to the Universe," she explains. "Like, I'd have a thought and then something would happen connected to that thought, and I felt like the Universe was talking back to me. It was an amazing feeling."

Samantha marked one of Henri's Covid-era birthdays by visiting the beach where they had spent so much carefree, joyful time together. She picked up a stick, drew *Happy Birthday Henri* in the sand, and offered a silent tribute to her dear friend. Just then, Samantha looked up at the sky and noticed something strange—a bright rainbow spot in the sky. She'd never seen anything like it, and when another woman walked by, Samantha alerted her to the phenomenon.

"I said, 'Look at that, isn't it amazing?' And the woman said, 'Oh yes, that's called a sun dog rainbow,'" she says. "A *sun dog.*"

Meteorologically speaking, a sun dog is caused by sunlight passing through a thin curtain of ice crystal clouds, which refract the light and create the bright encircling rainbow effect. It's technically called a parhelion, though most people who are aware of them know them only as sun dogs. If you look at a picture of one, you'll see that they are mysterious and heavenly and beautiful.

For Samantha, though, the fact that a weather phenomenon known as a sun dog appeared to her for the first time on Henri's birthday was more than a coincidence. "It was a sign from Henri," she says. "I wished him happy birthday, and he sent me a sun dog."

After that, Samantha was more attuned to potential messages from Henri. During Halloween season, she visited a grocery store that featured a display of three small mechanical witches that howled and cackled when people walked by. When she saw the witches—from a distance of dozens of feet—"I remembered how the same witches once started moving in front of Henri and he jumped up and down and barked in front of them and I'd filmed it," she says. "The memory made me feel sad." Just then, though not a soul in the store was anywhere near them, the witches came to life, their eyes lighting up and flashing bright red. "No one had triggered them, yet they got activated just when I thought of Henri," Samantha says. "I dug in my phone for the video I'd taken of Henri and the witches, and I saw that this was three years to the day of when I took the video. *To the day.*"

After that, Samantha began asking Henri for specific signs.

"The first one I asked for was a bear," she recalls. "The reason I asked for a bear is that I used to use this goofy little baby voice when I talked to Henri, and my friends said it sounded like I was saying the word *bear* and calling him Henri Bear when all I was really doing was just making a weird sound."

On vacation in New York City, just two days after she asked Henri to show her a bear, Samantha was walking on Manhattan's Upper West Side when she turned a corner and saw something on the sidewalk outside a store that stopped her cold—a life-size, elaborate wooden carving *of a bear.*

But that wasn't all. Beside it was a smaller carving of a baby bear. Samantha asked for one bear; Henri sent her two.

But *that* wasn't all, either.

A second small carving sat on the other side of the large bear.

Inexplicably, and incongruously, this one was a *French bulldog.*

"I mean, I turn the corner and I see a momma bear, a baby bear, and a little French bulldog," Samantha says. "I have no idea why the

Frenchie was there with the two bears, he just was. It made no sense, but there it was." When Samantha looked at the carvings a little closer, she noticed the baby bear had a rock with writing on it placed in its lap.

The inscription?

YOU ARE LOVED.

Henri continued sending Samantha little signs to show he was still around. On another visit to their favorite beach, Samantha asked Henri to send any kind of message, and soon after she saw two French bulldogs frolicking together by some tide pools. She walked over to them, focusing on the one who reminded her of Henri. The Frenchie was busy playing with his paws in the water. The dog's owner saw her watching and said, "That's Henry." The very first words spoken to Samantha after asking Henri for a sign were "That's Henry."

Samantha broke into tears.

In the years since Henri's death, Samantha has continued shining his love out into the world. Committed to raising awareness and helping prevent other animals from suffering Henri's fate, Samantha brought his case to trial, and in a state where animals are viewed legally as property, a jury found the vet hospital liable for negligence and the specific veterinarian liable for concealment. For her first day in court, she once again asked Henri to send her a bear. As soon as Samantha walked into the courtroom, she saw, mounted on the wall, three large, framed photograph prints of bears. The judge for her case was a nature photographer, and the specific courtroom for Henri's case was the only one in the courthouse with these pictures. The photos were so prominent that when Samantha nervously took the stand to testify in her case, she could look out beyond the jury and see all the bears on the walls.

Samantha knows what she will do with the money the defendants owe her. She has always known what she would do with it, and that knowledge motivated her throughout the lawsuit. "My favorite sound in the world was the sound of Henri drinking water in the middle of the night from the little bowl I had for him on the balcony off my bedroom," she says. "Hearing him nourishing himself made me feel so peaceful and happy." Her dream is now to use the money from the case to fund the building of a watering hole for elephants and other animals dealing with drought in Africa. "I want it to be Henri's water bowl and for it to be something that nourishes elephants and other wildlife. I like the idea of Henri's tiny water bowl becoming something huge, something that helps so many others."

Finally, Samantha has kept Henri's legacy of love alive by finishing *Henri and the Magnificent Snort*. The Universe, it turns out, has been helping her with that, too. The story found its way into the hands of the Dr. Seuss Foundation, which is now funding Henri's book to be used to teach bullying prevention in schools. Today, people reach out to Samantha to tell her the book is their children's favorite bedtime story—or that their child wants to name their next dog Henri.

And while Samantha doesn't have Henri by her side at readings, as she'd planned, she knows that Henri is still with her, still around. And she knows this because Henri worked so hard to convince her it was true.

"I don't think we ever really lose someone we love, even though we go through the experience of feeling like we have," she says. "What Henri has done for me is help me see the big picture, where everything happens for a reason, and everything has this absolute beauty to it, even the hard stuff. Henri taught me so much about love when he was alive, and now he has taught me so much about the meaning of existence."

Most of all, she says, "Henri showed up to assure me that we will always be connected at the heart, like we always were."

Margaux Perrier was raised in a very religious environment; her grandfather was an Episcopalian priest, so her grandparents were heavily involved with their local church. Margaux enjoyed the community aspect of church events, but at the same time there was something about organized religion, she says, "that just felt so misaligned, and made me think, *I don't feel this is it for me.*" She developed a curiosity about other ways to experience and interpret existence, a pursuit that was influenced by her move to a 1920s apartment in Hollywood, California, that, according to Margaux, "was pretty seriously haunted."

"I started having some strange experiences there, and I was like, *Okay, let me figure out how to deal with this,*" she says. "They didn't feel like negative spirits, but some stuff was definitely happening.' Lights going on and off, doors opening and closing, blow dryers that mysteriously switched on—all that led Margaux to a well-known Los Angeles metaphysical shop whose owners took her under their wing and taught her how to gently guide her unwanted spirit roommates away. The experience kick-started what has become Margaux's lifelong pursuit of a spiritual life. "I was continually interacting with things I couldn't see, but that I could very viscerally feel," she says. "I opened myself up to a whole new metaphysical realm and I never looked back."

Margaux's then boyfriend, Iain, shared her spiritual curiosity—as well as a deep love for all animals. One day, with time to kill before a meeting, they went for a walk along Santa Monica's Montana Avenue and stumbled across an Adopt a Dog booth. "We weren't shopping for a dog or anything like that, but when Iain saw the booth he said, 'Let's just take a look,'" Margaux says. "My thought was, *Are you kidding? No one ever just looks—they end up going home with a dog.*"

Sure enough, Margaux was browsing around on her own when she heard Iain call her name. "You have to come here!" he yelled. Margaux walked over and saw what she calls "a huge fluffy black mop of hair. I mean, he had so much fur you couldn't even see his eyes." The dog was a twenty-five-pound, roughly two-year-old Schnauzer–Tibetan terrier mix who'd been abandoned by a previous owner and clearly needed some loving care. Iain looked at me and said, 'Yeah, this is our dog,' and I said, 'Wait, what? We're not getting a dog. We don't have time for a dog.'"

"We'll make time," Iain responded. "This is the one, I know it. This is our dog."

Margaux crouched down to the dog's level and gently brushed the fur away from his eyes. "When I really looked at him, he had the most human eyes I'd ever seen and they pierced into my soul," she says. "The feeling I had was like, *Oh, there you are. There's our little teddy bear.*"

And that's how Margaux and Iain went home with a new family member they named Teddy.

The first question: Would Teddy get along with Margaux's two cats? When they got home Iain set Teddy down near the felines, one a Russian blue short-hair and the other a former feral barn cat, and said, "Okay, Teddy, these are the cats. If you want to live here, you have to get along with them." Teddy approached first, tenderly sniffing the cats, careful not to come on too strong. The cats performed the equivalent of a shrug and went on with their days. Teddy had passed the test.

"Very quickly we realized just how incredibly smart and special and unique Teddy was," Margaux says. "He was so loving and gentle and kind, and he learned things so quicky. He could understand exactly what we were saying. He just wanted to be with us and share our lives with us, and he was happy. He wasn't a dog's dog. He was a people dog."

Margaux and Iain took Teddy to the groomer and freed him from his tangly mop of fur. "It was a complete transformation," Margaux says. "Suddenly he was free. It was like he magically moved on from his past." Then they took him to the pet store to round up supplies and let him wander down the toy aisle. Margaux told him to pick any toy he liked. Teddy was deliberate and considered all his options, sitting with a toy for a while before moving on to the next one.

"Finally, he fixated on a little squeaky whale," Margaux says. "He pulled it off the shelf and marched it straight up to the register. From that point on he had a real affinity for whales. One of his blankets had whales on it and he always had to take that one with him, and he'd always bring his whale toy with him when we went to the beach. I told Iain, 'He must have been a whale in his past life.'"

It was one of those wonderfully happy merging of souls that belong together, as if Teddy had always been part of their lives, as if it were all preordained, the bond between them far beyond simply owner and pet. "We both realized Teddy was basically our child at that point," Margaux says. "When Iain and I went through some really tough moments in our relationship, Teddy was the glue that held us together."

The couple eventually got married and moved into a non-haunted house in the Hollywood Hills, tucked away on a small leafy street. It was the perfect arrangement—more room for them all, grass for Teddy to romp on—except for one thing. "There was this one elderly neighbor who was always speeding up and down the street in her little sports car," Margaux says. "It's a narrow street, and there was no footpath, and Iain flagged her down many times and told her she had to slow down. There were toddlers and babies in the area, kids learning how to walk. But she just kept driving too fast."

One day, Iain went for a walk with Teddy and Bambi, a small, wiry-haired Chihuahua-terrier-dachshund mix they'd adopted as company for Teddy. Margaux stayed behind in the house and took a business call. "Suddenly, I heard this bloodcurdling scream," she says. "I ran outside crying and saying, 'Oh my god, oh my god.'"

There was a commotion, and several neighbors were gathering. In the middle of it all there was Iain, screaming and trying to lift a car.

It was a small sports car. The neighbor had run over Teddy.

It unfolded like a nightmare. Margaux and Iain rushed Teddy to an animal hospital and pleaded with the vet to perform a miracle. Teddy held on for three days before finally surrendering to cardiac arrest, crossing over while in Margaux's arms. Iain was inconsolable, blaming himself because he'd been the one walking Teddy. Margaux sank into a bottomless pit of sorrow and disbelief. Their home, once so joyful and boisterous, felt empty and drained of life. "I sat on the bathroom floor holding Teddy's little whale and crying and pleading to my spirits, 'Just give me Teddy back,'" says Margaux. "I was so depressed. I couldn't think of anything that could possibly ever make me feel happy again. I lost all hope in the world."

The horror of what had happened put an enormous strain on their marriage as well, with Iain fighting off self-blame and Margaux struggling to find any meaning behind the tragedy. Numbness, guilt, PTSD, depression—there was no apparent way out of the awful spiral they'd found themselves in.

Until a therapist Margaux was seeing told her a version of the story of Pandora's Box.

In this telling of the Greek myth, Pandora—a woman fashioned out of earth by Hephaestus, a god of fire—was entrusted with the care of a mysterious jar, which she promptly opened out of curiosity. The jar contained all the world's great evils—sickness, death, madness, violence, greed—which flew out and escaped to forever plague humanity. When Pandora slammed the lid shut, only one gentle thing remained trapped inside—hope. "The message really moved me," Margaux says. "It was, 'You still have hope, you always have hope, if you choose to let it out.'"

Hope can take many forms, and in this case hope had fur, four legs, and a tail.

As the weeks passed Margaux and Iain discussed the possibility of getting another dog, not to replace Teddy—Teddy could never be replaced—but to provide a companion for Bambi. "Poor Bambi was just as depressed as we were," Margaux says. "We'd take her for walks and you could see how sad and sluggish she was. And her depression made me ever more depressed. So we talked about another dog, not for us, but for Bambi."

And yet they still weren't sure. Something about putting a new animal in Teddy's place just didn't feel right. "That's when Iain said, and I'll never forget it, 'If the Universe sends us a very clear sign and guides us to another dog, then we'll get one. Otherwise, we'll just leave it with Bambi.' So the standard was, the Universe had to be very, very clear with its message."

The very next day after that conversation, Margaux was working in her home office when she heard Iain yelling from the kitchen. She rushed over and saw him sitting on the floor, staring at an image on his iPhone. "He looked like he was in shock," she says. "His hand was trembling holding the phone."

Iain showed her a text he'd just received from a friend. The friend had been out with his wife and their dog for a stroll in the park when they saw a dog running wildly past them, in and out of the park and even into traffic. Several parkgoers tried to get ahold of the dog, with no luck. It was like he was running for his life. Iain's friend joined in, and the group was finally able to corral the dog.

He had no collar or leash, and was badly neglected and malnourished. Iain's friend brought him to a vet, who did not find any identification chip. The animal had just appeared out of nowhere, untraceable, alone in the world. Iain's friend took him home, intending to find him a permanent family. The first people he thought to contact were Iain and Margaux. "Mate," read the text sent to Iain, "I hope I'm not being insensitive, but we found this dog in the park today. Take a look and I think you'll be able to see why we thought of you."

Margaux looked at the photo attached to the text.

"I was shocked at a cellular level," she says. "This dog looked *exactly* like Teddy. Not a little like him, exactly like him. We'd never seen any other dog who even resembled Teddy, and here was a dog who looked like his twin. We were both just so utterly shocked."

Margaux sat on the kitchen floor alongside Iain. They talked it over. It wasn't like this stray that suddenly appeared in their lives was a big German shepherd or Rottweiler or any other breed that wasn't a Schnauzer–Tibetan terrier mix—this dog could have been Teddy's *clone*.

"I told Iain, 'You just finished saying the Universe has to send us a very clear sign, and we get this. If we don't at least go meet him, we'll literally be kicking the Universe in the face.'"

At Iain's friend's home, the stray was waiting for them, "sitting on a bench exactly how Teddy used to sit, with his head cocked to one side,"

Margaux says. "I just lost it. I started sobbing hysterically. I was like, 'I've got to cool it or I'm going to frighten this dog.'" Margaux gathered herself and sat next to the stray and watched with wonder as the dog instantly snuggled up against her, totally calm and at ease.

"That was it," Margaux says.

They called him Archie, a name that had been tumbling around Margaux's head since she saw the text—and it turned out that Archie was also the name Iain's friend and his wife had randomly given the dog when they took him home. Iain and Margaux figured out that they met Archie three months to the day of when Teddy crossed.

When Bambi saw Archie, she ran over excitedly, thinking, perhaps, that this was Teddy. She sniffed him for a while and realized it wasn't Teddy, but she stuck around anyway, happy to have a new partner in crime. The two cats saw Archie and shrugged.

As for Archie? "He just became this super-snuggly little thing," Margaux says. "He clings to you like a baby koala. He needs to be touching you at all times. It was like he just knew this was his home."

Margaux and Iain still wrestled with feelings of guilt, as if bringing in Archie was a betrayal to Teddy. "It *was* weird having a dog around who looked exactly like Teddy but wasn't him," Margaux says. "At the same time, we felt like we'd been divinely guided. We didn't go out looking for Archie. The Universe brought him to us."

When Margaux posted photos of the new dog to her Instagram account—which was packed with friends who'd fallen in love with Teddy, just like Margaux had—the sentiments that came back helped assuage any guilt or regret that lingered. "Everyone was so positive and sent such beautiful messages. They were like, 'This has restored my faith in God' and 'Miracles do happen.' I answered that they'd all been part of harnessing this miracle and bringing Archie to us. I really don't think it would have happened without the collective energy of all the people who loved Teddy. It made me realize there was a reason for this happening, though I didn't know what it was. It was just Teddy's time to go, and Archie's time to arrive. I don't know why, but somehow this had all been dreamed of and wished for and finally manifested."

In the end, Margaux feels certain that, even more than dreams and energy and the Universe, it was Teddy, their beloved Teddy, who steered Archie into that Los Angeles park and into the arms of Iain's friend and finally into their lives. "One hundred percent I believe that this was Teddy responding to our request to be sent a sign," she says. "It made me realize that Teddy was going to do whatever he could to make sure we were okay without him. Archie made me feel like Teddy was still with us, and that Teddy was never going to leave."

I first met Margaux during the Covid pandemic, when we both joined a Friday-night sales event called Crystal QVC, hosted on Instagram Live by an amazing shop called Open Eye Crystals, based in L.A. The shop's owner, Madison Young, taught participants all about crystals—and if you saw one you liked, you could purchase it by "claiming" it. Often, many people would try to claim the same crystal at the same time. Week after week it created a beautiful little community of connection and kindness—all thanks to Madison! I noticed that Margaux and I tended to like the same crystals, and when I bought one and had it shipped to my home, I got a strong download that it actually belonged with Margaux, not me. I mailed it to her and soon discovered that she is an artist who designs her own beautiful jewelry "inspired by all that is dreamy, pastel and Rococo." She also authors a blog titled *Being*, on which she shares her thoughts on topics such as embracing everyday miracles. "Life is a mosaic of moments," she writes in one blog entry, "and within each one lies a tiny miracle waiting to be uncovered."

What a truly beautiful encapsulation of what the Universe has to offer us every day.

I learned about Teddy the same way I learned about Henri le Frenchie—on their owners' Instagram pages, where communities had sprung up around the shared love for these magical creatures. (You see? Social media can be used for good!) I wanted to share their stories with you because, in a time of unthinkable tragedy and heartbreak, both Samantha and Margaux remained open to the healing wonders of the Universe—to the immense reservoir of love and energy that is accessible to us just when we need it most.

Most of all, their stories affirmed for me once more that our animal companions never really leave us, but rather stay with us in our hearts, and in the air and sky and space all around us, determined to ease our sorrow and bring us all the joy we thought we'd lost.

"I now believe Teddy and Archie were both part of the same universal energy, and that Teddy gifted us the chance to do with Archie all the things we wished we'd done with Teddy before he crossed," Margaux says. "It's been four years since he passed, and I can still feel him with me every day. When I go through something difficult, I can feel Teddy nudging me, letting me know it will be okay, and I say, 'Oh, hi, Teddy, thank you so much. Thank you for hugging my heart.'"

Guidance to the secret path to an illuminated life can come in many forms, including from our pets who have crossed but who, I have seen, still love us very, very much.

30

Stars That Light Up the Darkest Night

L isa Wolkind stood in the wings of the Majestic Theater in Gettysburg, Pennsylvania, waiting to go onstage. Her heart raced and she took deep breaths, trying to stay calm. She'd been anticipating this moment for many months—longer, even, if you go back to the beginning of the story. There were hundreds of people in the glorious old theater, and soon she'd be in front of them all, doing something she'd never done before.

But really, everything she was about to do, everything she'd prepared for, was all for one person—a person who wasn't in the crowd.

Or rather, to be accurate, a person you couldn't *see* in the crowd.

The audience grew silent, and Lisa listened as the master of ceremonies introduced the next act.

"Ladies and gentlemen, we have a very special dance for you."

Then it was her moment, and Lisa walked into the light.

If you want to go back to the beginning of the story, you have to admit that, at least on paper, they weren't a very good match.

Lisa Wolkind was a veterinarian who was so into health and fitness that she moonlighted as a spin class instructor. Scott Waybrant was a U.S. Air Force veteran, a partner in his family fuel oil business, a sales executive, and later a real estate agent. A onetime formidable volleyball player, he preferred lifting weights and competing at golf. Scott grew up in conservative Adams County, Pennsylvania. He liked bow and rifle hunting and eating venison; Lisa was a New Jersey–born liberal who'd never shot a gun and was a vegetarian. Scott was six foot two; Lisa was five foot nothing. "We were polar opposites," Lisa remembers. "People who knew us would never have put us together. And besides, I was dating someone else."

Still, when Scott signed up for an indoor cycling class at his local Y, he took an immediate shine to the instructor—Lisa. "I guess it was one of those 'having a crush on your teacher' things," Lisa says. "I liked talking to him, but I really didn't think we were a match."

Then Scott took a chance—he decided to send a bouquet of flowers to Lisa at her office. Before he did, he called his sister for advice.

"I'm gonna do it," he told her. "I'm gonna send her flowers."

"Are you really gonna do it?"

"I'm gonna do it."

"I don't know if you should do it."

"Neither do I. But I gotta do it."

So he did it.

And it worked.

Not right away, but eventually. It took a few years for Lisa to finally accept his offer to go on a date, but after that, they were pretty much instantly an item. Lisa moved in with Scott in his home in Gettysburg, the city where he was born and raised, and they became a popular couple in town. "People were just so entertained by how different we were," Lisa says. "I guess it was kind of funny that we meshed together so well."

Scott kept his real estate business going while Lisa kept working as a vet. She'd loved animals her whole life (her mother helped her write little books about squirrels and birds), particularly dogs, ever since she fell in love with Poodle Puff, her first pet and best childhood friend. As a veterinarian, however, she eventually made the care of felines her specialty. "It just sort of happened," she says. "I didn't have a cat as a kid because my dad was allergic, but suddenly I realized I really liked being around them." That was yet another difference between Lisa and Scott—the cat veterinarian and the guy who hated cats.

Despite his issue with cats, Scott understood how gifted Lisa was with them and prodded her to start a volunteer trap-neuter-return program, hoping to help local free-roaming cats. Along the way, the number of deaths among unwanted kittens Lisa had to confront convinced her she should start fostering some of them herself. She decided to foster one particularly scraggly cat to see if she could make a difference. When she brought it home, Scott—perhaps reluctantly—agreed to help her care for it.

Scott went out and bought the supplies they'd need—syringes, bowls, kibble. He gave the cat medicine and affection. "He was so sweet with him," Lisa says. "Now, as a kitten, this cat wasn't easy. He was a toe biter, and he liked to pounce on you at night. He could be kind of crazy, actually. But Scott came to love him." The plan, however, was never to keep the cat as their own, only to foster it to better health. When Lisa suggested they keep it instead, Scott balked.

"How about if I let you pick the name?" Lisa asked.

Scott thought about it for a moment.

"Okay," he said. "Boomer."

Boomer?

But that was the deal, and that is how Boomer the toe-biting, night-pouncing, short-haired tabby became the family pet, and Scott became an honest-to-goodness cat daddy.

It wasn't always easy. In 2020, Boomer was diagnosed with a heart condition and required special medicine every afternoon. Lisa couldn't get away from her practice, so it was Scott who came home at lunch every day and took care of Boomer. "Scott and I worked really well together," Lisa says, "and we kept Boomer going."

Then, everything changed.

. . .

It was June 23, 2021, a beautiful, balmy summer day, and Scott was playing a fun round of golf with some friends and family. He teed up on a hole and hit the perfect drive, right down the middle of the fairway. Just a few seconds later, Scott collapsed to the ground. No words, no warning, he just fell. His golf partner, a good friend, rushed over to him and tried CPR, along with his brother-in-law, who was part of the foursome. But sadly, it was no use.

Scott passed away on the golf course. He was just sixty-four.

Lisa was devastated—"just *destroyed*," she says. More than anything she felt numb, except for bouts of sheer panic at night. A million thoughts raced through her head, and her focus steered itself toward Boomer, who still had his heart condition. "I was thinking how I'd be able to keep Boomer alive without Scott there to help me," she says. "I work forty-five minutes from home. Who was going to come home at lunch to give him his medicine?" That mattered so much because, Lisa understood, Boomer was going to be her main source of support through her grieving, curling up with her at night and allowing her to fall asleep.

"I was depending on him," she says. "He was the one."

But it was not to be. Just one day after Scott's passing, Lisa was awakened from a fitful, thrashing sleep at three in the morning by a loud thump. She saw that Boomer had fallen from the bed. "I thought I'd kicked him off by mistake," Lisa says. "But it wasn't that."

Boomer was having a cardiac event. On the floor, he couldn't walk and was struggling to breathe. Lisa knew what was wrong—it was a saddle thrombus, or a blood clot that lodges at the bifurcation of the aorta and hinders blood flow to the legs. The situation was dire, and all Lisa could do to end Boomer's agony was to put him down (she had what she needed for that in the house).

"I couldn't believe it," she says. "I felt a lot of things when Scott passed, but I never felt anger for him leaving me. But then it was Boomer, too. And I thought, *Come on, now. What's going on?*"

The next day, Lisa struggled with the sudden and profound absence of Scott and Boomer, and to escape her sadness she got on her bicycle and went for a ride, as she and Scott used to do on every wedding anniversary. She went to their favorite spot, the scenic Chesapeake & Ohio Canal, along the Potomac River. "I didn't want to see or talk to anyone," she says. "I just wanted to be left alone."

At the end of a long ride, she sat down near the canal, put her backpack on the ground, and pulled out her cell phone to look at photos of her and Scott together. Just then, a very odd thing happened.

A dragonfly appeared out of nowhere and settled comfortably on the top edge of her cell phone as she held it. "I looked at it, and it just sat there, looking straight at me," Lisa remembers. "We just looked at each other for a while, and then I decided, *Well, I might as well talk to it.*"

The words that came out of her mouth surprised even her.

"I'm okay," she told the dragonfly. "I'm gonna be okay. Don't worry about me."

The dragonfly cocked its head to the side, as if it were listening intently. Lisa kept talking.

"Look, I'm gonna cry and I'm going to be down. That's going to happen. And I know you are here to make sure I'm okay. I know that's why you came. Well, I want you to know—I *am* going to be okay."

Lisa and the dragonfly spoke for what seemed to her like an hour. "People were walking by and looking at me while I talked to this insect on my phone," she says. "We were having a full-on conversation. But it was all organic. It just kind of happened. The dragonfly appeared, and then it just stayed, and I knew right away it was Scott."

The next few days were a blur. There was a memorial for Scott, who was known for his casual demeanor and upbeat spirit, and the invitation declared: *No black attire allowed. Hawaiian shirts welcome.* In lieu of flowers, mourners were asked to send donations to a trap-neuter-return program for free-roaming cats, set up in Scott's name. After the memorial, when all the guests had gone, Lisa lingered at the site and heard her cell phone ping over and over. "It was all of our friends text-ing me and reporting the same thing," she says. "A big, beautiful dou-ble rainbow. They all saw it. We agreed it was Scott letting us know he was there."

First the dragonfly. Then the double rainbow. Lisa never had a mo-ment's doubt these were Scott's ways of sending her messages. "He was always good at communicating, so I wasn't surprised he was so good at it even after he passed," she says. Yet as heartening as his messages were, it was Scott's physical absence that tore away at Lisa's heart. Even a listening insect and a rare weather phenomenon weren't enough to erase the terrible reality: Scott wasn't there anymore.

But Scott wasn't finished.

Scott's niece and nephew traveled to Gettysburg for his memorial and stayed in a local bed-and-breakfast. The morning after the memo-rial, they packed up and were leaving to go home when they noticed something small tucked into a tight ball at the bottom of the entrance coor. Scott's niece bent down to look at it and saw that it was a tiny little kitten, soaking wet from the rain outside and terrified.

She asked for a towel, gently picked up the kitten, and wrapped it up and dried it. The first person she thought to call was Lisa. "It was prob-ably one of the feral cats in town, and I told her to bring it to the local rescue shelter," she says. "I called them and told them I was sending over a kitten, and they said they had no room. No cages left, no place to put him, nothing. So I said, 'Okay, I'll take him for a night or two until we can find a place for him.'"

At home, Lisa cleaned up the kitty and brushed out his few long hairs. "He was adorable," Lisa recalls. "Really beautiful. I thought, *Well, at least we'll have no problem finding him a home.*"

Scott's niece, however, had other ideas.

"This is supposed to be your cat," she told Lisa over and over. "Scott sent this cat for *you*."

But Lisa didn't want to hear it. "I kept telling her, 'No, no, I don't want it, I'm not ready, I can't handle this,'" Lisa says. "I tried every-thing I could to find that little guy a home."

Lisa called the rescue shelter again, and this time they had room. But before Lisa could drive over, someone at the shelter called her back. They told her they'd just had an outbreak of infections, and it wasn't a good time for a fragile, unvaccinated little kitten to show up. Lisa kept the kitten for a while longer, all the while searching for a foster family. "I really didn't want to keep him," she says. "I just kept saying no."

Until she finally said yes.

Lisa kept the kitten. No room at the shelter, a sudden outbreak—i was like the Universe had put up a series of roadblocks to keep the kitten with Lisa until, inevitably, she fell in love with it. She even came to agree with Scott's niece—who, perhaps not coincidentally, was named Kat—that it was Scott who sent him.

"I tried not to keep him, but Scott wouldn't allow it and, I think, neither would the cat we shared, Boomer," Lisa says. "So I decided to name my new kitten after them both."

That's how a little lost kitten named Scoomer found his forever home.

Another remarkable moment awaited. Scott and Lisa had many friends who were part of the social scene at their local YWCA. One of them was Alex Hayes, the Y's director of fundraising who, a year after Scott's passing, approached Lisa with an idea. The Y was hosting its annual fundraiser based on the popular TV show *Dancing with the Stars*. Would Lisa be interested in being a participant?

"Whenever we went to the Y fundraiser Scott would always tell me, 'You'd be so good at that,'" Lisa remembers. "He'd say, 'I'd be so darn jealous, but I know you would be great.' I never thought I'd get the chance, but when Alex asked me to be on the local version of it, I knew it was something I had to consider. I wound up saying yes before I had a chance to talk myself out of it."

She had two issues. One, would Scott be okay with her dancing with another man? And two, whatever song she danced to had to tell a story—the story of Lisa and Scott. "It was never just a dancing competition for me," she says. "I saw it as a way for art and dance to help me through Scott's loss. It wasn't about dancing—it was about *life*."

Lisa kept on the lookout for signs from Scott that he was okay with her taking part in the show. She finally got one at a weekend conference she attended—a workshop where I was teaching. One of the exercises I had everyone in the audience do was draw a random card with a symbol on it out of a basket. Lisa's card depicted a star, and she took it as a sign. "The star said it all to me," Lisa explains. "I knew Scott was sending me a message that he approved of me dancing in the show."

Lisa agreed to be teamed up with Bruce Moore, a former Broadway actor, singer, and dancer. Now she had to find the right song. She and Bruce considered several classics by Michael Bublé, Barry Manilow, and others, but nothing felt right. Lisa wanted something that conveyed the ongoing connection she felt she had with Scott. After a few weeks, Lisa stumbled across a song she'd never heard before by a singer she didn't know. "The song was called 'Address in the Stars' by a duo named Caitlin and Will. It was about all the things you want to say to your loved one every day, the little things, the big things, and what do you do with all those things you want to say? Well, for me I *did* have an address in the stars. I always had a way of communicating with Scott. And the song captured that longing beautifully," Lisa says.

Lisa and Bruce practiced on and off for about half a year. Lisa had an athletic background, but she hadn't taught a class in years, and she'd never danced in front of an audience. She was nervous but she pushed through her nerves, until the big day finally arrived.

And as she stood in the wings of the Majestic Theater, waiting to go on, she thought about her intention for the night. "I didn't just want to dance," she says. "I wanted everyone to take the ride with me. I wanted everyone to feel what I felt. I wanted us all to honor Scott."

A panel of three judges sat impassively stage left. Two well-known local personalities danced their dances ahead of Lisa—a high school principal and a hospital president. Then the emcee announced Lisa and Bruce. The lights dimmed and the stage went dark. Suddenly,

Lisa's voice could be heard—she'd pre-taped a poem she wanted to read before the dance. It was by Hannah Szenes, a Hungarian Jewish poet killed during World War II and considered a hero:

There are stars up above so far away we only

See their light long, long after the star itself is gone.

And so it is with people we have loved—their memories

Keep shining ever brightly though their time with us is done. But the stars that light up the darkest night, these are the lights that guide us. As we live our lives, these are the ways we remember.

The lights came up, and there was Bruce, in white tie and tails, and Lisa, in a sparkling dark blue gown, her curly hair tied up in an elegant bun. The song began to play, and Bruce and Lisa danced.

What a dance it was! I've watched it on YouTube, and I felt the emotion of their performance right through my laptop. Lisa was graceful and fluid, and she devoted heart and soul to the dance. When it was over the audience applauded loudly, and the three judges shared their feelings.

"It went straight to my heart," one judge said.

"It was beautiful and you really touched my heart," said another

"The steps were flawless," said the third judge. "Still, you can have great steps, but you have to really *feel* the dance in your heart, and you did that tonight, and I think you touched everyone's heart."

Later, Lisa gave all the credit to Scott.

"I feel like he picked the song that I danced to, and I feel like he was there with me when we danced," she says. "We didn't win that night, but that was okay. I think we honored Scott well."

Living an illuminated life does not mean living a life free of grief; it means that you live vibrantly even in the face of grief—and in doing so, you honor the love that is there, shining through your grief. It is know-ing that the physical world is not all there is; there is an invisible world of love and connection and guidance shining the path for us always — every step of the way. And it is staying open to the language of signs that our loved ones on the Other Side send us. And there have been other signs from Scott to Lisa, as their conversation continues un-abated.

One time, when Lisa entered a gas station she knew Scott detested (it had been a competitor of his family's business), all the power sud-denly went off. "I immediately thought, *Good one, Scott*," she says.

Another time, while chatting with a former student on her laptop about how she and Scott met, an old song playlist of hers inexplicably popped up—from a spin class in 2011, the very year Scott first sent her flowers. He has appeared in dreams, in dragonflies that linger forever, and, of course, in those ever-present rainbows. During one recent har-vest moon Lisa spent the day at the beach by herself, reading and con-templating and talking to Scott. A lone seagull appeared and kept circling her and simply refused to leave. "He was pestering me and I didn't have any food, so I just kept my head in my book," Lisa says. "Finally, I gave in and I looked up at the seagull, and right behind it there was a bright, beautiful rainbow. I might have missed it if it weren't for that seagull. I knew that was Scott."

Not a day goes by when Lisa doesn't miss Scott—his larger-than-life presence, his sense of humor, his loyalty, and loveliness. But not a day passes either without Lisa feeling like Scott is some-where nearby. The signs he sends have changed over the years, from dragonflies ("very reliable messengers") to the number 11, which was Scott's number in volleyball. "I'll wake up at 11:11 all the time, or I'm rushing to get to work in the morning and it's 11:11," Lisa says. "I see 11s everywhere."

Her continuing connection to Scott has taught her a profound les-son she wishes to share with others. "My message to anyone who has suffered the loss of a loved one is to stay open to receiving messages from the Other Side, because if you keep your heart open, you can keep the connection going," she says. "It may be a little different connection. But it's still a *great* connection."

That vital connection guides us to vibrant, illuminated lives—lives in which we can dance, even in the dark, knowing that light shines from within us, and that our loved ones are shining their light down on us as well.

Spirituality is recognizing and celebrating that we are all inextricably connected to each other by a power greater than all of us and that our connection to that power and to one another is grounded in love and compassion. Practicing spirituality brings a sense of perspective, meaning, and purpose to our lives.

BRENÉ BROWN

31

Honoring the Soul

We've talked about honoring the body because the body houses the soul. Yet while we acknowledge and celebrate and honor our physical presence on earth, we must also acknowledge that *we are spiritual beings connected to and part of something far greater than our singular lives.*

The very first story I told in this book was about two strangers who discovered they were intimately connected as human beings in a way they could never have foreseen. The way I like to look at it is that we are all different leaves on different branches of the same tree — sprouting separately, growing in different ways, yet inextricably bound to one another. And because that is true, we cannot define success or failure in our own lives through only our own myopic view of our individual selves — we must define it in terms of our connection to the greater Universe, and the impact our souls have on the Universe.

I'm reminded of an episode of the British sci-fi TV series *Doctor Who*. In the episode, Doctor Who, traveling through time in a machine called the Tardis, picks up the famously gloomy Dutch painter Vincent van Gogh and brings him back to a modern-day exhibit of his paintings at the Musée d'Orsay in Paris. Van Gogh, vastly unappreciated in his lifetime, is astonished to see an entire exhibit devoted to his paintings and a crowded room of admirers. When Doctor Who asks an art critic at the exhibit to rate where Van Gogh stands in the history of art, Van Gogh listens in as the critic says:

> Certainly, the most popular great painter of all time, the most beloved. His command of color, the most magnificent. He transformed the pain of his tormented life into ecstatic beauty. Pain is easy to portray, but to use your passion and pain to portray the ecstasy and joy and magnificence of our world—no one had ever done it before. Perhaps no one ever will again. To my mind, that strange, wild man who roamed the fields of Provence was not only the world's greatest artist, but also one of the greatest men who ever lived.

Listening to this, the fictionalized Van Gogh dissolves into tears. In his lifetime, he could never have conceived of the positive impact he'd have on the world. His life, he realized, would not be measured by the perceived lack of success he had while he lived, but rather by how much joy and magic and beauty he created and spread for centuries and centuries to come.

In the same way, we cannot always conceive of the role we play in the Universe, or the impact our actions have on the world. As the TV Van Gogh learned, our souls are more far-reaching than our brains can comprehend.

The Other Side has guided me to see and understand that the most beautiful way we can honor and feel this soul connection is by being of service to others. When I was still an English teacher at Herricks High School, I had my students participate in an annual project through our local social services department, in which we'd "adopt" a family in need and buy them gifts and necessities. But the best part, after learning all about these families—names, shoe sizes, likes and dislikes—was when the class and I drove boxes and boxes of presents, food, and supplies to them, and got to spend time with them. These connections were always deeply moving and meaningful. Years later, I heard from former students who told me how much that experience changed their view of the world and impacted their souls. I came to realize that this Adopt-a-Family project was perhaps the most important part of my teaching, because its lessons didn't come out of a book, they came out of service to others. While we could read about choices and struggles and connections and compassion in books, putting it into action in real life was transformational.

We cannot be whole human beings until we acknowledge that we are all part of a larger whole—branches of the same tree. We canno live truly illuminated lives until, I like to say, we "get our spiritua selves on." The truth is that we are all spiritual beings having a human experience in which we're being taught the same collective lesson of love. Every thought and every action contributes either to the light or to the darkness.

Try, at all times, to get your spiritual self on. Being of service to others encompasses an endless array of possible actions, from donating millions as a major philanthropist to offering a stranger a smile. All of our actions matter; all of them have an impact. We may not always see what that impact is while we are here, but, if we are open to and trust the guidance the Other Side gives us, we can be greatly enriched by knowing that our impact on others is real and far-reaching. (Later, when we do our life reviews on the Other Side, we will learn, in a millisecond, how we affected the collective energy of life on earth.)

Honor your soul, honor your spiritual self, and honor your connection to the Universe. Know that we all belong to one another. When you do, you will be walking on an illuminated path. And you'll realize the secret path has been yours to walk on all along.

May we raise children
who love the unloved
things—the dandelion, worms
& spiderlings.
Children who sense
the rose needs the thorn
& run into rainswept days
the same way they
turn towards sun.
And when they're grown & someone
has to speak for those who
have no voice
may they draw upon that
wilder bond, those days of
tending tender things
and be the ones.

NICOLETTE SOWDER

32

Nature as a Path Home

Did you know there's an official World Bee Day?

That's right, ever since 2018, May 20 has been World Bee Day, designed to raise global awareness of bees and their role on earth. Some may wonder: Do we really need a whole day just for bees? There's already a World Wildlife Day (March 3), so why single out bees? The tiny honeybee, for example, buzzes about weighing just a tenth of a gram.

The reason is simple: One out of every three bites of food we eat depends on animal pollinators like the bee, which is the most efficient and productive pollinator of all (pollination allows crops to fertilize). Bees can pollinate as many as one thousand flowers in a single outing, and they are the main pollinators of roughly 80 percent of all flowering crops—apples, cucumbers, nuts, berries, broccoli, asparagus, and many more.

In the last few years, however, bees have been dying off in huge numbers around the planet, due mostly to parasites, pesticides, habitat loss, disease, and climate change. In 2023, the mortality rate among all bees was close to 50 percent, with whole colonies wiped out by the millions. Should these tiny buzzing bees ever disappear from the planet, our global food ecosystem would be gravely disrupted, with unthinkable consequences.

So, yes, we need a World Bee Day.

I bring up bees and their outsize role in a much larger ecosystem to illustrate one of the key elements of living an illuminated life—*honoring our profound connection to nature.*

If you've been wondering what you can bring into your life path that will elevate your energy and intensify your connection to the Universe, here is one suggestion: Think about and explore the way all organisms everywhere, including the human species, are inextricably bound to one another in the natural world.

Honoring our connection to nature is one of the clearest and easiest ways we can rebalance our energy, ground ourselves, and connect to something greater—yet the pressures of modern life often *distance* us from nature. We become bound to our desks, locked in our comfortable homes, glued to our TV and iPad screens. Gradually, we lose our sense of connection to nature altogether.

Which is tragic, because nature offers us so many amazing opportunities to embrace our interconnectedness and get closer to living illuminated lives.

Consider the wolf. In the 1800s, thousands of packs of gray wolves roamed the area in northwest Wyoming that is now Yellowstone National Park, which became the world's first national park in 1872. But the wolf population was devastated by hunters, who made the species the most hunted animal in U.S. history. By the end of the 1920s, the very last gray wolf disappeared from Yellowstone.

For the next seventy years, no wolves roamed the park. In that time, we grew increasingly aware of how ecosystems work. Biologists noted that the loss of wolves upset Yellowstone's delicate ecosystem by allowing the elk population to explode, which in turn led to more grazing that killed off young bushes, plants, and trees and caused dangerous erosion. On top of that, wiping out Yellowstone's wolves left the species in danger of extinction. Scientists and biologists felt something had to be done.

So, in 1995, eight gray wolves from Jasper National Park in Alberta, Canada, were driven by truck through the stone Roosevelt Arch at the north entrance to Yellowstone and released in the wilds of the park, reintroducing wolves to their former habitat. What happened next was astonishing.

The return of wolves to Yellowstone caused what is called a trophic cascade of ecological change. The park's wolves (there are now somewhere around 80 to 120 of them) lowered the elk population, which allowed young willow, aspen, and cottonwood plants to thrive, which brought beavers back into the ecosystem, which altered the course of some of the park's rivers. The impact on the ecosystem was so deep and varied that it took biologists by surprise. "It's like kicking a pebble down a mountain slope where conditions were just right so that a falling pebble could trigger an avalanche of change," explained Doug Smith, the wildlife biologist who ran the Yellowstone Wolf Project. Fully understanding that avalanche of change will, biologists predict, take decades.

What a beautiful, vibrant example of our interconnectedness! Every creature matters; every creature profoundly affects its environment. We are all part of the same universal ecosystem, and all of our thoughts and actions are like pebbles that ripple in rivers and tumble down mountains and cause changes we can't hope to foresee.

This is why honoring our connection to nature is so important to an illuminated life: because experiencing nature infuses us with a greater sense of our place in the Universe. Breathing fresh air, counting the rings on a tree trunk, marveling at majestic animals in the wild—all of this nourishes us immeasurably, and strengthens our sense of connection to one another and to the world.

In 2017, Scottish doctors, in conjunction with the National Health Service and the Royal Society for the Protection of Birds, began writing what they called nature prescriptions for patients. These prescriptions were exactly what they sound like—instead of giving patients pills, doctors prescribed spending time out in nature. They provided yearlong calendars of simple outdoor recommendations, including:

- Appreciate the wind.

- Borrow a dog and take it for a walk.

- Make beach art from natural materials.

- Touch the sea.

- Bury your face in the grass.

- Talk to a pony.

- Feed the birds in your garden.

- Appreciate a cloud.

The belief is that such activities help reduce blood pressure and anxiety, and benefit patients with diabetes, heart disease, stress, and depression. A wealth of scientific research has shown that "there's a robust relationship between mental health and nature exposure," Matthew Browning, director of the Virtual Reality and Nature Lab at Clemson University, said in an interview. The same is true of how nature can reduce stress and lower high blood pressure.

Why? Because the experience of nature is multisensory, inviting us to appreciate colors, scents, sounds, and textures and making it easier to acknowledge the beautiful communion of all elements in existence. For instance, dozens of scientific studies, many published in the *Journal of Environmental Horticulture,* have shown that proximity to plants is surprisingly beneficial to humans. Just by being in the presence of flowers, we can reduce stress, improve our mood, and accelerate healing. One study found that patients who had flowers in their hospital rooms reported less pain, anxiety, and fatigue. Specifically, flowers, like humans, have vibrational energy that can be measured in frequency: the rate at which our body cells vibrate. A healthy human body has a vibrational frequency of 62 to 70 megahertz (MHz). By contrast, roses have a vibrational frequency of 320 MHz, significantly higher than we humans. Simply holding and smelling a rose creates a mingling of our vibrational frequencies, with the result that our own frequency is increased—which in turn strengthens our ability to heal, physically, emotionally, and mentally.

Other studies have shown that flowers are very good at "hearing" vibrational energy. The sound of honeybees, for instance, causes flowers to quickly sweeten their nectar to attract the pollinating bees. It's not surprising, therefore, that flowers can also "hear" us, pick up on our vibrational energy, and in turn share their energy with us.

Japanese researchers developed a concept called shinrin-yoku, or forest bathing, which holds that time spent in a forest, or otherwise immersed in nature, has an exceptionally positive meditative effect on our minds and bodies. Forest bathing ecotherapy can be structured (breathe in the aroma of evergreen trees as they release high concentrations of phytoncides, or airborne essential oils that provide an immunity boost) or unstructured (take a simple hike in nature and marvel at its beauty). But shinrin-yoku and other eco-therapies all have the same aim—to reconnect us to nature as a way to improve our health and well-being.

Animals, too, are part of this, and better appreciating our unique relationship with animals is part of honoring nature. For instance, did you know that a cat's purr produces a frequency of vibrations that can help heal wounds and reduce inflammation *in humans*? Vibrational therapy with frequencies between 10 and 15 MHz can, studies show, strengthen bones, tendons, and joints, and enhance overall well-being. A cat's purring also releases endorphins—not only in them but in us, too. And these endorphins lower stress levels and blood pressure. Our little cat buddies, it turns out, do more than just scratch up sofas—they help heal us.

Richard Louv, the chairman emeritus of the Children & Nature Network, has written extensively about what he calls "nature-deficit disorder" and its negative effects on children. He describes how we live in two worlds—the outer habitat of the world around us, and the world of our inner private lives. To these he adds a third world—"the shared habitat of the heart." As Louv writes in his beautiful book *Our Wild Calling*, there "is a deep connection between a person and another animal. It is the permeability of empathy. It is the connection that extends from within us, across the mysterious between, and into the other being. If we're lucky, we feel something almost indescribable in return."

This profound connection to and communion with other creatures, Louv writes, "is fragile, and needs nourishment to survive, as do they and we."

This is another truly beautiful idea. Our connection to animals is an exercise in *empathy*—honoring our inherent connection to another being, and to the Universe we both inhabit. Empathy is the secret language that binds us to animals, across, as Louv notes, "the mysterious between" that separates species, and can separate us from one another. Spending time with animals, either domestic or, when safe and possible, in the wild, is another clear, simple, yet profound way to honor our connection to nature.

Louv's idea of the permeability of empathy extends beyond animals, too—it can encompass art and music and literature and anything else that serves to reveal to us the experiences of others. All these beautiful creations—a brilliant painting, a delicate melody, a powerful book, or a flower or an animal—put us in proximity with other entities that share or have shared existence with us and now offer a vision or perspective that is universal, enlightening, and binding.

The more we exercise this inherent empathy for others, especially through nature, the more illuminated our path through life becomes. So go ahead: Touch the sea. Talk to a pony. Feed a bird. Find a way in your life to honor nature.

Art is when you hear a knocking from
your soul—and you answer.

TERRI GUILLEMETS

33

The Power of Art

As you've seen, I've included some poems in these pages, because I love poetry and I think it's uniquely moving and inspiring. Here are a few lines from the poem "High Tide" by one of my favorite poets, Christine Osvald-Mruz (who also happens to be my sister):

> Against a distant cliff, a tiny sailboat wafts.
>   Seagulls drift.
> Near the shore, a small wave rises.

Okay, now that you've read it, I want you to know that you have just improved your mental and physical health.

We spoke about how honoring our connection to nature can benefit us in meaningful ways. The same is true of art. Scientific studies have established a strong connection between creating and enjoying art and our overall wellness as humans, and as a result, healthcare providers are incorporating the arts into their treatments. According to the World Health Organization, "Including the arts in health care delivery has been shown to support positive clinical outcomes for patients . . . Benefits are seen across several markers, including health promotion, the management of health conditions and illness, and disease prevention."

Imagine that! Simply enjoying works of art—going to a concert, visiting a museum, reading poetry—alters our brain in a way that is extremely beneficial to us and to the world as a whole. But how can merely gazing at the *Mona Lisa* make us healthier? Exposure to the arts, or "art intervention," as some scientists call it, "showed more functional connectivity in the frontal and parietal brain cortices," determined a study published in the Public Library of Science journal *PLOS*. "This correlated with increased psychological/stress resistance . . . and demonstrated the neural effects of visual art production on psychological resilience in adulthood."

Simply put, art is good for us.

This, of course, is neither news, nor new. "For thousands of years, people have been using arts like singing, painting and dancing for healing purposes," declares the Mayo Clinic. "Modern healthcare settings continue to use art to help treat specific conditions, contribute to overall well-being and even help prevent diseases." Many of us integrate art into our lives instinctively and sometimes without even realizing it—we doodle on a margin to relieve stress, or we sing in the shower to unwind. To live a life free of art, even if you don't think of yourself as an artistic person, is to deprive yourself of an enormous stream of resources that can enrich your life.

One way to tap into that stream is to be an artist yourself. I'm not talking about becoming a professional artist, though if that is your calling, then by all means you should heed it. I'm talking about creating a work of art that comes from your heart. Perhaps you've tried to paint a landscape, or sculpt clay, or write a short story, and the results have dismayed you enough to make you quit. But producing something great is *not* the point of making art.

The act of creating—letting that art flow through you—leads you on a path of connection and illumination. Because the Other Side has shown me that *no artist ever works alone.* We are connected to a team of Light that works through and with us, and in turn we shine brighter because of them. Art is an expression of this guided act of creation.

There is a story I found on the internet that is usually attributed to the writer Kurt Vonnegut and that is, whoever it comes from, a beautiful, timeless lesson for us all:

> When I was 15 I spent a month working on an archeological dig. I was talking to one of the archeologists one day during our lunch break and he asked those kinds of "getting to know you" questions you ask young people: Do you play sports? What's your favorite subject? And I told him, no I don't play any sports. I do theater, I'm in choir, I play the violin and piano, I used to take art classes.
>
> And he went WOW. That's amazing! And I said, "Oh no, but I'm not any good at ANY of them."
>
> And he said something then that I will never forget and which absolutely blew my mind because no one had ever said anything like it to me before: "I don't think being good at things is the point of doing them. I think you've got all these wonderful experiences with different skills, and that all teaches you things and makes you an interesting person, no matter how well you do them."
>
> And that honestly changed my life. Because I went from a failure, someone who hadn't been talented enough at anything to excel, to someone who did things because I enjoyed them. I had been raised in such an achievement-oriented environment, so inundated with the myth of Talent, that I thought it was only worth doing things if you could "Win" at them.

The point of art is the pleasure and joy it brings us, either through creating it or simply by exposing ourselves to it. Attending an artistic event is just as beneficial as sitting down to create art. These benefits are so well documented that Penn State University began a medical humanities program that requires medical students to take a class such as Impressionism and the Art of Communication in their fourth year. At Yale and Harvard, medical students need to visit museums and write reports describing the works of art they saw in detail. Studies have found that art improves critical thinking and empathy, builds bias awareness, and eases pain and depression—all of which explains why the world's top universities and colleges have integrated art into a variety of disciplines. Meanwhile, the American Congress of Rehabilitation Medicine says that just observing art can:

- Increase serotonin levels (which positively affects mood and emotion).

- Increase blood flow to the part of the brain associated with pleasure.

- Foster new ways of thinking.

- Help you to imagine a more hopeful future.

We can introduce these benefits into our lives by bringing art into our paths. The art we choose to enjoy doesn't matter—it can be dance, music, poetry, drama, sculpture, paintings, performance art, and on and on. London's Global University did a study that found that just sitting in a theater with other theatergoers and watching a show not only affects you emotionally through the performance but brings you the pleasure of being in an audience atmosphere, where everyone is connected by the performance.

This connection to your fellow theatergoers is not just conjecture. The LGU researchers monitored the heart rates and electrodermal activity of twelve audience members enjoying a live performance of the musical *Dreamgirls*. To their surprise, they discovered that the theatergoers' hearts were beating in unison, and their pulses were slowing down and speeding up *at the same rate.*

Watching a show synchronized everyone's heartbeat! What an astonishing display of the power of art in our lives. The same researchers earlier discovered that watching a live theatrical performance has the same stimulative benefit as performing twenty-eight minutes of cardio-vascular activity.

Enjoying art is not a passive thing. It engages us mentally, spiritu-ally, emotionally, and, yes, biologically. (This truth is explored more in the book *Your Brain on Art*, by Susan Magsamen and Ivy Ross, which I highly recommend.) The pure and absolute beauty of a perfectly crafted note of music, or of a sublime brushstroke across a canvas, or of the simple stringing together of thirteen words (as in the poem that opens this chapter) can reconnect us to our humanity, open our eyes to the splendor and magic of existence, make us feel more vital and alive, and illuminate our paths through life.

The message, then, is to invest in creativity—to bring art into your journey. That investment doesn't have to be massive or even time-consuming. You can begin by picking up an artistic hobby—journaling, sketching, collaging—and working on it for a few minutes a day. Or you can go bigger and join a local chorus or theater group. Or buy a canvas and some paint and indulge your imagination. What's clear is that opening your eyes and mind to your own creativity, and to the creativity of those around you, is a deeply meaningful and beneficial way to honor your connection to the world. It is a way of connecting to something that is greater than yourself—and to the great swirl of col-lective energy.

So maybe instead of "an apple a day," you can try "a poem a day." The payoff, I promise you, will be worth it.

I wish I could show you when you are lonely or in darkness the astonishing light of your own being.

JAFIZ OF SHIRAZ

PART FOUR

TURNING UP
THE LIGHT

H ere's the truth: you are a light being. Living an illuminated life means honoring that truth.

It means living a life of connection, knowing that you are guided by a Team of Light on the Other Side. It also means knowing that your role here on earth is more meaningful and powerful than you can fathom.

It is embracing the truth that you are a spiritual being. It is honoring the reality that you are here on earth right now in a body for a reason — and that reason is about collective love. And while we may not always be able to see and understand the many ways that we are part of each other's journeys, living an illuminated life means *knowing* that we are tied to others in profound ways. It is a life that honors the oneness.

But it's about more than that. It's about how we carry our energy in this world.

We've talked about how an illuminated life is one in which you are guided to understand the important role of nature and art, but what does an illuminated life look like, in practical terms? How can we turn up the light in our own practices? How can we use our free will to steer the ship of our soul in our bodies onto an illuminated path? How can we then use this understanding to navigate each day as we embrace our paths, as well as the longer, winding paths of our lives?

Our Teams of Light are always trying to reveal to us this simple truth: the answers are not outside of us, they are within. We hold the light inside of us.

Nothing can dim the light which
shines from within.

MAYA ANGELOU

34

A Little Handbook to an Illuminated Life

There are many things I have been guided by my Team of Light about over the past many years when it comes to understanding, living, and embracing an illuminated life, and I'd like to share them here with you. You can think of this as a secret handbook to life, gifted to you by the Other Side.

The Power of Embracing a Positive Mindset

> Whether you think you can, or you think
> you can't, you're right.
>
> *Henry Ford*

Both our attitude and our mindset are of utmost importance when being guided to the secret path of an illuminated life. Living an illuminated life means paying attention to what we give our energy to, what we give our attention to, and the intentions we set, because they matter more than we realize.

What will you give your attention to?

Will you dive into every argument that comes your way—and take anger and negativity into your energy field? Or will you make a choice to release it?

Did you know that studies have shown that just one minute of anger weakens your immune system? And researchers at Penn State University found that negative moods not only change the way in which the immune response functions but also increase inflammation throughout the body.

By contrast, a positive attitude and mindset can be game changers on your external path, as well as on your inner path to happiness.

And this happiness can be achieved without the money mindset so many of us feel pressured to embrace. For we can be truly wealthy without money. In fact, researchers from the University of Barcelona concluded that the old adage is true: Money does not, it turns out, buy happiness. Instead, what they found is that the key to happiness is a connection with nature, a sense of community, and having time to relax.

"When people are comfortable, safe, and free to enjoy life within a strong community, they are happy—regardless of whether or not they are making any money," states Chris Barrington-Leigh, one of the co-authors of the study. This supports earlier research that shows how when societies grow richer, there is actually no overall increase in happiness! In fact, a lot of wealthy Western countries are plagued by high levels of depression. Psychologists point to envy about money as a significant contributing factor to this depression. Couple that with the workaholic mindset distancing us from one another and nature, and you'll see how focusing your attention only on money as a path to an illuminated life will leave you feeling empty and depressed. In fact, another study of more than twelve hundred Americans found that those who valued time over money were actually happier!

So—what should we be focusing our attention and intention on?

The Power of Gratitude

Studies show that adopting a gratitude mindset can help people feel significantly happier. This applies even to people already struggling with mental health issues, who, research shows, can lower levels of anxiety and depression through this mindset. Gratitude is a bit of a magic formula. It is inherent to embracing an illuminated life. Its effect is far-reaching. It has also been shown to help people build strong relationships and improve sleep, thus boosting their immune system. Gratitude can even change your brain-wave activity in positive ways!

One way to get into a gratitude mindset is to simply write down five things you are grateful for each day. Or just before falling asleep, think of five things you are grateful for.

Researchers have found another truly effective way to embrace a gratitude mindset is by writing a letter of gratitude to someone you are grateful for. The mere act of writing it can help you appreciate people in your life, and shift your focus and mindset from negative to positive. (But by all means, go ahead and send it after you write it! You never know how your words might impact someone else and shift them into the positive as well! You might even start a great chain of positivity!) In fact, one study revealed that the brains of people who wrote gratitude letters showed greater activation in the medial prefrontal cortex (measured with an fMRI scanner) three months after writing those letters — revealing that gratitude may have lasting effects on the brain!

> When I go to bed and cannot sleep,
> I don't waste time by counting sheep;
> I count all my blessings one by one.
>
> **Bing Crosby**

Embrace Being a Lifelong Learner

Be a critical thinker. Be open to ideas.

Share your experiences with others.

Share feelings, stories, worldviews, ideologies. This is how we learn from one another and grow!

Be a seeker. Seek out new information. Read. Join organizations that interest you. Go to the library!

Honor Your Ongoing Connection to Loved Ones Who Have Crossed

Ask for reassurance of presence through signs and messages.

We can create a language with our Teams of Light. We can ask for specific signs—and there will also be times our loved ones will establish signs of their own. I talk about this a lot in my earlier book, *Signs: The Secret Language of the Universe*.

Take, for example, the way Sarah Graham's father let her know he was still with her, loving her and guiding her, after he crossed.

Sarah, an artist living in the UK, wrote me a message on Instagram, and shared a very special story:

> I've just started reading *Signs: The Secret Language of the Universe* after a friend recommended it. WOW! It's everything I've believed but been unable to fully articulate for a long time, beautifully expressed in black & white!
>
> I have to tell you the point in my life when I stopped being skeptical.
>
> In 2004, my beloved Dad died of cancer. I was only 26 and I was heartbroken. Dad was incredibly intelligent, loved literature and language & of course his favorite game was Scrabble.

A month after he died, I took his Scrabble set back to the home I lived in with my then boyfriend and said I wanted to play Dad's Scrabble.

I went first and felt for 7 tiles in the bag. I took them out & opened my hand, they spelt

DADDY_X

I've also had many incidences with dragon flies, and I see 11.11 all the time and know it's a sign I'm on the right path. I look forward to seeing the signs all around me each day. They enrich my life and make me feel unafraid.

Thank you 🙏
Sarah Graham xx

It's magical to get signs of reassurance and guidance from those we love who have crossed. Embracing an illuminated life means honoring this connection and allowing it to be an active part of our lives. This can include talking to our loved ones who have crossed (either in our thoughts or out loud), talking to others about them and about our love for them, as well as sharing the signs we get from them, celebrating their ongoing presence in our lives (birthdays, anniversaries, crossing dates) and doing things in their name (they especially love this!).

So speak to them.

Tell stories about them—laugh—be joyful.

And also know relationships can still heal (often those who have crossed have new perspectives). Anytime we ask for forgiveness or grant it, it is given and received.

Invite your loved ones who have crossed into your dreams.

Acknowledge the signs/messages they send, thank them, and share the story of connection with others.

Do something beautiful in their name. Run a marathon. Pay for a stranger's ice cream. Give someone flowers. It doesn't matter what it is. Big or small. It all matters.

And if you think it is a sign, it *is*.

Look for ways to give and receive love.

Be kind. Because as Aesop's Fables remind us: "No act of kindness, no matter how small, is ever wasted."

Forgive.

Honor the value of all life.

Be a Light Worker: Find and honor your own unique gifts, and help others do the same. Support others' light and growth!

Celebrate positive-energy people here. Gravitate toward them. Avoid the ones who are negative.

Part of living an illuminated life is protecting, honoring, and preserving your light. Just as you can be guided *to* people, you can be guided *away from* people, too.

Avoid people who devalue your light and act in disrespectful ways. People who are constantly negative or belittling. People who are stuck in anger and limiting beliefs.

Follow your passion (whatever lights you up).

Trust your pulls, because you are part of a great chain of light. Think of the butterfly effect. You do not know what you will put into motion: You might bring about meaningful change and even save lives!

You never know when a small act you do or a positive word you say will have powerful and reaching consequences.

You just may create a great river of light.

First Lesson

Lie back, daughter, let your head
be tipped back in the cup of my hand.
Gently, and I will hold you. Spread
your arms wide, lie out on the stream
and look high at the gulls. A dead-
man's-float is face down. You will dive
and swim soon enough where this tidewater
ebbs to the sea. Daughter, believe
me, when you tire on the long thrash
to your island, lie up, and survive.
As you float now, where I held you
and let go, remember when fear
cramps your heart what I told you:
lie gently and wide to the light-year
stars, lie back, and the sea will hold you.

PHILIP BOOTH

35

Home Base

I've often hoped that everything I've taught my own three children about being connected to the Universe and guided by a Team of Light would help them navigate their own paths in life, especially during the challenging and dark times. These periods of hardship are as much a part of the journey as the light and joyous times. As parents, we strive to create a safe home base for our children to grow in, which includes, in the material world sense, a home. But we also strive to help them create a safe inner world for themselves. One where they have the tools and know that they can, as the writer and Light Worker Glennon Doyle likes to say, "Do hard things." Doing hard things often means dealing with hard things. Things that throw us off our equilibrium, things that challenge our soul, things that make the illuminated path sometimes a little harder to find.

We all want to protect those we love from the harms and sadnesses of the world, but obviously none of us can do that. Still, as parents, we hope our children's journeys are gentle, and that they get to preserve the innocence of their childhood as long as possible, for it is sacred and pure. The best we can do is prepare them for whatever journey they go on and have confidence in knowing that they, too, are guided.

But it is so hard when the darkness comes.

My youngest daughter, Juliet, is a truly stellar human being—smart, considerate, and giving—and, though this is something parents tend to say, she is wise far beyond her years. She is also deeply empathetic. I am constantly impressed by her poise and curiosity and kindness.

I was out of the house on an errand at 3:00 P.M. on a Monday when my cell phone rang. I could see from the screen that Juliet was calling. Fifteen years old and a sophomore in high school, Juliet typically called me for a ride home around this time. But when I picked up the call, someone else's voice came on. It was Juliet's high school administrator, telling me that Juliet couldn't talk because she was too upset and that she had asked her to call me. I could hear Juliet crying in the background. The administrator explained that one of Juliet's good friends, Clara,* had died.

A wave of absolute sadness came over me. Clara, who was one year ahead of Juliet at the high school, and Juliet were amazing friends. They'd connected and become fast friends the year before, when they had both volunteered to run a face-painting booth at a charity event benefiting a mental health group called Sounds of Silence (SOS) that one of their teachers had founded. They were in the Art Honor Society together (a tight-knit group of wonderful kids), and they were always talking, always laughing, sharing their own little language of girlhood and friendship. They also connected on a deep, spiritual level and shared a sensitivity and uncommon compassion for others. They both brought so much light and kindness into the world.

The physical crossing of anyone in a teenager's life can be momentous. The death of a peer, especially a close friend, can change your view of the world forever. So I knew Clara's death had to be absolutely devastating for Juliet.

Juliet managed to get on the phone with me. She asked if I could come to the school and pick her up, along with several of her friends

---

*Name and identifying details changed to protect anonymity.

whose parents were still at work, and bring them all to our home so that they could be together.

I put the third row up in my SUV, picked them up at the school, and brought everyone to our house. There, these innocent children, weeping and raw with grief, tried to make sense of the tragedy. My son, Hayden, eighteen, who knew Clara from school, was there, too, also distraught. Clara's older sister, a senior at the high school whom Juliet had been friends with for years, came along to the house as well. She was outwardly calm but clearly in shock, and she told everyone what had happened.

Clara had taken her own life.

Any death is painful and difficult to comprehend. But suicide is especially traumatic and complicated for those left behind. How were these teenagers supposed to deal with their friend crossing in this way? What could anyone possibly say to help them cope? On top of all that, Juliet had a huge Advanced Placement test coming up in just two days, a test she'd spent a year preparing for. How on earth was she supposed to take that test after what had happened?

This was one of those times when I wondered, *Have I given Juliet enough tools to handle this? Can any parent? Can anyone?* Practically, all I could do for Juliet now was tell her that I was there for her whenever she wanted to talk, and that her friends could stay with her in our house for as long as they all wanted.

Well, there was one other thing I could do, though I resisted doing it. Eventually, though, I caved, because later that evening, when everyone had left and Juliet and I were standing together in the kitchen, I felt someone pushing through from the Other Side, and I knew it was Clara trying to pass a message to Juliet. The message came through clearly, though I didn't understand it. She showed me chewing gum and, more specifically, a gum wrapper. She then showed me herself drawing pictures on Juliet's arm. She made me feel she was in a place of love, and that she was fully healed. I told Juliet that Clara said all this and explained what I'd seen.

Immediately, Juliet stopped crying.

"Mom," she said, "that was our thing. In Art Honor Society we'd always sit together and she would play with my gum wrappers and draw on my arms." Then, quietly, she said, "Wow."

And a small, quiet smile emerged on her lips.

Hayden was there in the kitchen with us, too. He was deeply moved by the message Clara sent.

"You guys know you never need me in order to connect with her," said. "You know you can ask her to send you signs, right? To confirm that she is safe and in a place of love and still with you and present. You can still talk to her. She will hear you. What's more, she will help guide you on your grief journey. You never need me in order to communicate with her."

A day later, I got a package in the mail. It was a decorative room spray I'd ordered weeks earlier on Etsy and forgotten about. I opened the package, took out the spray, and then noticed, at the very bottom of the box, the tiniest bit of paper folded up into a shape. I held it in my hand and saw it was a delicate little origami crane, no bigger than my pinky nail. (The company I ordered the spray from was called the Paper Crane Apothecary.) For some reason, I knew this little paper crane was meant for Juliet.

"This may sound odd," I told Juliet when she arrived home from school, "but this came in the mail today and I know I am supposed to give it to you." I asked her to put out her palm and in it I placed the tiniest of origami cranes.

She stared at it for a moment, and then smiled again. "Oh my god, Mom," she said, "this is my sign with Clara. It's the sign I asked her to send me, an origami animal. It's because she used to make them for me and our friends out of Post-it notes. She would make them for all of us and give them to us as little presents. That was what she always did."

We both sat quiet for a long moment, thanking Clara for the love and guidance.

Shortly after that, Hayden texted me, *You're not gonna believe this.*

He sent a picture of a blue deer with antlers, standing on the windowsill of a classroom.

I called him right away.

His voice was excited on the phone. "Mom, when we were in the kitchen the other day and you said we could ask Clara for a sign, I did. And I made it really, really specific. I told her in my thoughts that I wanted her to send me a blue deer, but it had to have antlers and it had to be standing. I didn't tell anyone about it. Today, when I got to IB Politics class, my teacher called me up to her desk to talk to me about a project I have to complete. While we were talking, I looked over to the windowsill right next to her and there was a little figure of a blue deer with antlers standing, just like I'd envisioned it in my mind!"

Talk about specific!

"Hayden, that is amazing!" I told him.

"I know," he said. "It worked! It's wild! I just texted the picture to Juliet, too—and told her! It's so comforting!"

But I'd noticed something else in the picture, something Hayden hadn't picked up on yet. It seemed to me that Clara had sent a double sign, in case there was any doubt left that it was from her.

The window the deer stood against had a sign posted on the outside with the room number: 205. But because the sign was inverted from our view (the numbers facing the courtyard outside), it appeared in reverse in the picture as 502, and it was positioned directly above the deer on the windowsill.

The number 502—or May 2—was the date of Clara's crossing.

More signs followed. Hayden went to a fishing supply store with some friends, and when he got to the register, there were boxes and boxes of a certain brand of fishing lures piled up on the counter and impossible to miss. The brand name included Clara's name, and the logo included THE BEST. (Juliet laughed and said that was absolutely Clara's sense of humor.)

Juliet and her friends continued to encounter Clara's name repeatedly, including on a national test that one of the friends took the week after Clara crossed. On the test, only three random names were used as an example for one of the prompts, and one of those names was Clara. The name appeared numerous other times on the test as well. This was Clara letting her friends and classmates know that she was right there with them.

Then there was the Friday night that all of Clara's friends gathered in one friend's yard to have their own informal memorial ceremony. While they were sharing memories of Clara, Clara's favorite animal, a bunny, appeared and sat crouching nearby for the entire two hours.

Juliet decided to up the ante and asked Clara to send her not just any generic origami animal as a sign, but specifically a purple origami butterfly. The next day at school in one of Juliet's classes, there were student presentations. One was about suicide prevention. Juliet felt too raw and overwhelmed to sit through it. The teacher allowed her to leave the classroom and go for a walk during the duration of the presentation. Juliet walked the quiet hallways of the school, going downstairs, passing through a silent wing where testing was taking place. She was trying to focus on her breathing, keep calm, and remind herself that Clara was in a place of love, when she noticed what looked like a small scrap of paper discarded on the floor. Her eyes narrowed onto it. It was purple. She walked closer and picked it up.

It was a purple origami butterfly.

It made no sense. She had no idea where it came from or why it was on the floor. It almost seemed too unlikely to be real. It seemed like something out of a movie script, or part of a magic trick. And yet there it was, in her hand.

A purple origami butterfly from Clara.

Just like she had asked for.

Somehow, Juliet made it through her important AP test, and two other AP tests she had to take the following week. How she managed to pull that off, in between preparing a eulogy and delivering it at Clara's private memorial, I'll never know. But the body keeps score, and at

10:00 one evening shortly after Clara's memorial, Juliet, who had been resting in her bed, came stumbling down the stairs and into the family room where her father and I were sitting.

"Mom, Dad, I think something is really wrong," she said as we helped settle her on the couch. "I was just lying in bed and all of a sudden I got so dizzy. Dizzier than I've ever been in my life. I had a hard time walking down here, but I was scared I was going to die in my bed, so I came down. Something is wrong. I don't know, I just feel really confused right now, like my brain isn't working right."

My mind raced. Dizziness, disorientation.

"You're going to be okay—we've got you," I said.

And then the left side of her face started to go numb.

Now, migraines run in our family, and Juliet had gotten one once before when she was in eighth grade—an optic migraine (like I get), during which her vision fizzled out to white. These migraines can make you feel disoriented and confused. Hayden had gotten one before, too, but this was different. All these signs resembled a stroke.

We needed to go to the hospital.

"Everything is going to be okay," I told her. "We need to go and get this checked out. But I'm right here with you. I've got you." I tried to reassure her, my voice remaining calm so as not to betray the myriad places my mind was going.

We helped Juliet into the car and got to the hospital quickly. Thankfully there was no traffic. When we arrived, hospital staffers immediately did an intake and sent us to the pediatric emergency waiting room. The room was almost empty. There was only one other child there, a little girl who appeared to be about four years old and was with her mom and grandma.

We sat in the chairs, waiting. "I'm really scared, Mom," Juliet said. "I can't feel the left side of my face anymore. My thoughts feel all confused. Something is really wrong." The pace of her language was slowing, too. She almost sounded the way someone would sound if they were drunk and trying to act sober. But she hadn't ingested anything.

"We are in the best place possible," I reassured her. "We are going to find out what is wrong and get you help. Everything is going to be okay. I'm right here." Simultaneously I directed a silent prayer to the Other Side requesting help from both our Teams of Light. A sign, anything, something to let us know things would be okay.

At that moment, the receptionist called in the little girl, the only other patient in the waiting room.

"Clara," she called out, clear as a bell.

I looked at Juliet and she looked at me. In that moment we knew that everything would somehow be okay. We knew we were being guided. We knew we weren't alone. And, Juliet knew, Clara was right there with her, letting her know that everything was all right. I mean, what are the odds that the only other person in that waiting room would be named Clara? It is not that common a name. And yet, in the exact moment I'd asked for a sign of support and guidance and comfort, that was the name we heard.

Juliet later told me, "My first urge was to text Clara when that happened and say, *Oh, ha ha, this is so funny, I keep hearing your name everywhere,* but I remembered the text wouldn't go through. But still, I thought it was just a beautiful nod to me, just as I was feeling so miserable and so scared. It was just very comforting to hear Clara's name. I knew it was her telling me I'd be okay."

It turned out—after the ER doctors called an urgent pediatric stroke code and requested an immediate CT scan, an MRI, and overnight monitoring with an EEG for a possible seizure—that Juliet *was* okay.

But the Universe wasn't done sending me signs. The doctor who came into her room in the morning to deliver the final prognosis? Well, although he was wearing a mask (as was protocol at the hospital even now that Covid had eased) and his face was mostly obstructed from view, I knew immediately who he was. Dr. Marzuk Masub had been one of my students, a stellar student in fact, when I taught English at Herricks High School. It was so beautiful to see him in that moment decade and a half later, as a poised, thoughtful, well-spoken doctor ... the news that my daughter was going to be fine. When he recognized me, we had a great hug.

According to the prognosis, Juliet had a severe migraine with an atypical aura but was otherwise okay—just as Clara had assured her while we were waiting to be seen at the hospital.

I've heard about thousands of amazing signs sent from loved ones who have crossed, and they all dazzle me in some way, but the signs that came to my children from Clara touched me in a way no other signs have. I was so worried about how Juliet and Hayden would handle their friend's tragic passing. I worried that the darkness and the sadness of it would stay and seep in, crippling them emotionally and making it impossible to function. I worried that a loss so tragic and profound might send Juliet, who is very sensitive, into a hopeless depression. I worried that I hadn't prepared them for such an enormous and saddening event.

What I learned, however, is that by talking to them about signs and other facets of our enduring consciousness, I had helped them be open to the signs Clara sent them. I know Clara's messages changed their grief journey. The signs let them know that Clara is in a place of safety and love, and that she is now guiding them from the Other Side.

We are all guided by those we love who have crossed. I've learned that, especially with crossings by suicide, those who passed have missions that include helping their loved ones here on earth with their grief and healing journeys. I shared this very personal story with you with Juliet and Hayden's blessing, because we all want to convey to you that the Universe is constantly trying to light our path through life, to guide us, to help us through all the harms and sadness of life. The Universe, our Teams of Light, our loved ones who have crossed, all want us to live the best, happiest, most joyful lives we possibly can. All we have to do to receive that guidance is be open to seeing and feeling it.

"For me, it was just really nice to get all these signs from Clara because it feels like she's still here," Juliet says. "When you get signs like that, you realize they're not actually gone, they're just somewhere else that we can't comprehend. Somewhere where we can't reach out and physically touch them, but where they can somehow reach out and connect to us. And it makes you realize that they're okay and it's going to be okay for you even if you feel at the time that you can't deal with it.

"But the ultimate importance of Clara's messages is that they showed me that she is okay and comfortable and at peace. They were just her saying hi to me in her funny little humorous way. And I think that's just such a beautiful thing to happen, you know?"

36

The Secret Path

I have this dream where I'm flying.

Not in a plane—just me in the sky. I'm still my human self, still in my body, except I'm defying all logic and soaring through the air like a bird. Sometimes the dream is a lucid dream, which, as I described earlier, is a dream that you are conscious of having and that you can often control. In these dreams, when I become aware that I'm flying, I feel total elation. I feel like flying is the most fun I've ever had or could ever have, and I don't want the dream to end. Flying is simply the most incredible feeling I can imagine, and I've been shown that this is what it feels like when we leave our bodies and become pure consciousness and are no longer bound by earthly constraints.

I love my flying dreams.

In our actual, physical lives, our awareness of our actions and abilities is equally lucid yet far more limited. We cannot, of course, fly on our own just because we want to. Yet we *can* control everything we do and every action we take by being mindful of our thoughts and intentions. We can design our lives just as we sometimes get to design our lucid dreams. This is an awesome power to have, and it's what allows us to steer our paths and shape our lives.

We have the ability to actively make choices that align with our goal of living vibrant, engaged, guided, illuminated lives.

That is what this book is about: seeing, exploring, and owning the light we shine out on the world, and the light that is shined back down on us to illuminate our paths. Nothing is ever guaranteed, nor can we expect to have stress-free, pain-free lives. But we always have the choice of how to embrace the beautiful, precious life we've been given. We decide how we want to navigate the hazards and pitfalls and challenges of existence, and how deeply we appreciate the beauty and wonder and blessings of life, and how much we honor our connection to one another.

We have the power to make forgiveness, gratitude, empathy, and love the currency of our lives, and to pay attention to, and allow ourselves to be led by, the signs and guidance we all receive from the Universe and our Teams of Light.

I hope that the examples in these chapters have inspired you to always be open to the gifts available to you. The Universe is always, always sending us the guiding lights we need to find our highest paths, and all we have to do to see these lights—*all we have to do*—is be open to seeing them.

And once we see them, we realize the illuminating guidance we need and hope for existed within us all along.

How can we be open to this light? What does being open mean? In one way, it's as easy as asking for, looking for, and accepting signs from the Other Side. For example, ask for an orange dragon with a short tail, and be ready to see one. Yet there are any number of ways we can keep ourselves prepared to receive guidance from the Universe, and actively taking these steps sets us on a course to live a truly illuminated life.

Chief among them, I believe, is striving to remain an inquisitive person. A perpetual student in the school of life. The invitation in these chapters is to embark on a lifelong quest of learning and not shy away from the mysteries of existence. Be open to everything, but be critical in your thinking. There are so many yet-to-be-fully-accepted phenomena—past lives, reincarnation, life after death—that challenge some of the scientific beliefs we tend to cling to. But we should re-member that there were similar concepts that humanity initially ridi-culed but that have become sacred and honored truths. For centuries we believed the earth was flat, until we came to accept it's a sphere. The notion that humans evolved from apelike ancestors was sacrile-gious until it became scientific fact. The idea that germs cause disease was a fringe viewpoint until everyone started washing their hands.

Science probes, learns, and corrects itself.

And so can we. We are all on a journey together, and everything we do or think has a ripple effect on the tide of our existence and the col-lective lesson in love we are here to learn. Living an engaged, guided, and illuminated life means always being open and curious and seeking and accepting of the bonds we share as beings, and the ways we are all tied to the Universe.

I wish you great success and joy in your journeys, and I wish you luck in staying true to these ideals, because, if you do, even in the dark-est of times, you will find that you are already on the secret path to an illuminated life.

Author's Note

Every person whose story is included in this book granted me express permission to feature them. I have used the individuals' real names and identifying characteristics by their request, except in one instance when I was asked to exclude a last name and one instance when I noted that I changed a name for anonymity. I am deeply grateful to all of them for sharing their experiences with me, and for encouraging me to share them with you here, in the pages of *Guided*. I hope you will find their stories as moving and inspiring as I do.

Acknowledgments

Alex Tresniowski: Your light, kindness, and talent are immeasurable. Thank you for journeying with me again on this book—and for all the time, energy, and light you have brought, and always bring, to all you do. This book wouldn't be here without you.

Whitney Frick, Dial Press publisher and editor-in-chief: How lucky am I that the Universe guided me to you? You are an extraordinary editor and friend. I am so grateful for your patience, encouragement, and guidance—they have been a gift to me on this journey. You shine so brightly and carry it all with such humility!

To the rest of my incredible team at Dial Press:

Avideh Bashirrad, deputy publisher; Debbie Aroff, marketing director; Corina Diez, marketing manager; Michelle Jasmine, publicity director; Hope Hathcock, publicist; Talia Cieslinski, assistant editor; Rebecca Berlant, managing editor; Sarah Feightner, production manager; Ralph Fowler, interior designer; Donna Cheng, cover design and art direction; and Evan Camfield, production editor—it truly takes a village and I am so grateful for the ways you have offered your light and talent to bring this into the world!

To my team at Little, Brown UK, Jillian Young, Aimee Kitson, and Narjas Zatat—thank you for your light, energy, expertise, and kindness! I feel so fortunate to have such an amazing team across the pond!

Margaret Riley King: Thank you for your constant guidance, love, kindness, and support. Your light makes such a difference in my world!

Jennifer Rudolph Walsh: fairy godmother to all, but especially me. This book would not exist in the world without the light of you. You continue to inspire me every day. I just might be your biggest fan ever. . . .

To my amazing, inspiring mom, Linda Osvald—anything good I do here on earth is because of your love. You are the strongest and kindest person I know, and I have always known how blessed I am to be your daughter. I hit the mom jackpot. I learn from you every day. You have always been, and will always be, my greatest inspiration. I love you so much more than I could ever express.

To my husband, Garrett, a man of character, integrity, and kindness: Journeying through life with you is a great gift. You have brought so much light to my life, and you continue to.

To Ashley, my first born—the light you brought with you transformed my heart and life forever. You have already changed the world in extraordinary ways, and I know you will continue to do so. May you feel all the love and guidance surrounding you always. May you see the dazzling light of your own being.

To Hayden, my Bubba—you have grown into an insightful and eloquent young man. May you continue to grow in kindness and love and always trust and honor your intuition. May you create a life of beauty and meaning. You have brought so much beauty and meaning to mine.

To Juliet, my bottled sunshine—you bring light and kindness and creativity wherever you go to whatever you do. How lucky we all are that you are part of this world; how blessed I am to get to be your mom. I learn from you every day.

To Cam—you have brought a new layer of light and love and joy to my world and I am so grateful that I get to be your Oona. You are a force of love, full of joy, with an incredible sense of humor. You are a gift of light in our lives.

Christine Osvald-Mruz: Having you as a sister has been a gift from the start. Your empathy and all that you observe in life are incredible. You are one of my favorite poets. May your poems reach out into this world, carrying the light of you.

John William, brother extraordinaire: The spark of light you bring to things is contagious. Being your sister is a gift.

Ann Wood, my incredible, classy, beautiful, strong aunt: I am blessed to be your niece!

To the rest of my wonderful family—my wonderful nieces, nephews, and in-laws—John, Mat, Willy, Henry, Peter, Natasha, Maya, Zoey, John, Angela, Angela, Jason, Lucille, John, Emily, Jay, Johnny, Jimmy, Kerry, Joey, Brian, Kevin, and Danny: I am so grateful for the light of each of you!

Dad/TT/Omi/PopPop/DundeeYette/Nani/Vicki/Apa—and the rest of my TOL: Thank you for all the signs and all the love. I feel your guidance every day.

To my extraordinary friends, old and new—you know who you are and I am so grateful the Universe connected us. Being on this journey together and exploring it all is a great gift. Your laughter, light, insight, kindness, and joy transform my world. There are no coincidences in life; friendship is sacred. I honor the light of each of you!

To you, the reader—may you always feel the love, guidance, and support of your team of light—and may you see the light of your own soul's beauty, always. Never forget, you are connected to everything . . . you matter, and the world is a better place because you are here.

Suggested Reading
Based on Books Mentioned

Childs, Samantha. *Henri and the Magnificent Snort: A Children's Book About Bullying, Belonging, and Love.* Samantha Childs, 2024.

Dimmick, Christine. *Detox Your Home: A Guide to Removing Toxins from Your Life and Bringing Health into Your Home.* Rowman & Littlefield, 2018.

Kelly, Edward F., Emily Williams Kelly, Adam Crabtree, Alan Gauld, Michael Grosso, and Bruce Greyson. *Irreducible Mind: Toward a Psychology for the 21st Century.* Rowman & Littlefield, 2010.

Lewis, Sarah Elizabeth. *The Rise: Creativity, the Gift of Failure, and the Search for Mastery.* Simon & Schuster, 2015.

Louv, Richard. *Our Wild Calling: How Connecting with Animals Can Transform Our Lives—and Save Theirs.* Algonquin Books of Chapel Hill, 2020.

Magsamen, Susan, and Ivy Ross. *Your Brain on Art: How the Arts Transform Us.* Random House, 2024.

McTaggart, Lynne. *The Intention Experiment: Using Your Thoughts to Change Your Life and the World.* Atria, 2013.

Miłosz, Czesław. *A Book of Luminous Things: An International Anthology of Poetry.* Harcourt, 1998.

Ober, Clinton, Stephen T. Sinatra, and Martin Zucker. *Earthing: The Most Important Health Discovery Ever?* Basic Health Publications, 2014.

Osvald-Mruz, Christine. "Against a Distant Cliff." *Atlanta Review,* Spring/Summer 2025

Powell, Diane Hennacy. *The ESP Enigma: The Scientific Case for Psychic Phenomena.* Walker, 2009.

Rosenberg, Liz. *Children of Paradise.* University of Pittsburgh Press, 1999.

Rosenberg, Liz. *The Laws of Gravity.* Lake Union Publishing, 2013.

Notes

8   *an average of twenty-two vets:* Janet Kemp and Robert Bossarte, "Suicide Data Report—2012," Department of Veterans Affairs, 2012. va.gov/opa/docs/suicide-data -report-2012-final.pdf.

45   *"The criterion is failure"*: William Faulkner, quoted in Stephen Railton, Faulkner at Virginia: An Audio Archive, Virginia Colleges Conference, tape 2, April 15, 1957, tape T-122b. faulkner.lib.virginia.edu/display/wfaudi007_2.html.

47   *"Accidents are important in science"*: "The 'Accidental' Nobel Laureates: 10 Years On," University of Manchester: Graphene, December 6, 2020. sites.se.manchester.ac .uk/graphene/2020/12/06/the-accidental-nobel-laureates-10-years-on.

83   *"We still do not know one thousandth"*: Albert Einstein, quoted in "Some of Einstein's Reflections, Aphorisms and Observations," *New York Times*, March 29, 1972. nytimes.com/1972/03/29/archives/some-of-einsteins-reflections-aphorisms-and -observations.html.

145   *"Research shows that [traumatic] events can trigger"*: "Overcoming Abuse-Related Trauma," Wellmore, January 29, 2021. wellmore.org/post/overcoming-abuse-related -trauma.

146   *"Some research suggests that trauma can affect a person's DNA"*: Rachel Zimmerman, "How Does Trauma Spill from One Generation to the Next?" *Washington Post*, June 12, 2023. washingtonpost.com/wellness/2023/06/12/generational-trauma-passed -healing.

146   *"an emerging area of scientific research that shows how environmental"*: "What Is Epigenetics? The Answer to the Nature vs. Nurture Debate," Center on the Developing Child at Harvard University, February 19, 2019. developingchild.harvard.edu/ resources/infographics/what-is-epigenetics-and-how-does-it-relate-to-child -development.

146   *"the positive psychological change that some individuals"*: Richard Tedeschi, "Transformation After Trauma," *Speaking of Psychology* (podcast), episode 96, American Psychological Association, December 2019. apa.org/news/podcasts/speaking-of -psychology/transformation-trauma.

147   *"can influence the properties of that particle in the past"*: Lisa Zyga, "Physicists Provide Support for Retrocausal Quantum Theory, in Which the Future Influences the Past," Phys.org, July 5, 2017. phys.org/news/2017-07-physicists-retrocausal-quantum -theory-future.html.

193   *"felt the experience of losing a child is by far the worst"*: U.S. Institute of Medicine,

Committee for the Study of Health Consequences of the Stress of Bereavement, "Re actions to Particular Types of Bereavement," in *Bereavement: Reactions, Conse-quences, and Care,* ed. Marian Osterweis, Frederic Solomon, and Morris Green (National Academies Press, 1984), 71–98. ncbi.nlm.nih.gov/books/NBK217848.

193   *"All parents have hopes and dreams"*: U.S. Institute of Medicine, Committee on Palliative and End-of-Life Care for Children and Their Families, "Appendix E: Be-reavement Experiences After the Death of a Child," in *When Children Die: Improv-ing Palliative and End-of-Life Care for Children and Their Families,* ed. Marilyn J. Field and Richard E. Behrman (National Academies Press, 1970), 533–79. ncbi.nlm .nih.gov/books/NBK220798.

223   *Today, the average U.S. citizen spends 86.9 percent:* Mateja Dovjak and Andreja Kukec, "Health Outcomes Related to Built Environments," in *Creating Healthy and Sustainable Buildings: An Assessment of Health Risk Factors* (Springer, 2019), 43–8= ncbi.nlm.nih.gov/books/NBK553922.

227   *"From the beginning of time"*: Clint Ober, "Earthing—Additional Reading 2: Grounding the Human Body to Neutralise Bio-Electrical Stress from Static Electric-ity and EMF," Regenerative Nutrition, January 1, 2000. regenerativenutrition.com. friendly.asp?url=Grounding-the-Human-Body-to-Neutralise-Bio-Electrica-Stress-from -Static-Electricity-and-EMF.

227   *"Emerging scientific research has revealed"*: Gaétan Chevalier, Stephen T. Sinatra, James L. Oschman, Karol Sokal, and Pawel Sokal, "Earthing: Health Implications of Reconnecting the Human Body to the Earth's Surface Electrons," *Journal of Environ-mental and Public Health,* January 12, 2012. pmc.ncbi.nlm.nih.gov/articles/PMC 3265077.

228   *The article cited one recent TikTok video:* Alex Janin, "Stand Outside Barefoot or Better Health? 'I Feel Like an Oddball, But If It Works, It Works,'" *Wall Street Jour-nal,* August 15, 2023. wsj.com/health/wellness/earthing-grounding-wellness-tiktok -trend-c9d82ca5.

234   *"a lower rate of edentulism"*: Paula K. Friedman and Ira B. Lamster, "Tooth Loss as a Predictor of Shortened Longevity: Exploring the Hypothesis," *Periodontology 2000,* October 1, 2016. pubmed.ncbi.nlm.nih.gov/27501497.

235   *"Oral health is much more than"*: Caswell Evans, "The Connection Between Oral Health and Overall Health and Well-Being," in *The U.S. Oral Health Workforce in the Coming Decades: Workshop Summary* (National Academies Press, 2009), 5–8. ncbi.nlm.nih.gov/books/NBK219661.

236   *There is also a connection between oral health:* "Oral Health Across the Lifespan: Working-Age Adults," in *Oral Health in America: Advances and Challenges* (National Institutes of Health, National Institute of Dental and Craniofacial Research, 2021), 3A-1–3A-96. ncbi.nlm.nih.gov/books/NBK578294.

240   *"reduce public health risks to farm workers"*: "Health Benefits of Organic," Organic Trade Association, 2024. ota.com/organic-101/health-benefits-organic.

240   *"have shown a strong correlation"*: Marlowe Hood, "'Ultra-Processed' Junk Food Linked to Advanced Ageing at Cellular Level, Study Finds," ScienceAlert, Septem-ber 1, 2020. sciencealert.com/study-links-ultra-processed-junk-food-to-age-marker-in -chromosomes.

240   *"enter food through packaging"*: Sunil Sharma and Mani Kavuru, "Sleep and Meta-bolism: An Overview," *International Journal of Endocrinology,* August 2, 2010 doi: 10.1155/2010/270832.

240 *In 1998, 35 percent of American adults:* American Thoracic Society, "Sleeping Less Linked to Weight Gain," ScienceDaily, May 29, 2006. sciencedaily.com/releases/2006/05/060529082903.htm.

241 *"the brain totally changes function":* "Good Sleep for Good Health," National Institutes of Health, June 18, 2024. newsinhealth.nih.gov/2021/04/good-sleep-good-health.

249 *we must integrate all facets of the 3H model:* Johann Heinrich Pestalozzi Society. jhpestalozzi.org.

253 *an organization dedicated to psi:* Rhine Research Center. rhineonline.org.

254 *"devoted to the rigorous evaluation of empirical":* University of Virginia School of Medicine, Division of Perceptual Studies. med.virginia.edu/perceptual-studies.

260 *"maps representing and corresponding":* Ralph Lewis, "What Actually Is a Thought? And How Is Information Physical?," *Psychology Today*, October 7, 2023. psychologytoday.com/us/blog/finding-purpose/201902/what-actually-is-a-thought-and-how-is-information-physical.

262 *Are dogs psychic?:* Jessica Pierce, "Is Your Dog Psychic?," *Psychology Today*, November 19, 2018. psychologytoday.com/us/blog/all-dogs-go-heaven/201811/is-your-dog-psychic.

276 *The shop's owner, Madison:* Open Eye Crystals. openeyecrystals.com/collections.

279 *She also authors a blog:* Margaux Perrier, *Being* (blog), Margaux Perrier (website). margauxperrierjewelry.com/blogs/news.

291 *"Certainly, the most popular":* "Vincent and the Doctor," *Doctor Who*, season 5, episode 10, IMDb, 2010. imdb.com/title/tt1591786/quotes/?item=qt1219356.

294 *In 2023 the mortality rate among all bees:* Brian Fredericksen, "Death by 1000 Cuts—the Big Bee Loss of 2024," Ames Farm Single Source Honey, March 13, 2025. amesfarm.com/blogs/showcase-ames-farm-honey-retailer/death-by-1000-cuts-the-big-bee-loss-of-2025.

296 *"It's like kicking a pebble":* Richard Holmes, "Business Lesson from Yellowstone National Park Wolf Project," LinkedIn, March 9, 2018. linkedin.com/pulse/business-lesson-from-yellowstone-national-park-wolf-project-holmes.

297 *patients who had flowers in their hospital rooms:* Lara S. Franco, Danielle F. Shanahan, and Richard A. Fuller, "A Review of the Benefits of Nature Experiences: More Than Meets the Eye," *International Journal of Environmental Research and Public Health* 14, no. 8 (August 1, 2017): 864. doi.org/10.3390/ijerph14080864.

299 *"is fragile, and needs nourishment":* Richard Louv, "The Mind-Altering Power of Deep Animal Connection," Sierra Club, February 12, 2020. sierraclub.org/sierra/mind-altering-power-deep-animal-connection.

301 *"Against a distant cliff":* From the poem "High Tide" by Christine Osvald-Mruz. *Atlanta Review*, Spring/ Summer 2025. For more information, please see christineosvaldmruz.com.

301 *"including the arts in health care delivery":* "Arts and Health," World Health Organization. who.int/initiatives/arts-and-health.

302 *"showed more functional connectivity":* Anne Bolwerk, Jessica Mack-Andrick, Frieder R. Lang, Arnd Dörfler, and Christian Maihöfner, "How Art Changes Your Brain: Differential Effects of Visual Art Production and Cognitive Art Evaluation on Functional Brain Connectivity," *PLOS One* 9, no. 12 (2014): e116548. journals.plos.org/plosone/article?id=10.1371%2Fjournal.pone.0101035.

302 *"Modern healthcare settings":* "The Intersection of Art and Health: How Art Can Help Promote Well-Being," Mayo Clinic, October 16, 2023. mcpress.mayoclinic

.org/living-well/the-intersection-of-art-and-health-how-art-can-help-promote-well
-being/.

303   *"When I was 15 I spent a month"*: three--rings (user name), post on *Hardcore Emotional Smut* (blog), Tumblr, September 8, 2020. three--rings.tumblr.com/post/
625948601747636224/when-i-was-15-i-spent-a-month-working-on-an. (Note: This post
by three--rings is often misattributed to Kurt Vonnegut. The error was originally made
because the post is a response to another post that cites a letter by Vonnegut and includes a photo of him.)

304   *art improves critical thinking and empathy*: Shengyu Zhang and Lege Zhao, "The
Impact of Public Art Education on College Students' Mental Health Literacy," *Fron-
tiers in Public Health* 12 (August 26, 2024):1427016. doi.org/10.3389/fpubh.2024
.1427016.

304   *Increase serotonin levels:* "How the Brain Is Affected by Art," American Congress of
Rehabilitation Medicine. acrm.org/rehabilitation-medicine/how-the-brain-is-affected
-by-art.

304   *watching a show not only affects you emotionally*: "Audience Members' Hearts Beat
Together at the Theatre," UCL Psychology and Language Sciences, November 17,
2017. ucl.ac.uk/pals/news/2017/nov/audience-members-hearts-beat-together-theatre.

312   *one minute of anger:* Suzanne C. Segerstrom and Gregory E. Miller, "Psychological
Stress and the Human Immune System: A Meta-analytic Study of 30 Years of Inquiry," *Psychological Bulletin* 130, no. 4 (July 2004): 601–30. doi.org/10.1037/0033-2909
.130.4.601.

312   *negative moods not only change:* Samuel Brod, Lorenza Rattazzi, Giuseppa Piras,
and Fulvio D'Acquisto, "'As Above, So Below': Examining the Interplay Between
Emotion and the Immune System," *Immunology* 143, no. 3 (November 2014): 311–18.
doi.org/10.1111/imm.12341.

312   *also increase inflammation:* Marjorie S. Miller, "Negative Mood Signals Body's Immune Response," PennState, December 20, 2018. psu.edu/news/research/story/
negative-mood-signals-bodys-immune-response.

312   *researchers from the University of Barcelona*: "Surprising New Evidence on Happiness and Wealth," McGill, Health e-News, February 20, 2024. healthenews.mcgill.ca/
surprising-new-evidence-on-happiness-and-wealth/.

312   *those who valued time over money:* Ashley Whillans, Lucía Macchia, and Elizabeth
Dunn, "Valuing Time Over Money Predicts Happiness After a Major Life Transition:
A Preregistered Longitudinal Study of Graduating Students," *ScienceAdvances* 5,
no. 9 (September 18, 2019). doi.org/10.1126/sciadv.aax2615.

313   *revealing that gratitude may have lasting effects:* Joshua Brown and Joel Wong,
"How Gratitude Changes You and Your Brain," *Greater Good Magazine*, June 6,
2017. greatergood.berkeley.edu/article/item/how_gratitude_changes_you_and_your
_brain.

ABOUT THE AUTHOR

LAURA LYNNE JACKSON, an international speaker, teacher, and psychic medium, is the author of the *New York Times* bestsellers *Signs: The Secret Language of the Universe* and *The Light Between Us*. She lives in New York with her family.